FALLING APART

APART

Avoiding, Coping with &
Recovering from Stress Breakdown

DR. MICHAEL EPSTEIN & SUE HOSKING

CHEVRON PUBLISHING CORPORATION
ELLICOTT CITY, MD
USA

First published in Australia by: Matchbooks, The Magistra Publishing
                    Company Pty. Ltd.
First North American Edition © 1992 Michael Epstein and Sue Hosking

1992. First printing by: CRCS Publications/Sebastopol, CA.   Published
          simultaneously in the United States, Canada and Europe.
1998. Second printing (via subsidiary rights transfer) by:
                    CHEVRON PUBLISHING CORPORATION
                    Ellicott City, MD

1998.   Cover Design: Matthew D. Czapanskiy
            Interior Design: Caroline J. Zimmerman
            Editor/Proofreader: Jason B. Lawrence
            Printer: Victor Graphics, Inc.

Library of Congress Cataloging - in - Publication Data

Epstein, Michael, 1944 -
      Falling apart : avoiding, coping with & recovering from stress
   breakdown / Michael Epstein & Sue Hosking.
            p.   cm.
      Originally published : Australia : Matchbooks , 1989.
      Includes bibliographical references and index.
      ISBN 1-883581-10-9 (pbk. : alk. paper)
      1. Stress (Psychology) -- Popular works. 2. Job stress -- Popular
   works. 3. Stress management -- Popular works. 4. Adjustment
   (Psychology) -- Popular works. I. Hosking, Sue, 1945 -
   II. Title.
   RC455.4.S87E67   1998
   155.9'042 -- dc21   98-44201
                                                                                    CIP

Dr. Michael Epstein and psychologist Sue Hosking are two of the foremost experts in the field of stress-related illness and stress breakdown. Sue and Michael worked for two years on *Falling Apart* and have also done extensive interviews with the media to spread the word about this important subject that touches the lives of so many people today.

Sue Hosking spent a number of years working as a school psychologist and as a consultant to many school systems and teachers' unions, and since then has worked in private practice, mainly seeing people who have suffered breakdowns due to excessive work pressure. Since 1984, she has been involved in setting up support networks for those recovering from stress breakdown. She has written and lectured extensively on the prevention and treatment of breakdowns and has consulted with unions, employers, government agencies, and researchers in an effort to reduce the incidence of stress breakdown.

Dr. Michael Epstein completed his professional training at the University of Rochester Department of Psychiatry in New York, and since has maintained a private practice. He was a founding director of the crisis service at the Austin Hospital, which he ran for six years, and an associate in the Department of Psychiatry at Melbourne University (Australia). He is also a Fellow of the Royal Australian and New Zealand College of Psychiatry.

"Falling Apart is a penetrating examination of how excessive stress can push an individual to the brink of destruction. Unlike more academic volumes, *Falling Apart* examines excessive stress from the survivor's perspective. It is refreshing and insightful. Most of all, it provides us all with hope and leaves us impressed with the strength of the human spirit." **-George S. Everly, Jr., Ph.D., CEO, International Critical Incident Stress Foundation, Inc.**

"It tells the reader that out of pain and despair; comes hope and strength. And basically that's one of the best things about this book....

"Certainly, it's a great resource for people who may not be coping, or for families or friends of people experiencing a break-down. But it's also invaluable for anyone involved in a stress-prone career or life-style because it explains how you can avoid falling apart. And in this stress-ridden world, we can probably all do with that advice." **-Executive Woman's Report**

"This simple, very accessible book is a survivor's manual for the increasing number of people who either actually experience stress breakdowns, or reach the brink of collapse." **- Sunday Telegraph**

"Hosking and Epstein have formulated what I believe to be an excellent perspective on the topic of stress. Some authorities view stress and stress breakdown as the coming epidemic in health care and rehabilitation. This book depicts the features of frightening personal experiences termed collectively 'stress breakdown', known by other terms such as nervous, or emotional, breakdowns.

"I believe this book should be essential reading for practicing rehabilitation counsellors....

"This is a book with a profound message of hope tempered by a view that the effects of stress breakdown are personally devastating and tend to be long-term. I found it easy to read and well structured....I cannot put my support for this book more clearly than: read it, please read it." **-Bulletin of the Australian Society of Rehabilitation Counsellors**

"Essential reading for everyone in the helping professions, as well as anyone dealing with stress-related problems." **-Michael Mersman, MA., Board Member, California Assn. of Rehabilitation Professionals**

"Falling Apart tackles the subject from the heart, using case histories of people who have traveled the breakdown path and moved on to rebuild their lives... the book takes you, quite logically, through various symptoms of a breakdown and how you can pull yourself, or someone near to you, back from the edge."
-The Canberra Times, Australia

Publisher's Note

This important book addresses one of the most widespread health problems of our era, that of stress-related illness. Workplace stress is in the news a lot lately, and rightly so. Stress-related problems are epidemic in industrialized societies today, in both Western and Eastern countries. In the United States, stress-related Worker Compensation claims have soared over 700% in the last decade!

The reader should study closely the chart on the following pages and use the last line to evaluate the stress factors in his or her job if it is not already listed. This alone can be a valuable exercise in recognizing what sorts of things are affecting one's stress level. In addition, the following list from Dr. Epstein provides a concise summary of common signs of stress as well as ways to cope with stress that we can all benefit from. Recognizing the symptoms can help us to avoid and prevent the kind of breakdown that the authors describe so well in this superb book.

TEN SIGNS OF STRESS

1.	Crying easily.	6.	Muddled thoughts.
2.	Depression.	7.	Exhaustion
3.	Low confidence.	8.	Loss of interest in sex.
4.	Irritability.	9.	Sleeping problems.
5.	Poor memory.	10.	Fear of social situations.

TEN WAYS TO COPE

1. Rest.
2. Time off work.
3. Counselling; medication can sometimes be useful for sleep problems, anxiety and depression.
4. Make your diet more nutritious, with an emphasis on vegetables.
5. Cut out alcohol and cigarettes.
6. Keep a diary of how you're feeling.
7. Avoid anything upsetting which may include television and newspapers.
8. Only spend time with people who accept you.
9. Pace yourself, use your body's symptoms as a guide. for example, if gardening makes you tired, stop.
10. Think positively - people get better.

How stressful is your job?

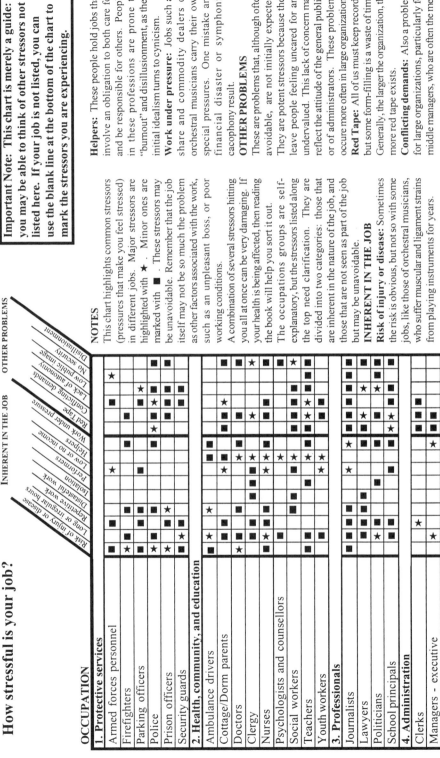

NOTES

This chart highlights common stressors (pressures that make you feel stressed) in different jobs. Major stressors are highlighted with ★. Minor ones are marked with ■. These stressors may be unavoidable. Remember that the job itself may not be so much the problem as other factors associated with the work, such as an unpleasant boss, or poor working conditions.

A combination of several stressors hitting you all at once can be very damaging. If your health is being affected, then reading the book will help you sort it out.

The occupations groups are self-explanatory, but the stressors listed along the top need clarification. They are divided into two categories: those that are inherent in the nature of the job, and those that are not seen as part of the job but may be unavoidable.

INHERENT IN THE JOB

Risk of injury or disease: Sometimes the risk is obvious, but not so with some jobs, like those of orchestral musicians, who suffer muscular and ligament strains from playing instruments for years.

Helpers: These people hold jobs that involve an obligation to both care for and be responsible for others. People in these professions are prone to "burnout" and disillusionment, as their initial idealism turns to cynicism.

Work under pressure: Jobs such as share and commodity dealers or orchestral musicians carry their own special pressures. One mistake and financial disaster or symphonic cacophony result.

OTHER PROBLEMS

These are problems that, although often avoidable, are not initially expected. They are potent stressors because they leave people feeling uncared for and undervalued. This lack of concern may reflect the attitude of the general public, or of administrators. These problems occur more often in large organizations.

Red Tape: All of us must keep records, but some form-filling is a waste of time. Generally, the larger the organization, the more red tape exists.

Conflicting demands: Also a problem for large organizations, particularly for middle managers, who are often the meat

The chart is divided into two main groups of stressors: those **INHERENT IN THE JOB** (Risk of injury or disease; Long or irregular hours; Repetitive work; Disastrous work; Isolation; Performers; Helpers; Low or no income; Work under pressure) and **OTHER PROBLEMS** (Red Tape; Conflicting demands; Lack of autonomy; Low public image; No security; Disillusionment).

OCCUPATION

1. Protective services
- Armed forces personnel
- Firefighters
- Parking officers
- Police
- Prison officers
- Security guards

2. Health, community, and education
- Ambulance drivers
- Cottage/Dorm parents
- Doctors
- Clergy
- Nurses
- Psychologists and counsellors
- Social workers
- Teachers
- Youth workers

3. Professionals
- Journalists
- Lawyers
- Politicians
- School principals

4. Administration
- Clerks
- Managers - executive

in the sandwich. It can also apply to those running a home, who must set aside their own needs for the needs of the family.

Lack of autonomy: People doing a job usually have a better idea than onlookers of how to do it efficiently. If their expertise is ignored and no channels of feedback are provided, they feel ignored and frustrated.

Low public image: The hard-working bureaucrat is often offended by the public's image of the lazy public servant. The honest cop is upset by the prevailing view of police corruption. Public attitudes change slowly and this burden is often part of the job.

No security: Lack of security in a job can come from lack of tenure for either the job itself or for its location. Both can be a constant source of anxiety. For example, many people leave the armed forces because of frequent forced transfers.

Disillusionment: Most jobs fail to live up to their promise, especially those in the helping professions. Over time, a potent combination of fatigue, lack of appreciation and low income can overwhelm the strongest vocation. Social workers and teachers are especially vulnerable.

Long or irregular hours: This category includes shift work, broken shifts, and overtime. Many people are surprised that teachers complain of long hours, ignoring preparation and correction time as well as involvement in extracurricular activities.

Repetitive work: This is emotionally demanding as there is little or no stimulation. Sports people, for example, are faced with long, tedious hours of practice.

Distasteful work: Work involving constant exposure to human misery, broken bodies, personal abuse, or 'dirty' industries.

Isolation: Some work must be done solo. This is especially true for creative people and can be very lonely.

Performers: Politicians, priests, ministers, actors, musicians and others are all, in a sense, performers. The are "on stage" and must ignore all personal problems. Threat of failure to communicate properly is always just a step away.

Low or no income: This is both an absolute problem - for, say, students, process workers, and others - as well as a relative problem for people like school principals and bank managers, whose salaries are often well below their counterparts in other industries and professions.

Occupation															
Public servants											★	■	■		■
Typists/WPOs/KPOs	★			■				★					★		
Union Officials	■		■	★	■	■	■	■	★						■
5. Transport and communication															
Air traffic controllers			■				★			■	■				
Drivers (train, bus, taxi, etc.)	★	■		■	★					■	■				
6. Wholesale and retail															
Convenience store cashiers	★	■	★				★	■							
Small business operators	■	■		■		■	★	■					★	■	
7. Agriculture and mining															
Farmers and rural workers	■	★	■	★		■		■					★		■
Miners	★	■	■												
Oil rig workers	★	■													
8. Manufacturing and construction															
Foremen/women	■	■	■	■		■	★								
Process workers	★	■	★	■	★					■	■				
Construction workers	★	■	■	■						■	■				
9. Financial services															
Bank officers	★			■			■								
Share and commodity dealers		■			★		★		■	■					■
10. Entertainment															
Actors	■		★	■		■		■			★	■	■		★
Entertainers, singers, media people	■		★	■		■					★		★		★
Creative artists, writers, composers	■		★	★		■					★		★		★
Orchestral musicians	★	■	★	■		■	★			■		■			■
Professional sports people	★	■	■			■	★								
11. Other															
Chefs and cooks	■			■		■			★		★		■		
Home duties people	■	★	★		■		★						■		■

vii

Preface

If you have had a breakdown or feel that you might be close to one, then reading this book from cover to cover will seem like an impossible task. We suggest that you use the chapter headings, the quotes from patients and especially the extensive index at the back of the book to find the sections that interest you most. Chapters 7 to 16 will be most relevant as they describe simple strategies for dealing with the many dilemmas that confront people during recovery.

This book is a tribute to the courage, sensitivity and determination of those with whom we have worked. We hope that it will help to ease the pain they and their families are enduring.

- Michael Epstein and Sue Hosking

Acknowledgements

There are many people who have helped to make this book a reality, but only a few can be mentioned by name. Our colleagues, especially Madeline Reid and Heather Cook, have been generous with ideas and support. Irma Harper, with the help of Lynne Massingham, typed the manuscript and Barbara Moriarty assisted with research.

Blanche D'Alpuget, Barry Smith and Gary Bell initially encouraged us to write and our special thanks go to Jane Arms, our editor, who showed us how to put our energy, our concern and our admiration for our clients into words.

This book has been a truly cooperative venture. Over the two-year writing period, we have had daily input from those who have had breakdowns as well as their families.

We would like to thank each other. Mutual honesty, trust and affection have enabled us to speak as one throughout the text and will result in friendship surviving co-authorship.

Finally, we would like to thank our friends and family for their patience, encouragement and love: Dell and Len Gamar, Josie and Frank Hosking and especially Daniel and Miranda Epstein, Rae Brady, and Peter, Shona and Lachlan Hosking.

- Sue Hosking and Michael Epstein

CONTENTS

PART ONE

BREAKING
DOWN

1

Falling Apart

My breakdown was the climax of a very bad period in my life. It was a terrible time for me but, in a way, I don't regret it. It has been the strongest factor in determining the person I've become. When I go through a rough patch, I simply think to myself that nothing can be as bad as that.

If you have had a breakdown, or know someone who's been through one, these words may be familiar. You may have found it impossible to explain to others what it was like and how it has affected your life. You probably felt isolated and, at times, totally alone as if no one but you had ever experienced this before. Yet this comment could have come from Walt Disney, Florence Nightingale, Bertrand Russell or Charles Darwin, for each of these famous people had a breakdown. They are part of a vast army of people who have had the same sort of experience.

You may have broken down from a combination of overwork and frustration, as was the case for the four famous people named above, or from some disaster such as a bush-fire or flood; you may have been the victim of a crime. Many people have been unlucky enough to experience both prolonged pressure and a crisis. Whatever the cause, or whoever is involved, the result is the same - stress breakdown.

This book is about stress breakdown and the way it can affect your life, or the life of someone close to you. You may find that you can no longer cope with yourself, your family, your friends or your work, and just getting through the day seems an impossible task. This is an event so far outside our ordinary experience that it may be hard to comprehend. Only those who have been through it can know what it's like, and yet it happens to ordinary people, people like you and me, who have coped well with the demands of life, people who would not normally need a psychiatrist or psychologist.

It happened to Andrew Parker, who was awarded the George Medal for bravery after the Zeebrugge ferry disaster in 1987. The British-owned car ferry overturned off the coast of Belgium, and 193 people died.

While Andrew Parker was below decks frantically helping other passengers to escape from the watery grave that awaited them, he was comforted by the knowledge that his wife, Eleanor, and daughter, Janice, were safe. Eleanor was not so fortunate: she had become separated from Janice and for more than 24 hours thought she had lost both her husband and daughter.

The disaster made him a national hero in Britain, but two years later, Andrew and his wife's lives have been shattered by that fateful day-trip to Belgium. Eleanor has been plagued by insomnia, phobias and depression.

After the disaster, Andrew became a workaholic at first but has since become progressively more irritable, depressed, self-centered and withdrawn. Both have been in therapy for some time and are on medication. Life has become a burden to them and the disaster is a recurrent intrusive nightmare.

It takes little imagination to see how the Parkers could have "fallen apart" as a result of their terrible experiences. The cause is obvious and the result understandable. Less obvious or understandable are breakdowns arising from more personal disasters, like a death or separation, or from a series of small disasters: illness, financial loss, or unemployment. And yet the same symptoms occur, the same problems in coping and the same experience of one's life being shattered.

Most of us know roughly what we mean when we use the word breakdown, although we would perhaps be hard-pressed to really define it. We use it to describe the sudden change in someone who has coped well before, but after a period of strain, has reached or passed the point of collapse. This is how the term is used in this book.

A breakdown can also mean a sudden outburst of emotion, often tears or rage, which is usually short-lived, and leaves people feeling drained but relieved. The word is sometimes used to indicate the development, or the recurrence, of a mental disorder like schizophrenia or manic depressive illness, and although we do not use the term in this sense, many people with mental disorders also experience the symptoms of a stress breakdown.

Despite the term "breakdown" being used so often in general conversation, doctors tend to scoff if you tell them you've had one. This is not a term they use or even acknowledge; after all, it's only used by people who don't know any better, the general public and the popular press. Doctors dismiss it out of hand, often with the glib explanation, "You can't have a nervous breakdown because your nerves don't break down."

Stress breakdown is a condition caused by stress in which the capacity for coping with life is damaged, not just strained but really damaged. This damage is shown by a number of symptoms and the damage takes a long time to mend.

We talk and write about it because we see the damage it causes people every day, with jobs lost, health shattered and families split. If you cross the divide that separates stress from stress breakdown, you have a lonely and exhausting battle to survive and overcome the crippling affects of your breakdown. This is a tragedy that can be avoided.

A breakdown is a mystery. It's difficult to comprehend; it's frightening because it could strike down anyone of us, and there is a great deal of shame attached to it.

Indeed, if you are in the midst of a stress breakdown, you may go to great lengths to cover it up, to put on a mask of coping, and you may even succeed, but only with outsiders and not with your family. The mask may be good - you dress normally, you can still putter around the house, visit friends or even party - for a while. You may even look really good, better than you have for years, because you are getting so much rest. But it's a charade and inside you feel a mess.

It is only occasionally that the mask slips. The bank teller wonders about the customer who bursts into tears and runs out of the bank after filling out the wrong withdrawal form. Passersby probably don't notice the confused expression on the face of the person who just backed into the parked car at the supermarket. Do others notice when someone has to leave the party because it has all become too much?

We may not find it odd that our taxi driver used to be a policeman, or that the local farmer was once a teacher, or even that our doctor suddenly gave up his practice in his 40s. The truth is that only very close family and friends see what happens when the facade crumbles and even then you try to hide it from them as much as you can.

Therein lies the problem. If you've had a breakdown, you don't want anyone to know because you're afraid, you're frightened of being rejected, of being thought weak or mad. You don't want to face questions about something you don't understand and find too difficult to explain. You don't want advice from someone who doesn't understand you.

But if others don't know all this and only see your mask, then they are likely to misjudge your behavior. If they see an apparently healthy man not working but going shopping or gardening, they might think that you are faking, especially if you are receiving worker's compensation or a pension. People often gossip and sometimes make cruel and nasty comments, calling you "work shy," lazy, selfish, or weak when they think you are cheating the system.

It would be much easier if you had broken your leg or developed anemia or diabetes. Then you would be allowed to be sick, to be less responsible. You would receive compassion and support rather than blame, because these "obvious" illnesses carry no morality; they're not your "fault." It is much easier to feel charitable to a child with leukemia and much more difficult to feel that same sympathy to a middle-aged person with a breakdown.

Stress breakdown raises all sorts of doubts in everyone's minds, even in those affected. Maybe it's a cop-out, maybe people are malingering. Couldn't some people be weak? How is it you can't work when you look so well? All these questions, and more, come to mind when people encounter stress breakdown, and yet, notice how we never ask these questions of someone who has a clear-cut physical illness. We are all reluctant to let someone play the part of being sick if they don't look sick, if they are not obviously disabled with a problem that can't be seen or be readily understood.

Sometimes it can seem that the only people who really understand are those who have been through it themselves.

For the past 10 years we have been seeing people who have had breakdowns. People like Tom, a middle-aged teacher who crumbled over a period of years as his department was destroyed by bureaucratic indifference and student vandalism; or Margaret, a proud resourceful woman whose daughter was murdered; or George, a fireman who never recovered from the injuries he received in a house fire.

These three are representative of all those we have seen who have had breakdowns. They have come from all walks of life. Some are near the end of a productive life and others are just starting out. There are those blessed by a stable, tranquil upbringing and others who have managed despite neglect, cruelty or even bad luck. In every way that a group can be different, this group is different and yet they share the same symptoms, problems and fears.

Stress is a constant, underlying theme for them all: stress from fear, loss, or exhaustion. The fear may have come from life-threatening situations like car accidents, assaults or disasters like floods or bush fires. Loss may have come from personal tragedy, bankruptcy or a serious illness. Some "crashed" because of exhaustion, often following a long period of frustration and disappointment. Some were exposed to overwhelming pressures that would have brought most of us down. Others experienced very mild pressure.

Most had experienced considerable pressure for a long time

before they "snapped." This pressure had arisen from frustration at their lack of power to alter the situation. It was not just pressure that was bringing people down, it was pressure involving frustration and powerlessness.

There were two things about the people we saw that we found disturbing. The first cause of concern was that many were "salt of the earth" people, the backbone of the community - sergeants in the police force, experienced nurses, school principals, and senior public servants - many in their mid-30s and at the peak of their productive lives, with a young family dependent for its stability on their continuing good health.

Our other concern was that these people were doing so badly. No one seemed to know what was wrong, and no one seemed to know what to do. They were given a myriad of labels, but the labels didn't help. So many were told that they were depressed, but they didn't feel depressed. It didn't matter; they were told that they were suffering from hidden depression and were treated with antidepressants; still they didn't improve. Some were treated with different drugs or electroconvulsive therapy; some underwent behavior modification therapy but without much success; others spent years in psychotherapy with no real gain.

None of this expenditure of professional skill, time and money seemed to make much difference. People still complained of the same problems. By this stage the therapist was becoming frustrated and, maybe, even a little irritated at the lack of improvement. Some therapists began to blame their clients for their failure to improve, which only made them more upset and bewildered than ever.

What is wrong if even a therapist can't help? After all, therapists, whether they are psychiatrists or psychologists, are trained to handle these problems. If they can't, who can? What is wrong if people who were fit, active and productive can't seem to work or can't even get out of bed because they feel so exhausted? Maybe they really are as weak and pathetic as they feel. Maybe if they were stronger they could overcome this crippling thing that has wrecked their lives. Maybe those therapists were right when they said that these people didn't want to get better.

So what was wrong? The answer lay in front of us the whole time. Every day we had people telling us that they had broken down, that they were damaged. Sometimes they didn't use the word "breakdown," but that is what they meant. They couldn't really define it but they were convinced that they'd had a breakdown, and were not able to cope. They had learned their survival strategies by trial and error: some things made them better, some things made them worse.

They were our teachers and we learned from their successes and their failures; in a sense they have written this book.

We have learned that our job is to provide clarification, advice and much support. We are coaches; our job is to inform, guide and give strength in fighting the battle for survival. This is a long-term battle, and it's easy to lose hope.

We are like athletics coaches in some ways: we can't run the race, but we can advise the runners on how to improve their performance so that they can do their best.

Sometimes the support we provide is simple and direct, particularly during the early stages of a breakdown. It might be help with pay problems, advice about lawyers, or a phone call to a co-worker. Our aim is to empower people, to help them see how they can regain control and influence, and to give help when it is really needed.

There are a number of questions we are usually asked. "What is wrong with me?" "How did it happen?" "How long will it go on?" "What can I do about it?" "Will I be able to go back to work?" "Will it happen again?"

We have written this book to provide the answers to some of these questions. The answers themselves have come from those who have suffered breakdowns as well as from their families and friends.

We have used the stories of Tom, the teacher whose department was destroyed; Margaret, whose daughter was murdered; and the stories of several other people to illustrate the points we are making. None of these stories is that of any one person; they are composite portraits all based on real stories from real people.

This book is an endeavor to distill the information we have gleaned over the years from the real experts, those who have been through it, and their families. We know that they have looked for such a book in vain. We hope the book helps in removing the stigma felt by those who have been through a breakdown.

The most compelling reason for writing this book is that we see so many people whose breakdowns were unnecessary and need never have occurred. We hope this book will help in preventing some of these in the future.

There is one other thing that must be said: many of these people have found that their breakdown was not an end but a beginning. The knowledge they have gained from this experience helped them reach a level of understanding and maturity that has enriched their lives.

2

Stories of Breakdowns

What is a breakdown, what does it feel like and how is it different from stress? The best way of describing it to you is by telling some stories of those who've had a breakdown, and those who've come very close to it.

Margaret and Tom are two very different people who experienced a breakdown. Helen came very close and was lucky to escape. In later chapters we will follow their progress, look at how they and their families coped, and what they did over a period of time to return to a normal life again.

Margaret

Margaret had been working as a freelance journalist in her small, semi-rural community when her daughter was raped and murdered. She had always been a strong-willed, committed woman. A local shire councilor, she had raised her three children alone after her husband deserted her.

She was 45 at the time of her daughter Melinda's death but she looked closer to 60 when she first came to the office. She had been persuaded to come by her old friend Ruth, who had been a client. Ruth had driven her to the appointment as Margaret had been frightened about getting lost on the way.

Margaret was a tall, rangy woman dressed in an elegant, black pantsuit. She had lost weight recently and was haggard and drawn. She had dark circles under her eyes, a sallow tinge to her skin and her brown hair was graying. Margaret was restless in the waiting room, pacing to and fro with loping strides. She was chain-smoking, butting out each cigarette when it was barely alight. Her glasses hung around her neck on a chain.

Margaret began her story in this way: "I feel like I'm going crazy, but I just don't know what to do. When the psychiatrist told me about the shock treatment, I knew I had to do something myself, it was sort of shock treatment itself, I suppose.

"I've had hard times before but this is different. I've never felt so terrible. I can't sleep; my clothes are falling off because I've lost so much weight.

"Everyone tells me I'm depressed, but I'm not depressed. I feel like I've had too much, and I've just broken down.

"Everyone says it's because of Melinda's death. I know that's really important, but it was what happened afterwards that really broke me and I feel like it was then that I lost the old me. I don't know if I'll ever get her back."

Margaret told her story hesitantly, jumping from one topic to another. Sometimes she stopped mid-sentence and seemed lost, then her face would redden and crumple as she tried unsuccessfully to stop the flow of tears.

From her story she emerged as a woman of unusual strength of character and energy. She had kept her family together after her husband left. Her wide circle of friends attested to her warmth and loyalty. And, in some ways, the qualities of warmth and caring that she saw in Melinda were descriptions of herself.

"Melinda is, or rather was, my eldest child. We'd always had a special feeling between us. I think it was because we clung to each other when my marriage broke up and Ron left. She was the only one I seemed to be able to talk to. Tim was only a few months old, Hannah was just two and I was desperate and I remember feeling so tired, I don't think I've ever felt so bad . . . until now.

"Ever since we had been more like sisters than a mother and daughter. She had a rare sweetness that everyone responded to, and she seemed to attract lame ducks wherever she went.

"I don't mean that she was a saint. She had a wicked tongue sometimes and she'd have me in stitches with the comments she'd make about the other shire councilors. She was the one who started calling John Letts "bottlenose." Letts, who lives nearby, is one of the shire councilors and he had an enormous red nose. Every time he got up to speak in the council I used to giggle inside; she was so right. I got so used to calling him 'bottlenose' at home that I used to worry I'd call him that in the meetings. Oh, that all seems a million years ago now."

Margaret's father had started an engineering business that had become successful. She could never remember any money worries when she was a child, although she did have monumental battles with her father as an adolescent over her determination to have equal rights with her brother who was one year older than her. Her mother was very much in the background during these struggles, and Margaret tended to despise her for being weak. When she was much older Margaret realized that her mother was quietly influencing her father to change his old-fashioned ideas.

Her brother went into the business with her father and took over when, reluctantly, he retired. Her parents had tried to help Margaret over the years, but she was resistant to handouts, although happy to accept the small income she received from her share in the family business. Her sister was three years younger than Margaret and had always resented her sister's dominance.

She had married a lawyer who had become wealthy and Pat was now very much the society lady. Margaret found her irritating and petty. In recent years Pat had come to patronize her sister and her mother.

Margaret's father had died five years before, and her mother appeared to have flourished once out of her husband's shadow. She had gone on long trips and had become much closer to Margaret than before. But she would only stay with her for a few days, saying that it was as much noise as she could stand. Her mother had a bad fall a year before and had fractured her hip. She was much less active and Margaret had felt guilty about seeing her so little. Her mother lived in an apartment very close to the city. Margaret's two younger children often stayed with their grand-mother and Tim, in particular, was very close to her.

"Hannah and Tim were just about inseparable as youngsters. They even had their own language for a while. Tim was always strong and graceful; he's a natural athlete although no scholar. He's very popular with the girls, but I think he'd really like to have a father around. He gets on well with Andrew, who's been in my life for two or three years.

"Andrew is a dear. I often wonder what he sees in me. He's 10 years younger than me and is the local butcher. His family has run the business for three generations. Andrew has spent all his life in the town and is very quiet and soft and strong. He comes around four or five days a week and has become part of the family. I think that's part of what he likes about me, although he hasn't been getting too much of that lately.

"I forgot to tell you about Hannah. She and I fight all the time, although sometimes I don't even know what it's all about. I think she's the one who resented the break-up more than anyone else, although, God knows, I've told her that Ron walked out on me and not the other way around. She's always got an answer though, and she said that I must have been impossible to live with; just lately I think she's right.

"I worry about Hannah because she never seems really happy. She's got a boyfriend now, but she's so possessive I don't know how long he'll hang around. Hannah's an artist; she has a real flair for color and design. When she's not arguing with me she likes to tell me what to wear, and she's really good. She made me buy this pantsuit."

Margaret had finished school and started a university course when she married Ron and abandoned her course to her father's displeasure. Ron was a few years older than her and he was a dreamer. She had great fun in those first few years even after Melinda was born.

She and Ron had hitchhiked around Europe and worked their way around the countryside doing all sorts of jobs. Margaret had worked as a cook, a housekeeper, a factory hand and even on a fishing boat for a week until she got so seasick they had to come back early.

Ron, it became clear, was a drifter, and although Margaret was devastated when he left, it was only a matter of time before she would have left him anyway. He turned up every now and then, still amiable, footloose and totally irresponsible. Occasionally money would arrive out of the blue with a short note: "Sorry I can't send more, I was lucky with the ponies."

She had always enjoyed writing, and after Ron left she began sending short pieces off to various newspapers. She had a funny, whimsical, slightly quirky sense of humor, and her pieces became popular. She developed a reputation as a zany, incisive writer who had the knack of articulating what many people were thinking.

She often received letters from people marveling how she was able to put into words so many of their thoughts and experiences. Eventually a collection of her pieces was published. She made a large number of friends from her writing.

She had lived in the old rambling farmhouse for 15 years. She had many plans to renovate the place but never seemed to have the time or the money. The house was two kilometers out of town on a winding bush road and she had only a few neighbors. She was very active in the local community.

"I seemed to get involved in just about everything. I was on the preschool committee, then the other school committees. I wrote some articles about the new housing estate, and I was asked to join the local progress association. I virtually ran that single-handedly for six years. I really became involved when the bushfires roared through town; that was an unbelievable time."

Bushfires had devastated the area five years earlier. Margaret's town was nearly destroyed; more than half the shops were burned to the ground and many of the farms were ravaged.

"I still get scared on hot, windy days and I don't like to leave home. As the fires approached that year, about 50 of us sheltered in the community center, which was in the middle of a large, cleared area. Some hosed down the outside for as long as they could while the rest of us huddled under sodden blankets on the floor.

"I remember the roaring of the flames - the fire was like a giant steam engine - the whimpering of the children; some of the women were praying. It was absolutely terrifying although we all tried to keep calm so as to not upset the children. Many of the women had husbands out fighting the fires and were agonizing over them. I think we all knew that we were going to die. It's the most amazing experience to accept death like that and then find yourself alive at the end of it."

The people in the center all survived, but some lost their husbands and sons. The fabric of the town was torn and the survivors were stunned and dazed.

"Ted, Ruth's husband, was killed when he and three of his friends in the volunteer fire brigade were caught when the wind changed and blew the fire back on them. I don't think Ruth had time to mourn then, she was so frantically busy looking after her two children and helping at the community center.

"The weeks after the fire were a time I will never forget. We worked day and night cooking, clearing, talking and building. I was roped into coordinating the catering, and Ruth had the job of distributing piles of donated food, clothing and even caravans.

"There was an influx of volunteers; we seemed to find superhuman energy at that time and we all became very close. Ruth and I were together day and night. I'd never really known her before as she'd always seemed such a private person, but we have become wonderful friends.

"I felt very guilty after the fires: my house was untouched, I'd lost no one. Some articles I had written were widely published and I think I was seen as a bit of a hero. I even got good money for the articles and quite a bit of extra work.

"I can remember wearing the same clothes for almost a week. Everyone else had lost so much that I felt uneasy about looking too clean. It took months for me to get over the feeling that people were resenting my good fortune. I think that guilty feeling made me work harder. Ruth eventually snapped me out of it when she told me that no one resented me, it was my imagination."

In the months that followed, Margaret seemed indefatigable. It was as a result of the work she put in then that she was asked to stand at the shire council elections and she won a seat. After the fire, there were massive dislocations in the community, and following the excitement of the first few weeks, the volunteers left and the burden of dealing with the vast social problems fell to a dedicated few. There was a lack of accommodation, a lack of work because farms and factories had been destroyed, and a lack of support for the many families coping with the loss of loved ones.

"I have never worked so hard. My place became a drop-in center and I would rope in everyone who came into doing something: some were helping people fill out forms, some were organizing accommodations, and some were just having a quiet weep in a corner. I remember working from dawn until midnight for days and weeks on end. I don't know how I did it; I seem to be looking at another woman when I think about that time.

"I kept it up for three months. I remember getting a sense of increasing urgency. I felt like everything had to be done yesterday and I was driving myself and everyone else mercilessly. I knew something had to give eventually, although I was so wound up I couldn't seem to stop and then I fell in a heap. For a while I felt almost as bad as I do now. I was beyond tiredness. I felt nervous all the time and I felt really uneasy about the kids' safety.

"The fights and bitterness over the distribution of the donated funds finally got to me. I felt like tossing it all in, but so many people were relying on me that I forced myself to keep going.

"I got a skin rash that just about drove me mental. I couldn't sleep, I was scratching all the time and then I came down with glandular fever and finally had to stop.

"I was in the hospital for a week while they were doing tests because they thought I had leukemia. After that I came home and did almost nothing for two months apart from belting out a few articles. I think the glandular fever stopped me from having a breakdown, because I would have just kept going if that hadn't made me stop."

Margaret quickly recovered her strength with the enforced break, although she felt she never had quite the same stamina that she had had before. Her daughter Melinda started her university course that year and was living away from home. Margaret missed her company and knew that she was drifting away as she was growing up.

Margaret became even more involved in community activities, although not at the same frenetic pace as before. She became active on a number of conservation issues in the council.

There were a number of councilors with a vested interest in some of the developments planned for the community. John Letts, the infamous "bottlenose," was one of this group. He was a near neighbor as well as being the local real estate agent. He was a heavy drinker, a bully and a bigot. Margaret found him very "slimy." He'd driven her home from the monthly council meeting one night and she had to fight off his wandering hands; Margaret made sure she had transportation arranged after council meetings from then on.

Margaret had opposed a waste treatment plant being built in the shire and was successful in arousing community awareness; the plan was rejected. She was told later that Letts owned the land that was to be used to build the plant and that he was very angry about her opposition, although his ingratiating manner towards her never changed.

"Letts was a real creep. His wife was a poor downtrodden thing who had been thoroughly cowed. His son Jack was a school friend of Melinda's. She took pity on him because he was a sad figure. He got odd jobs in the area but he was terrified of his father and frightened to break out.

"Jack was over at our place all the time and eventually I got sick of him hanging around and I told him to give it a miss for a while. He said he was sorry, just shrugged his bony shoulders and slunk away. Melinda was upset and angry with me for kicking him out . . . I'm sorry I'm crying, I feel so stupid."

Her story took several sessions to unfold and at times she seemed to talk about anything but her daughter's death. She cried bitter tears; she raged. At other times she sat very still for minutes and seemed lost; she seemed to physically shrink and her face was filled with pain.

"I hate talking about it and yet I never seem to stop thinking about it. I feel just about talked out. I mean, what's the point, nothing will ever bring her back. And yet I feel so terrible. I feel I have to do something otherwise I feel my life is over too."

Melinda was raped and strangled while walking home from a disco she had been organizing at the community center. Margaret had planned to pick her up but had been delayed by 30 minutes at a council meeting. When she arrived at the community center she was told Melinda had decided to walk home as it was a fine clear night.

Margaret was not concerned then, although there had been some attacks made on women in the surrounding districts in the previous few months. She drove home expecting to find Melinda there, but the other two children hadn't seen her. Margaret drove back to Jack's place expecting that Melinda had stopped in to see Jack, but no one was home. Margaret started to panic.

"When I could see that she had not stopped in to see Jack, I began getting frightened. I drove back to town calling out every few yards. "I got the police involved and a full-scale search was started. I was quite frantic because I really knew that she was dead.

"The whole night and the next day is a blur now. I can remember crying and faces looking down at me and voices reporting to the sergeant. Ruth was there and just held me; Andrew was frantic, and the two kids were dazed. Jack heard the commotion and came over. He was terribly upset and exhausted himself looking for her over the next day.

"Two boys found her body in a shallow grave next to the creek on the other side of town. It was almost an anti-climax for me because I knew she was dead. She was naked and had been raped and strangled.

"I made myself identify her body; I felt far, far away. She looked very tiny and gray, and her face was swollen and cut. The police had found a few clues, a tire mark near the creek, and a dirty handkerchief they think was used to strangle her."

The community was stunned. Margaret was a popular figure, and there was a large crowd at the funeral. Margaret coped as she had always done; she was strong for the kids' sake as well as for herself. Inside she was bitter and blamed herself for being late on that night. But she was surviving. She missed Melinda. It was as if a part of her was gone.

Jack, Melinda's friend and the son of her old adversary, was badly affected. He was crying on her shoulder and seemed pleased to talk about Melinda long after everyone else had lost interest. He seemed to lean on Margaret as much as anyone.

Three months later, another rape occurred in a nearby town and a few days after that there was an attempted rape in the local community. This time the girl involved had fought off her attacker and had given a good description to police. They were able to make an arrest later that day and subsequently charged her attacker with Melinda's murder.

"It was Jack. I couldn't believe it. I just couldn't believe it. After all that she had done for him and all I'd done for him after she died. He was crying on my shoulder, for God's sake, and all the time he'd killed her. And I know that his father had a pretty good idea it was Jack but did nothing about it. He'd grease all over me at those council meetings and say how sorry he was, and all the time he knew.

"That's when I started breaking down. I could feel myself sliding into an abyss and I couldn't stop it. I don't even know if I wanted to. I felt unclean, dirty. That anyone could do that! I couldn't comprehend it. I still can't."

Margaret suffered a breakdown. Her capacity for coping, already stretched, was overwhelmed by this fresh experience, by this contact with evil. She cried bitter, dry tears; she could no longer write; she lost interest in her surviving children and in Andrew. She sat immobile for hours at a time, seemingly lost in thought, although later she could not recall her thoughts. She had no energy and spoke in a tired; dead voice.

The local doctor had been sympathetic initially but then had "given her a good talking to." He thought she was being self-indulgent. Margaret lost confidence in seeing anyone else for many months. Andrew and her children became more and more worried by her behavior. She had no energy, was irritable and intolerant, and refused to see visitors. She wasn't eating, she was losing weight and she couldn't sleep. She was smoking constantly and developed a dry, racking cough. She was frightened all the time and couldn't shop or even leave the house by herself.

Andrew had nagged her without success for months to get help. One day, in desperation, he bundled her into the car despite her protestations and carted her off to see another doctor in a nearby town. He was very concerned about her condition and began treating her with anti-depressants, although Margaret told him she wasn't depressed. She saw him for a few months but she got worse.

"He was nice enough, but he didn't have a clue and he didn't seem to listen to me. I knew he was worried, but he kept telling me was depressed and that I had a pathological grief reaction, whatever that was. I knew I was heartbroken over Melinda's death, but this was different and I couldn't seem to get that through to him or the psychiatrist he eventually sent me to see."

Margaret was very apprehensive about seeing the psychiatrist, a tall, aloof figure who saw Margaret briefly. The psychiatrist said very little to Margaret or Andrew, but he was concerned enough about her condition to admit her to a psychiatric hospital. Margaret went along with all this until she realized that he was planning to give her shock treatment.

She left the hospital that day and contacted Ruth who arranged for her to see the therapist she had seen when her husband was killed. She was very frightened and antagonistic at first. Who could blame her! But as she gained some confidence she began to express her confusion and despair more freely.

"My brain just won't work. I forget things. I get scared of talking to people because I forget what I'm saying halfway through a sentence, or if someone asks me a question I don't know what to say. I feel such a fool.

"I can't read, although I used to read two or three books a week. I read a page and although I've read the words, I don't remember a thing. The worst thing of all is that I can't write. I've worked as a journalist for years and I've always written. I've used writing as a way of expressing my feelings, but now I can't put pen to paper.

"I try to make lists to do the shopping and come back with things I don't want and forget things I went to the shop to get; just going shopping is a nightmare. I've learned to go down early when there's no one around, but after five or 10 minutes I just have to get out of the supermarket. It all crowds in on me and I have to flee. Sometimes I'm so rude to the checkout girl because she's slow and I have to leave.

"I can't make a decision. I can't decide what to have for dinner, what to wear, how to spend my time. I can't drive, although I've tried a few times, but I get lost so easily. I can't seem to understand the street directory. I drove through a red light the other day. I feel like I'm a menace on the road and I keep getting nightmares about hitting some little kid.

"I'm getting aches and pains in my shoulders and neck; that skin trouble I had before has come back and I get dull headaches all the time. I feel like my body is falling apart.

"I'm hopeless with the kids. I know they feel terrible too, but I can't stand them around me a lot of the time. I can't stand Tim's music; he always plays his records loudly no matter what I say. And I keep screaming at Hannah.

"God knows how Andrew has put up with me. I can't stand him touching me and I keep snapping at him. I know he's trying to please and help me, they all are, but I just wish they would all leave me alone.

"My mother has been devastated by it all and I know she's worried too, but I don't want to see her. My sister, Pat, told me I should be ashamed of myself. I was invited to her daughter's engagement party, but I couldn't go. Pat called the next day and began abusing me. I just dropped the phone and curled up in bed.

"I feel like a physical, mental and emotional wreck with no control over my life. I feel as though I am living deep inside my body and everything outside my body is a dream."

Tom

Tom has the strong shoulders and the rough-hewn face of a man who instinctively inspires confidence in his strength. His hands are large, with thick, clumsy looking fingers that surprise you with their delicacy. You expect his hands to be ingrained with dirt, they are worker's hands, but they are fresh-scrubbed and the nails are cut square and clean.

Tom is a craftsman, and his hands are as carefully tended as any other of his tools. He has a large head on a bulky body with the beginnings of a small potbelly. His face is lined, and he has a firm mouth and a well-defined nose. He is like a mythical figure, the skilled craftsman who has achieved wisdom through his contact with things that matter: wood, fine tools, skill and experience. He represents old-fashioned values of honesty, reliability and pride. Your first impression is superficial and misleading.

His face tells a different story. Recent events have disturbed that sense of surety built up and reinforced over a lifetime. It reminds you of the ocean; in the midst of a squall you can feel the deep ocean swells moving on inexorably under the spume and foam of this latest spat.

Tom has a puzzled, bewildered expression: his mouth trembles a little and his eyes seem to lose focus and at times fill with tears. The confusion and perplexity on his face is disturbing. His very presence suggests strength, solidity and integrity. His facial expression seems as out of place as graffiti on a church.

Tom's appearance helps you sketch out the scant biography he provides when you first meet. He is very uncomfortable in the office and is clearly not used to talking about himself. His discomfort shows both in his naked despair and in his attempts to cover it with a jokey heartiness. He is contemptuous of himself. For him, seeing a psychologist is an admission of weakness and defeat. Having to seek someone else's help is bad enough but having to ask for that help from a psychologist is the ultimate insult to his pride.

His anger at his own helplessness and frustration in this unfamiliar role is patently obvious and bursts through his natural politeness very early during the first interview. A series of questions about his background prompts retaliation.

"Why do you need to know all that? I came to you for help and all you've done so far is ask a series of irrelevant questions. What have my mother and father got to do with it? What difference does it make if they got on well together or not? Next thing you'll be asking me about their sex life I suppose." You go through an explanation. "I need to find out your history so that I can get to know you. Your life's like a jigsaw puzzle and we both have to work at putting it together. The quickest way for me to do that is to ask these questions."

The explanation has a calming affect. It reassures Tom and gives him some control. He can understand what is going on and he visibly relaxes.

Tom's background is conventional enough. He was born in the country and his father and his father before him had been farmers. Tom was the middle son in the family of three boys and he spoke about his early life with affection and wistfulness. It was a time when, if there were troubles, the boys had seemed unaware of them.

"My elder brother and I were always great mates. We could drive the tractor as soon as we could walk, and we used to ride a horse to school. Butter was an old horse that would never canter. We two kids would sit up on the top of this tall, old horse, and we'd be kicking her and yelling, and she'd just amble, occasionally having a munch by the side of the road. The school was a one teacher school with about seven or eight other kids. We'd let Butter go in the school paddock and after school we'd have to catch her. That was the only time she'd ever run."

Tom had relaxed more by now. He was talking about a subject that was easy. He even seemed to forget who he was talking to most of the time, although every now and then you'd see him watching your face to gauge your reaction.

"My brother really loved the farm. He'd follow Dad everywhere. I remember him trying to pick up a hay bale when he was about six. He had no hope, of course, but he was a stubborn little bugger, and he'd never give up. He's never changed.

"I'd always be in the shed, puttering around, inventing things. Dad used to say, 'Bloody Tom's broken something again.' Mum was great though. She always seemed interested and, although she must have smiled to herself, she'd be very enthusiastic about my latest invention. I remember her trying to use my wind-powered butter churn. We never did get it to work, but somehow that didn't seem to matter. I'd just go on to the next thing.

"My other brother was 10 years younger than me. He was a quiet kid, always reading, a dreamer really; strangely, though, he loved farming too. He did an agricultural course and had a real passion for botany." Tom became an apprentice to a carpenter in a nearby town and continued working with him for 10 years. He enjoyed carpentry, even the mundane parts of it, like framing, because there was always something tangible and lasting that was produced at the end of a job. The intense, passionate side to his nature, although deeply hidden, was expressed in his workshop at home and was obvious even in the very way he turned the wood. He collected fine and unusual timbers, and after hours of total involvement, turned them into beautiful pieces. He described one of them.

"The rosewood was from an old mansion we were turning into offices - it was part of a banister - and I cut it up into thin planks with fine tongue and groove and made a chest of drawers, copying an old design I saw in a magazine. I dovetailed the drawers and carved the knobs and French polished it. The planks were only two inches wide, but I matched the grain and the joints are invisible. It's in the hall; I see it every day."

He built his own home over a number of years. His wife, Betty, basked in his strength and was contented with her husband, children and home.

But Betty was no pushover. She had always had a quiet confidence about her and whether it was organizing the mothers' club at school, playing catch with her kids or providing a shoulder for her friends to lean on, she was always reliable, sensible and efficient. Tom was luckier than he knew in his choice of partner.

Tom went back to the farm quite often. He enjoyed working with his two brothers, who sometimes suggested a partnership, but he wasn't interested. It was too restrictive, and he wanted to do more. He liked the country life in small doses, but he wanted to do more with his hands and his brain. He wanted to leave his mark on the world, and he didn't think he could do that with farming. His son Paul was the farmer.

"Paul, my eldest boy, loved the farm. He's a natural; he's doing agricultural science now. Every holiday he wanted to go to the farm. He could ride horses, help his uncles. It was a bit of a family joke, his two great big uncles with little Paul always tagging along. I've got a picture in my mind of one hot lazy afternoon, his little bum bouncing around on the tractor seat, he's driving this enormous tractor, pulling a cart filled with hay bales. He's dusty and dirty and tired but filled with self-importance and just loving it. I reckon kids like him who love something, doesn't matter what it is, are really lucky. Dennis, my other son, was always restless, a bit like me I suppose, never knew what he wanted. I reckon he wouldn't have gotten into trouble with those cars if he'd had something to focus on, like his brother."

Tom was offered a better job in the inner city and occasionally this new job led to his working on sets for theater productions. This experience awakened a longing buried within him, and he began doing voluntary work backstage on set construction and design. He had a flair for it and became more deeply involved, was given more responsibilities and was soon helping in production, even doing some acting. He had a strong tenor voice, it was raw, untrained, but appealing. He felt a passion he'd never experienced before and in his own inarticulate way he felt a "bursting out." He enjoyed the camaraderie of the theater company and found he had an unexpected gift for teaching some of his skills to the backstage workers.

His creativity, which had produced such clumsy inventions as a child, now came to the fore, and he discovered that he had a knack for bringing special effects into their productions.

"We did *My Fair Lady* one year. It's hard to do anything really different with that show because everybody's seen the film, but the producer and I came up with a great scene. In the ballroom set, I rigged up a set like one of those Hollywood musicals with different levels and mirrors on the walls. I had the mirrors moving slightly from side to side. It gave the impression of a vast space filled with light and dancing; it looked fantastic. I made a miniature set at home, and I experimented with light and mirrors. I used some electric motors out of my son Dennis's train set. He wasn't very happy about it at the time."

Tom had now totally forgotten where he was. This was his story and he had an interested listener. He went on.

"Two young blokes helped me with that set. Gee, it was tricky. We had to get all the mirrors at the right angles, and we had to synchronize their movements so they were out of phase with each other. It sounds very gimmicky, I know, but it worked. The two young lads couldn't believe how good it looked."

Betty had sensed Tom's restlessness for some time. He had glimpsed so many other possibilities through his work in the theater that his carpentry had become just a means to an end. He was excited yet apprehensive. Which way to turn? Betty suggested that he become a teacher. She'd heard some of the others comment on how patient Tom was with the boys on the set.

He ridiculed the idea at first because he was a little intimidated at the prospect, but the more he thought about it the more it appealed to him. He could use his trade skills, work with kids, and the money was quite good. The security aspect appealed too. He joined the Education Department and loved it. He stayed at his first school for three years.

Tom found that he had a natural authority; he had no problems with discipline. He enjoyed his students, who called him "Chippy" behind his back, and was highly regarded.

Tom was very pleased with himself when he got a promotion to an inner-city trade school. His pleasure was abruptly halted on the first day. The last person the school wanted was another woodwork teacher and those who were already there weren't about to move over for a newcomer.

As Tom described his feelings of displacement and rejection it seemed to trigger other disquieting thoughts. He passed over that time quickly and went on.

"The principal offered me a position in the new drama

department. I was really pleased. Each day was a joy. I used to tell Betty that no man could be luckier. I thought nothing of working until two in the morning or working over the weekend. I was doing what I loved."

Tom was the only teacher in the small drama department with any technical background, and he began to specialize in television production. This became a separate department, and eventually he had a staff of eight. Over the years he had borrowed from other departments, successfully put in submissions for extra funding and convinced the principal to buy some secondhand equipment. He installed much of it himself during holidays and weekends.

He was head of that department for 10 years and was enormously proud of what he had achieved. Two large studios with separate control rooms, a computer-controlled lighting system, a technical workshop and a record of achievement, with many of his former students imbued with his energy and enthusiasm.

Tom continued to teach, administer and be an advocate for his department. He had four other teachers, a secretary, a technical manager and two technical assistants.

"I started to get tired: it wasn't so much fun after a while. I felt like I was battling everyone. There was never enough money, and the new principal kept stealing my teachers. He was always ready to take credit for the department, but he would never back me up - not like the old boss, I could talk to him. This new guy would never look at you.

"I knew we could cut back in some areas, but we had to keep the equipment maintained. Well, they cut out one of the technical assistants, and the other two couldn't keep up, so I started doing some of the easy repair work myself. I also set up a program to bring across some of the kids doing electronics to help out, but the boss wasn't interested.

"We were being starved of funds, and he was stealing my teachers and my technicians. I could have handled all that, but the big problem was the students. My God, they'd changed! Most of them didn't even seem interested in learning, least of all what I was teaching."

Tom's manner changes and he gives this information reluctantly, distractedly, in disordered bits over several visits. He stumbles, becomes confused, rages, cries.

Tom's record contrasts oddly with his manner and appearance. He tells of his struggles and successes in a faltering, questioning manner as if he is describing the deeds of a stranger. He shakes, his mouth quivers, and he cries bitter, sad tears. He loses track of his story and becomes confused, his thick, sausage fingers intertwining restlessly. He now looks impotent and bewildered. He is surprised when the first session finishes and awkwardly confides that he couldn't sleep the night before and was shaking in the car on the journey to the office. He grasps my explanation for his trouble like a thirsty man gulping down water.

Over the next few visits Tom describes more about the events leading up to his breakdown.

"I hadn't felt right for the last two or three years. I was tired and cranky and kept making stupid mistakes. I wiped a kid's video that he had been working on for four months. I felt terrible. I'd done that job hundreds of times without any trouble, and I stuffed it up.

"The kids were different. They seemed to be there to keep them off the streets, and they didn't give a damn. We couldn't even put toilet paper in the bathrooms because they'd set fire to it. In one day, eight toilet bowls were smashed. They stole everything that wasn't nailed down.

"A lot of the teachers seemed to have given up. The last year was the worst because we were split into a secondary school and adult training section, and I chose to go with the school section because I felt I had more to offer them, but most of the equipment and all the technical staff went with adult training. I was back where I had started - a one-man band - and I had to do my own photocopying and even my own typing."

Tom could hardly speak at this point as he described his desperate search for a remedy.

"The student counselor was a good friend and in that last year she set up stress management courses. I did all of them:I listened to tapes, I did exercises, I did relaxation, but it was no good. I could feel myself slipping. I couldn't sleep, I wasn't eating. I was irritable all the time, and I couldn't remember things; silly things, like how to operate a machine I'd been using for years.

"I saw my doctor in October because my wife insisted I go. He said I should stop, but I thought I could hang on until the end of the year. A month later, I began crying at home, and I knew I couldn't go to work. I've never been back."

Tom expected to get back to work quickly and began planning to work in areas away from teaching. Over the first six months he alternated between periods of extreme exhaustion and frenzied efforts to restore his health. He had appointments with several doctors and was having naturopathy, herbal treatments and vitamin supplements. Nothing seemed to help.

At about the time that Tom had become so involved in his own drama department, Betty felt that she wanted to do more. When they first moved to the city, she missed her family and friends and had been a little disappointed and hurt that people seemed to go their own ways. There was no sense of community that she had grown used do. She half-heartedly tried becoming involved at the boys' school, but it was more of the same, a lot of hard work, but this time without the sense of belonging that she had previously enjoyed. She alternated between thoughts of study and paid work and, on impulse, applied for and got a job as a part time clerical assistant. Within a short time she was offered a law clerk's job. Her boss invited her to do some training courses, and she gradually became more involved in the management of the staff.

Betty was sympathetic to Tom's problems, but found his constant ruminations about the job and himself frustrating and boring, although she was reluctant to admit this to anyone, even to herself, because she knew he was in so much anguish.

His mood was such a contrast to her own enthusiasm for work, that coming home started to become an ordeal. She felt she was living a double life. As she came in the drive she had to put on her other face, be patient and listen.

At times her patience wore thin. She'd feel angry, with whom she was never quite sure, and then guilty. The boys quickly learned when to keep out of her way and this made her feel worse.

Betty was filled with concern for Tom but found that nothing she did seemed to help. She watched with a feeling of helplessness as he went from one treatment and one idea to another, all the time getting worse. News of yet another herbalist was the end. Betty decided she would have to shock him out of this useless activity and told him that unless he stopped, she would go. Tom was devastated.

"I think I was off my head in those first few months. I felt incredibly exhausted, but I kept thinking there had to be an answer. It was working in another job, in advertising, television or the movies. The doctors were telling me to go back to work, and I kept hoping I could, but I felt even sicker thinking about it.

"The main thing I remember - and I don't remember much about that time - was feeling totally exhausted. All I really wanted to do was sleep. When my wife put her foot down, I just folded up. For about three weeks I felt like a baby - I was helpless - it was like I had finally admitted to myself that I couldn't go on."

Over the next 12 months, Tom's recovery began. He was still exhausted, his sleeping pattern was erratic, he was irritable and kept to himself, he couldn't trust himself with people. His self-confidence was at rock bottom. He was frightened of leaving home, felt very dependent on his wife and, although he was grateful to her, he found he was irritable with her and rejected her affection. She felt confused and puzzled and several times felt close to leaving him.

Tom was bored and restless. He could read the newspaper and watch some television, but he couldn't read anything more challenging, and his concentration span was very short.

"The thing I found so hard during that year was how unstable and out of control I felt. I couldn't tell from day to day how I would feel. I learned that I had to avoid all sorts of things - birthdays, weddings, parties, reunions, even Christmas Day was an ordeal. I felt on show. I knew I couldn't escape, but I had nothing to say - I felt like such an idiot. I was frightened I'd disgrace myself by bursting into tears."

Tom's story is typical of someone who has had a stress breakdown. There is a pattern of a gradual build-up of stressful events culminating in a breakdown. Although there were warning signals, neither Tom nor his doctors realized their significance.

As Tom's stress symptoms became worse, he became less able to cope. He tried to work harder but became even more exhausted, thus compounding his difficulties. The downward spiral of fatigue, memory problems and a reduced ability to defend himself made him a less effective teacher, father and husband, adding to his despair and confusion. His breakdown was a logical consequence.

Helen

We have chosen to tell Helen's story because it represents a contrast to those of Tom and Margaret. Not because of her early life, which like theirs was filled with the usual dramas and joys present in most people's upbringing, or because of the series of events that brought Helen and her family to crisis point. The contrast lies in the fact that the downward spiral towards Helen's breakdown was halted.

As Helen spoke, her honesty was transparent. Her whole body mirrored her tale and, although her words were simple, she had come to understand a good deal about herself. She was in her early 30s, a small sparrow-like woman with an alert, chirpy manner who was in constant motion, cleaning, cooking, fussing. Her burly husband Peter had a casual manner and seemed resigned to Helen's frenetic activity, although clearly he was proud of his wife and proud of the way she coped with him and their two children, Michael and Sophie. Their house was small and in need of repainting but was always clean.

The garden had also responded to Helen's energy. She mowed the lawn, trimmed the edges, killed the weeds and regimented the flowers.

There were no trees; she thought them too messy.

Peter was content with the house, but Helen had plans to move to a larger house in a new suburb. She was always pushing Peter to get a promotion at his job, to get more money, more status; she was planning for their future. Peter was a leading hand in a car factory. He worked night shift, which he enjoyed because the factory was quieter.

There was a lot to admire about this woman - drive, ambition, care - but you could see why Peter had chosen the night shift.

Helen, like other migrants suddenly thrown into an unfamiliar environment, had a mixture of feelings about her early life, but regret was not one of them.

"I came from Greece with my family when I was 10. My parents came from a little village a long way from Athens. They've known each other all their lives. My Dad's father was the village blacksmith, and my Mum's father was a farmer. I can remember the school and small white houses. My Dad's family stayed there, but my Mom's brothers and sisters came to Australia. They were the ones who got Mom and Dad to come here too.

"I can remember going to school here in Australia and not speaking any English. There were some other Greek girls there, but we were teased a lot and called names like 'Wog' and 'Glicks.' My brothers were all older than me, and they used to fight kids who talked bad to me.

"I went to high school for a couple of years, but then I left. My Mom and Dad were working in factories, and I had to do a lot of the housework. They're from the old country, and they didn't think girls needed much school. I'm going to make sure my kids go to the university. I don't want them doing factory work!

"I stayed home for a year or two after I left school. It was a bit lonely, but then I got a job as a machinist in a factory. I liked that job and stayed there for a few years. I was really fast and the boss used to say, 'I wish I had twenty Helens'."

Helen's face softened as she spoke of weekly family gatherings at her uncle's house. They were obviously still a close family. Aunts, uncles, cousins and friends got together to enjoy lots of eating, drinking and dancing. Helen's cousin started to bring Peter along.

He was a leading hand at the car factory where her cousin worked. Her parents observed Helen's interest in Peter and approved. Why not? He was Greek, seemed nice and had a good job. Helen recalled her first impressions.

"Peter was so big he used to scare me. He had a big, deep voice and he'd laugh louder and dance longer than anyone. I used to flirt with him. I don't think he noticed at first, but then he became interested. We were engaged for a long time and we bought the house then with help from our parents. We had a wonderful wedding - we had 400 guests. My Dad used to say he was glad he only had one daughter."

Helen continued working until she became pregnant with Michael, returned to work for a while and then stopped again when Sophie was born.

There were obvious differences in Helen and Peter's approaches to life. While Helen pushed for something better, Peter resisted her efforts. He was happy with the way things were and was resistant to change; he was quiet while she was a "chatterbox" and she had enough energy for both of them.

"The house is all right. I think it's a bit small and old, and I wish we could live away from the city more. I've always dreamed of a big brick house with lots of garden out in the suburbs. Peter didn't seem to care where we lived. I was always the one pushing him. He used to say I was too fussy, even though he'd tell our friends what a great little woman I was. But he used to make me so angry! He'd just wander around. He wouldn't do any work on the house. I'd nag him and he'd just laugh at me. He was happy just dancing and drinking wine. He'd say, 'Helen, you're too serious, you've got to laugh more.'

"He'd go fishing with my Dad; he used to love it. They'd sit on the pier for hours and he'd take the kids sometimes. They'd go early in the morning sometimes and stay all day. I'd go sometimes, but it was boring. I had things to do at home. I think he liked the peace and quiet. I know he thought that I'd be telling him to do things at home. I would too, I wanted to get the house painted and the garden fixed.

"I went to another factory for a while after Sophie was born, but the factory closed down, and I lost my job. I was really lucky to get the cleaning job with the council. Peter didn't like it so much because he'd get home from work and have to look after the kids before they went to school. I used to start work at five in the morning and work for four hours. My boss, Vincent, was Greek too. He was a good man; he knew I was a good worker. The city manager was nice too. I used to clean his office and he'd be really pleased. I used to bring flowers from my garden and put them in a vase on his desk." Helen's eyebrows rose, again the note of surprise. Why wouldn't you bring flowers for a nice man like Mr. Thomas? With this job, Helen could see that her plans might become realities.

"I really liked my job there. While I was working, I used to dream about the house we'd buy and how I'd fix it up. I didn't say much to Peter because he'd laugh at me. I wanted a swimming pool for the kids and I wanted them to go to a good school. I don't think the school they go to now is very good for them, especially for Michael, he's the one I worry about. The doctor says he's hyperactive. Peter says he got it from me! He gets really worked up and then he'll carry on like a baby: he'll kick and scream. Sometimes, I swear to God, I want to kill him. Peter used to just pick him up and carry him around the house over his shoulder until he went quiet. If Peter wasn't there, I got mad at him and I started yelling and that made him worse.

"I worry because he's got asthma too and when he yells like that he can have an attack. I don't know how many times I've had to take him to the hospital in the middle of the night. They say he's too fat and I should make him diet. How do you do that with a 10-year-old? I think he's going to grow big and fat like his father."

Helen was bustling and ambitious. A little dynamo at her job and at home. She was demanding of herself and her family, but she was happy. Her dream might come true.

Peter's accident at work changed all that, not all at once, but slowly, bit by bit. Peter was doing a job he'd done a thousand times before when he slipped and fell back awkwardly, landing on the corner of a large press. He injured his back and couldn't move at first because of the pain. He was taken to the factory medical center where he had X-rays and then he was brought home.

Over the next year or two he went through the familiar round of specialists, physiotherapists, examinations, more X-rays, a back brace, promises and pain. He received workers' compensation but this was only half his normal income because of his shift work and overtime. The prospects of the new house receded. Helen's dreams began to fade and only a loan from Helen's parents enabled them to keep their house.

Helen became very upset as she described the change in Peter. At first they thought he would get better quickly but, when he didn't, he became a different person. Her big, smiling husband became an angry, demanding recluse. He yelled at Helen, he yelled at the kids. He refused to go out, even to her uncle's place and resented Helen for leaving him. She suspected that there were lots of things he could do for himself but he was constantly asking for help to get dressed, to bathe, even to shave and to go to the toilet. She was angry.

"He'd stay home all the time, but he'd never help; he'd just complain all the time. 'The vacuum cleaner is too loud, the kids are making too much noise, turn off the television.' I swear to God!

Sometimes I was shaving him and I'd think, 'You make one more complaint and I'll cut your bloody throat!' just like that and I'd shake his old cut throat razor behind his head. He used to expect me to take him to all his appointments. I'd have to drive, and I'd get nervous in the city, and he'd yell at me, and then I'd drop him off and try to park, and he'd complain because I kept him waiting. I'd get so tired but he wouldn't seem to notice."

Signs of stress were rippling through the family - Peter's anger, depression and helplessness, Helen's irritability and exhaustion. The children started to show it too. Michael's asthma and his demanding behavior got worse. There were huge yelling matches between Peter and Michael, with Helen being called in to "get Michael out of the way." Michael's teacher even contacted Helen about the deterioration in his work and his attitude at school. Sophie, normally so placid, became querulous and cranky. It didn't finish there either. Helen's Mom and Dad got upset because Peter wouldn't speak to them and then Helen's brothers got cross with her for upsetting them. Helen didn't know which way to turn.

"My job was the only place I could go where I could get any peace - no one yelled, and people liked what I did. I was so tired. Everyone seemed to get on my back - Peter, Michael, my Mom and Dad, especially when my Dad retired. They kept coming around.

"I'd have a cup of tea with them in the kitchen. Peter wouldn't speak and he'd turn the television on in the lounge room and Michael was running in and out with Peter yelling at him. Mom would cry and say to me, 'What have we done wrong, why does he hate us?' It was terrible, but even with all that going on I was okay. I knew I was tired but I was okay - until Vincent went away."

At this stage, although showing some signs of stress, Helen was still coping remarkably well. Her job was particularly important to her because it gave her relief and confidence. She knew that even though she had less energy, she was still more efficient than most of the other cleaners. That all changed when Vincent went on leave for two months and one of the other cleaners, Max, who'd been there for about 10 years, was made acting supervisor. Max was a surly, dirty man who was lazy and divisive. Max resented Helen because Vincent had kept praising her to the other cleaners, using her as an example of how they should do their work. Max saw his chance to get even; Helen was now very much at risk.

"That Max, he was a pig, he'd trap me on the stairs and he'd tell me, 'Helen, I'm in charge now, you must do what I say.' He kept making me do other people's work. Some of them wouldn't turn up or would come late and he'd make me do their jobs. He'd say he could sack me. I was scared, we really needed the money.

"I had two or three more offices every day and then he'd walk over my mopped floor in his dirty boots or he'd empty ashtrays on the ground. He was just a pig! One day I told him I wouldn't do the extra work, I'd had enough."

Max reported her to Mr. Thomas, the city manager. Ron Thomas was new to the job and was not familiar with Max and he'd noticed that Helen wasn't as thorough as she had been. He didn't question Helen about it, he simply told her that she was not doing her work properly and if her attitude didn't improve, she would be sacked.

"I was so angry, I thought I would burst - that nice Mr. Thomas - he was so horrible to me. I cried and ran out of the room. I swear to God I would have quit right then, but I was so worried about money."

Within six weeks, Helen's condition deteriorated rapidly and she was showing all the signs of severe stress. The stress had built up gradually at home since Peter's accident and now work, her only source of relief, had become a further burden. She had severe headaches, didn't eat and lost eight kilos. Each day she was feeling more exhausted and less able to manage. Even Peter noticed how morose and jumpy she was, although she hadn't told him what was happening at work. What was the use, she thought, it would only make him feel worse.

Her mother, fearing that Helen had cancer, made her go to the family doctor for tests, but nothing was found. Helen felt betrayed at work and trapped at home. She had to work to keep her family together.

"I knew I couldn't do it. I'd sit on the stairs and wonder how I could keep going."

Helen was on the verge of a breakdown. She saw no way out. Vincent returned and took action as soon as he saw how sick she looked.

"Vincent took one look at me and said, 'Helen what's happened?' I began crying and told him the whole story. I told him about Max and Mr. Thomas. I told him about Peter and Michael and my Mom and Dad. I told him everything.

"He went to see Mr. Thomas straight away and told him the whole story. He told me later that Max had been telling Mr. Thomas that I was stealing money from the offices. Vincent told Mr. Thomas the truth. Mr. Thomas called me in and apologized. He drove me to the doctor who gave me four weeks off work."

Vincent's intervention went further. He called around to see Peter to tell him what had happened and to let him know that he had arranged for someone to come and help in the house two or three times a week while Helen was off work. He also had a few words with Peter about not helping his wife and, surprisingly, Peter seemed to listen. The whole event had shaken Peter. He even agreed to see Vincent's back specialist when Vincent made an appointment for him.

Helen spent the first two weeks in bed, just resting. She had been shocked too at how ill she felt.

"Peter began doing a bit more. Vincent came around a few times and he'd give him a pep talk. The best news was that the new back doctor thought he could really help Peter with an operation. Peter went into the hospital a few weeks after I went back to work. We still have to see if it's been successful or not but he feels much better. One day I heard him laugh in the old way. It was the best sound in the world.

"He started talking about going back to work. They had a dispatch clerk's job there they thought he could do."

Helen recovered quickly once the pressure on her eased, but she had learned a good deal about her family and herself. The urgency had gone out of her housework, the ambitions now forgotten. She had her family back again.

"I think that Vincent is a beautiful man. But for him I would be dead or in the hospital with a breakdown.

"I often wondered what a breakdown must be like. It must be terrible to be even worse than I was."

There are several differences between her situation and those of Tom and Margaret. Helen never really lost her capacity to cope, even though she was slipping at the end. As soon as she was away from pressure and able to rest, she began to improve. And she improved very quickly. Within three months she was almost completely well again. Her symptoms had never become as severe or as chronic as those of Tom and Margaret.

3

Breaking Down - What Happens

"Breaking down" is a dramatic term and a shocking experience for those involved. Understandably, it is the focus of our attention. The event itself, however, has usually been a long time brewing, although some disasters are so massive they can suddenly overwhelm even the strongest.

The drama of the moment of "falling apart" fades with the painful re-adjustments that inevitably occur over the next few months and years. A breakdown has a time of build-up, a time of impact and a time of resolution. Although we will focus on the impact in this chapter, we will also look briefly at the build-up and the resolution.

The build-up involves mounting strains for weeks, months, sometimes years. The breakdown itself can be triggered by new pressures or may occur gradually, inevitably.

Impact is the moment of breakdown and is a highly charged time for most people. For some, there is an explosion of intense emotion, crying, raging or shaking with fear. Others find they have gone blank, as if their minds have switched off. Sometimes people feel as if all the circuits in their brains have become entangled; they feel totally confused. Breaking down for some is akin to dying.

The resolution is the time following breakdown; it is at once intensely painful and extremely demoralizing. People feel totally dependent on their family and friends for even the simplest of life's demands.

Some people recognize that they have had a breakdown immediately. For others, however, this awareness may only come after weeks, months, sometimes years. Some fight it until they are totally exhausted; others find a curious peace in letting go and allowing themselves to crumble.

All agree that their lives have changed irretrievably. Some find their breakdown has forced changes in their lives, which make their existence richer and more rewarding than before.

The build-up

Most breakdowns occur after a long build-up. This may be caused by such factors as ill health, relationship difficulties, work pressures, financial setbacks and excessive alcohol or drug use.

Together they produce unpleasant feelings of tension and anxiety. Some people endeavor to reduce this anxiety by using alcohol or drugs. These kinds of "solutions" may aggravate other problems and a vicious circle can be set up.

The build-up to a breakdown is obvious to some. Tom knew that he was in trouble for at least a year before he broke down, but he had no idea that the consequences would be so severe. Other people seem oblivious to their insidious decline, although it is perfectly clear to their family and friends. Some people are so closed, so guarded that their breakdown comes as a complete shock to everyone.

Some, like Margaret, expect to cope with everything and see themselves as invincible. Others, by contrast, seem to be in a race. Which will happen first, their retirement or their breakdown? Many are frightened of leaving the job that is "killing" them because it is the only trade they know.

Trapped

Tom was feeling pressure from a lack of help, a lack of appreciation by the administration and a lack of interest shown by his students. He was angry at the school, at the students and even at himself. His life had become a burden and nothing he did seemed to improve his situation.

"I knew something was going on inside me, but I thought that if I could just get through to my holidays, I would be okay. I'd tried relaxation and stress management courses so I could keep going. I hoped they would miraculously fix everything up. But I realize now that I was too far gone."

It was only many months later that Tom was able to recognize that he had been in trouble for three years at least and his efforts to remedy the situation in that last year now seemed desperately ineffectual.

Burn-out

There are some whose decline is so gradual that feeling bad seems very familiar. Although clearly they don't enjoy it, they are not motivated to make any changes. Their decline, however, is usually obvious to the people close to them because their moods and their behavior alter.

Brendan, a 28-year-old unmarried social worker had been working with young people since his graduation. He had an outgoing, cheerful personality and at first he had a great deal of success with many of the adolescents he supervised.

He had lived with his girlfriend for several years and their home had become a drop-in center for many of the youngsters in the area. Jeannie, his girlfriend, worked in the same department. Gradually, Brendan found it more of an effort to keep going.

"The case load kept increasing and the kids I was seeing seemed to have insoluble problems: rape, incest, car theft, prostitution - you name it - and one of my kids had seen it, injected it, done it or had it done to them. I know it sounds really cynical, but they all seemed such losers and I kept thinking, why do I bother? Jeannie tells me now that I've been a misery for two years. I knew I wasn't enjoying my work, or my life really, but it seemed impossible to change. Nothing really dramatic happened. I just seemed to slide downhill. Over the past year it has seemed harder and harder to get out of bed in the morning.

"I remember laughing ironically when someone at work said they had woken up one morning recently not looking forward to the day. I thought that was the way everyone felt."

Brendan applied for a transfer to the head office where he would be away from direct contact with people. Jeannie had pushed him to take this step, but his heart was not in the move when he was interviewed and when his application was unsuccessful, he seemed to visibly diminish and go into his shell even more. Jeannie was becoming very frightened.

Concealed build-up

Some people, many of them men, are so unaware of their inner life and so reluctant to show any "weakness" that they conceal from everyone, including themselves, that they are in any sort of trouble. They are often loners who have always been emotionally isolated.

Stan was a police constable who was stationed in a country town. He'd been in the force for 12 years and had moved to the town with his wife and two children. They had been there five years and his wife was happy for them to stay there until he retired.

Stan was a mystery to his colleagues as he was a loner. He was competent but showed no real flair. He'd always been in uniform and had no ambition for promotion or for criminal investigation work. He seemed to enjoy routine police work: patrolling the streets, picking up drunks and keeping the peace. During his off-duty hours he liked fishing and shooting. He usually went alone, leaving the socializing and parenting to his wife.

There had been unrest at the station because of under-staffing.

It should have had a senior sergeant, two sergeants and eight men, but sick leave, staff away on training courses and lack of recruiting had halved that number. This was a particular problem during the fruit-picking season when the district was flooded with pickers who were determined to have a good time after their hard days in the fields. "Keeping the peace" became an exhausting process of 12-hour days for weeks on end. They were dealing with drunks, fights, occasional murders, car smashes and rapes. The police were abused, spat on and threatened.

Stan seemed to take all this in his stride and did not join in the grouching and resentment of the other men. He seemed unaffected until he was badly beaten in a pub brawl. This hotel was notorious as a trouble spot and it was the policy for police to go there with a partner.

This time there was no one available and Stan had to go in alone. He was scared although determined not to show any signs of fear. He waded into the fray with his truncheon and fists. He was never one to shirk a fight. On this occasion, the mob in the pub turned on him and he was punched, kicked around the head and body and knocked out.

He could have been killed and was lucky to escape with cuts and bruises. He was in the local hospital overnight and was home for a few days. He went back to work a little quieter and a little more withdrawn.

A few months later Stan was involved in another dangerous incident. He was working alone again and he was sent to a farm where a deranged dairy farmer was holding his family hostage in the dairy. Stan spoke to the farmer for a few minutes and then jumped him. In the scuffle the gun discharged and the farmer was wounded.

The incident was investigated and although Stan was commended for tackling the farmer, he was reprimanded for being too impatient. He was told that he should have waited longer before moving in.

The other men were angry about the lack of support Stan got from the "bosses." It was after this investigation that his workmates noticed that Stan seemed more withdrawn than ever and a certain grim intensity had crept into his manner.

He finished work one day and drove to a nearby town. He checked into a motel and drank a bottle of whisky and took a handful of sleeping tablets.

He woke up in the motel two days later, showered, dressed and went back to work as if nothing had happened. His family was frantic, his colleagues worried. He seemed surprised by their concern and resisted getting any help. He saw the local doctor reluctantly. He began to cry in

Dr. Wilson's office and was placed off work. He was never able to return to police work.

Superwoman

Some people are so unaware of the extent of the build-up of pressure within them that they expect to continue to perform at high levels of tension indefinitely.

Margaret knew that she was a strong, capable woman. After all, she had coped with a marriage failure, solo parenthood and a devastating bushfire and its aftermath. She had even coped with her daughter's murder. She kept pushing herself to the limit - she knew no other way - and it had always worked for her before. But she was very close to her limit and when she exceeded it, she "fell apart."

"I was mourning Melinda, I was filled with a longing for her and I was drained and empty. But I was working and still going to council as well as looking after my other two kids.

"I think that if her murderer had been a stranger I would have been okay. The fact that it was Jack seemed to tip me over the edge. Once that happened I seemed to plummet."

"Soldiering on"

Many people know that they are heading for trouble but feel they have no other options. They hope that something will turn up to "make it all better" and, in the meantime, they soldier on.

George had been a fireman for 35 years, that was all he knew. Until his accident, he had loved the job, but since then his working life had become an endurance test. He could only try to hang on until he could retire with honor. Now he lives alone, separated from his family and unable to work. He stays on the family property, a few hectares on the outskirts of the city where he had worked for so long.

George is a solidly built man with a battered, "lived-in" face and a gruff manner. He had married young and his children were now fully grown. He and his wife had been close. They had bought the small farm to keep their children's horses and to satisfy George's yearning to have a piece of land for himself and his family to share. He had been a fireman since he was 21.

The fire service had given him more than his job. He'd met all his friends through the service and it dominated his life. He was a respected figure, although a little too stern to be popular.

Like most firemen, he'd had his share of narrow escapes. He received a bad acid burn in one fire and another time he was wearing breathing apparatus in a smoke-filled factory and became disoriented, close to panic. Firefighting is a dangerous job and he'd had innumerable cuts, sprains and other small injuries for which he had taken some time off.

He was made a station officer eventually and placed in charge of a small suburban fire station, where he worked for five years before he was forced to stop.

"I was a few years older than most of the men. They were a good bunch but they were inclined to be a little careless at times, so I kept a pretty tight check on them. I knew a few tricks of the trade, so they knew they couldn't pull any swifties on me.

"I liked the station and I was looking forward to working there until my retirement. I was injured on the day we were called to the house fire in Station Street. The little timber house was well and truly alight when we got there.

"Those house fires can be quite tricky because the fire can look like its out but it's actually still smoldering up in the roof and a bit of extra draft can set it off again.

"We had the fire well under control, but we were worried about one of the occupants, a young woman who had been staying with the family. I went in to have a look. I was in the living room and it looked safe enough and then, crash, the roof fell on me."

George was crushed under the debris. His men frantically dug him out. He woke up in hospital later that day, with a massive headache and extensive superficial burns.

"I felt really stuffed. The burns were okay; it was that hit on the head! They let me out two days later and I went back to work after a week at home. I couldn't seem to settle down. I felt fuzzy, I couldn't seem to think straight and that headache was like the worst hangover you've ever had."

George insisted on going back to work early. He hoped that as soon as he got his health back he would improve.

"I still felt confused, the headache was better, but my nerves had gone. I was hanging back; suddenly I'd gotten scared. It was terrible, I remember seeing it happen to other blokes and thinking what bloody wimps they were.

"I was uptight going to work and I'd jump whenever the phone rang. I worried about letting the other blokes down because I was so bloody scared I thought I'd do the wrong thing and some poor bugger would be killed."

George was unable to keep this hidden and he realized that his men were covering for him. He felt deeply ashamed and started to drink heavily to settle his nerves and to help him sleep.

He was unable to share any of his despair with his family or friends. His family found him cold, angry and unpredictable. His wife tried to talk to him and was repeatedly fended off. He hated her telling him he had to get out of the job. He just hoped something would happen, some miracle.

Blotting it out

Many people deal with anxiety by reaching for a glass or a tablet. The moderate use of alcohol and tranquilizers to dissolve tension, at least temporarily, can usually be justified, but when alcohol or drugs become the sole way of trying to cope with pressure, more problems result than are solved.

Alcohol and drug abuse certainly dim the pain temporarily, but they also reduce your work performance and cause havoc in families. The pattern we see is that alcohol begins to be used as a tranquilizer, often by someone who has never had a drinking problem before. Their alcohol consumption builds up to a crescendo until the point of breakdown and then rapidly dies away again afterwards.

Ultimately, the "breaking down" process is accelerated by heavy drug or alcohol use so that physical health declines and chronic intoxication further erodes the body's already depleted coping skills. After the point of breakdown occurs, people find that their alcohol and drug tolerance has fallen considerably so even small quantities make them feel ill.

Swamped

The combination of frustration and fatigue are particularly potent in leading to a breakdown. Dawn, a young, energetic woman, came to this point with the burden of being a young mother. She had been an executive secretary with a large oil company, where she had met her husband. They had both been transferred to work in the head office in another city. Dawn and Andy were both ambitious and had great plans for the future.

"This was my dream. The lovely house, the nice furniture, the three, cute kids all smiling and playing happily together, the immaculate kitchen. It was going to be so wonderful. Andy and I put off having a family so we could buy a good house and furnish it well and have our own nest ready for our family. No one told me how exhausted and cranky I would get, how Andy and I would fight over nothing and how I'd feel like screaming with frustration at having to change another nappy or clean up another mess."

Dawn smiled ruefully in the midst of the chaos of the living room. The television set was blaring out Sesame Street music and her two toddlers were gleefully dragging cushions around the room. Magazines were scattered over the floor and her youngest, sitting in his high chair like Lord Muck, was banging his spoon and spraying the kitchen with baby food all the while laughing, gurgling and messing his pants.

"No one told me about babies crying all night or breast feeding until I thought my nipples were being chewed off. Oh, I know there are good times, but just lately they've been few and far between. I'm not interested in sex, and I know Andy feels hurt, but I don't care at the moment."

Dawn had coped well with her first two children although young Robbie, her second child, had severe eczema and asthma and was a squally, crying, irritable child. His asthma was severe, and he was in and out of hospital for years. He was very sweet but a picture of misery at times with his skin red, roughened and weeping with sores all over his body and his wheezing just loud enough to wake Dawn at night with a start.

Andy did what he could to help Dawn and, although money was tight at first, on just his income alone they survived quite well, although they couldn't afford to run two cars. Dawn would bundle the two young ones into baby seats, drive her husband to the station and have the use of the car during the day and pick him up in the evening. Sometimes she couldn't be bothered with all the fuss just to keep the car during the day and then she would be stuck at home.

Dawn had all sorts of plans for things she could do at home. cooking exotic dishes, running up curtains and cushion covers on her sewing machine, if she could learn how to operate it! But, she never had the time or the energy.

"I was just coping with Sally and Robbie. Robbie's health was really a worry but I was getting by. Then I became pregnant again. I dreaded this one; I didn't know how I could possibly cope. Andy tried to reassure me, but he had no idea and I didn't want to talk to my mother or sisters. Anyway, they were all interstate and, after all, they seemed to cope. My grandmother had eight children and I was worrying about three. Andy told me I was being silly and that I would find it a breeze!"

Andy received a promotion during Dawn's pregnancy and he was frequently away interstate. He was becoming a little tired and irritable himself and he was annoyed that the house was always such a mess. He wanted to organize home help and couldn't understand Dawn's reluctance - she felt embarrassed about needing assistance.

Timmy was born after a prolonged labor in which Dawn used up the last of her energy. She insisted on breast feeding him and refused any extra help. He had colic for the first few months; Dawn's life became one long nightmare of screaming babies, asthma, eczema, food, laundry and despair.

"I didn't feel like I loved them any more - they just seemed to be consuming me - even Andy. I just wished they'd all go away and then I'd feel like I was a wicked mother and I would force myself to be nice to them when I was feeling like I could hurt them. I don't think Andy knew how bad I was so I don't really blame him for what happened."

Unexpectedly, Andy was sent on an overseas business trip for two weeks. Dawn was too tired to protest and anyway she was even looking forward to him being away because he seemed to have become so critical of her.

Three nights after Andy left, Robbie's asthma worsened; his wheeze became much louder and he was starting to go a bit blue. Dawn became frantic and rushed the other two into the car and strapped them into their baby seats. She bundled Robbie in a blanket and drove to the children's hospital wearing a stained dressing gown over her nightdress and bare feet.

"I remember panicking. I knew he was going to die - I just knew it. I don't know how I avoided crashing the car. We got to the emergency department and I couldn't get out. I was crying and Robbie was blue and I just leaned on the horn and sobbed and sobbed."

Robbie survived. In fact, he was not particularly ill but Dawn had "cracked" and she was crying, incoherent and confused. She and the children were admitted to a convalescent home on an emergency basis. Dawn slept around the clock that first night and she stayed in the home for another two weeks. She remained upset and felt very guilty.

Andy cut short his business trip and arrived home within a few days. Dawn's family also rallied around. The crisis, the acute breakdown, was over but Dawn took many months to improve.

"I had to lose some of my stupid pride. My family really pitched in and I had home help twice a week. It took months for me to feel really close to Andy again, but I felt better about the children after I'd had a rest."

The social worker at the family home put Dawn in contact with a young mothers' support group, which gave her a social outlet and some contact with other women who had had similar experiences. She learned to become more realistic about her own expectations of herself and the children and to accept her limitations. Andy had had a terrific fright and he took responsibility for the children on two nights a week and one day on the weekend.

Dawn said later, "I've never really got myself back again the same. I still get exhausted and rattled and I worry about how I'll cope. I'm much better at letting the kids go and make a mess instead of trying to keep everything clean. I tell myself it's only for a few years. Robbie's asthma still gets bad and he has a special diet for his eczema, but I don't seem to panic about it now."

The impact

Many people recall the moment of breakdown with anguish, although for some, this recollection is confused or even a blank. Others find it etched on their memory with such vivid clarity that it haunts them forever.

This moment is often triggered by some extra pressure that is just enough to finally overwhelm their ability to cope.

Personal trauma

Modern life poses all sorts of dangers and every day some people are exposed to the possibility of sudden, violent death. Such incidents as bank hold-ups and car accidents seem mundane to the general public, but to those exposed to deaths from them, the affect is often devastating.

A bank robbery usually last about 90 seconds. The disguised bandit walks into the bank, produces a gun from a shopping bag, demands money, fills the bag and dashes to a getaway vehicle.

The trauma of an armed robbery, however, can last years. Some bank tellers who have been victims of hold-ups have suffered guilt, anxiety, sleeplessness and physical illnesses for months afterwards. Many will be unnaturally suspicious of people for years.

For these people, the sight of a shopping bag on the counter will be terrifying. A person wearing a motorbike helmet, knitted cap or sunglasses will have them ducking for cover. Eighty per cent of staff who have been victims of holdups suffer symptoms including headaches, insomnia and anxiety. It can take years for someone to recover from an armed hold-up, and in the meantime they will find it hard to cope with work.

The trigger

The triggering event for a breakdown may appear trivial, some minor incident that would otherwise go unnoticed. Brian was a parking attendant at the government offices. He was leaning through a driver's window answering a question when another car sped around the parked car, narrowly missing him.

He saw the wheel of the car as it passed within 10 centimeters of his foot. Similar situations had happened many times before but this time he was caught unawares and it shocked him. "I got a terrific fright and I couldn't stop shaking," he said. His recovery took many months.

For most of us the 'final straw' lies somewhere in between an event like this and a catastrophe.

George, the fireman rescued from the burning house, was just managing at work and at home. Eventually he could no longer maintain his precarious position and he broke down. The trigger was an incident at work.

"I was just hanging on, hoping something would change it all. One day something did. Nowadays we get called to a lot of accidents because we have the heavy equipment to cut people out of wrecks. It's a part of the job I've always hated.

"I really broke down when we were called to a car accident. A car had slammed into the back of a truck and the roof had been taken off at door height. The driver was thrown out and a young guy in the back was drunk and lying down; he was okay too.

"The two girls were badly injured. We only had one respirator, and I began using it on the girl in the front. I got a pulse, and I was just holding her steady when my mate in the back said the girl there was fading. She wasn't as badly injured as my one so I had to make a hard decision.

"I got in the back with the respirator, and we saved her, but I had to watch the girl in the front die. She was just a kid: barely 19 years old.

"I kept thinking of her parents and how they would feel and how I would feel if it was my daughter. Maybe I could have saved her. I couldn't tell anyone. How do you tell your wife that sort of thing? I felt like I was going to explode."

Slow motion breakdown

Sometimes there is no clearly defined trigger that tips the balance. Instead a point of recognition is reached that a breakdown has occurred.

Jerry, a bank manager, was only vaguely aware that something was amiss. He had enough reason to be stressed. In the four years he'd been working in the job, he had dealt with two staff walk outs over industrial issues, lack of support from management in instituting changes to improve staff conditions, two armed hold-ups, and a large number of business failures in the farming community that put strains on the bank managers in the area.

One day, the bank's accountant, disenchanted by Jerry's irritability, confronted him in his office and demanded that he get help. He saw his local doctor that afternoon and began shaking and crying in his office. He was placed off work and has never returned.

The "weekend breakdown"

An extended holiday or long-service leave will sometimes prompt the recognition of a work-related stress breakdown. After resting for a time, people recognize how exhausted they have been and how much they dread returning to work.

To survive in their job, they have been pushing down their symptoms. Tears and anger are close to the surface but are held back because of the shame and embarrassment at exposing their feelings to their workmates and to the public. They feel terrified of letting go and they are unaware that, despite their best efforts to control unpleasant feelings, their colleagues find them irritable, forgetful and unreliable.

When they are on holiday or on extended leave, there is not the same constraint on behavior so that when they are with their families, or alone, those feelings that have been bottled up for such a long time burst out. Then the floodgates open and feelings pour out unchecked. The holiday has provided the time and freedom to feel bad, to feel the misery held inside for years; it is safe for feelings to emerge.

Raging breakdown

It's like the eruption of a long-dormant volcano when this mixture of feelings explodes. Men, in particular, tend to break down with outbursts of rage and violence. They have far more difficulty in recognizing their inner state and fewer acceptable outlets for expressing it.

Tears and other expressions of sadness or despair are shameful to many men who pride themselves on being tough. George, for example, had been deeply distressed by the death of the young woman in the car accident.

"When I arrived home, there was no one there. I knew I needed help, but who could help me and what could they do? I started drinking to try and settle the raging feelings within me, but the booze just made me worse.

"I was sitting at the table and when the bottle was finished, I threw it against the wall. Then I really lost control. There was so much sadness and anger and confusion coming out. I tipped the table over and threw the chairs about. I kicked the TV over and smashed the mirror. By the time I'd finished, everything in the room, apart from Nancy's special pieces, had been overturned or smashed.

"Then I sat down and cried for a couple of hours before curling up in the chair. That was how Nancy found me. She dragged me off to the doctor.

"I think that if I hadn't destroyed the lounge room I might have killed myself or hurt someone else. I suppose, in a way, I did have control. After all I didn't smash Nancy's stuff, but I was really close to the edge."

George went off work for a few months. During this time, Nancy had quite enough of George's moods, his heavy drinking, his dependence on her and his jealousy.

He resented her leaving him to go shopping and he would question her at length about her activities away from home. Nancy felt she was living with a time bomb, one that would occasionally erupt and, in the end, Nancy left George. She could not tolerate his violence.

He drank more heavily when she left and was eventually admitted to a hospital to "dry out." He was in the hospital for three weeks and improved remarkably. Nancy and he began talking again although she was still frightened of his temper.

Nancy pleaded with him not to try working so soon, but he was determined and returned to his job. He lasted a week. He was shaking, sweating and very anxious. One of his oldest friends on the job arrived from headquarters and told him to "give it away." He was a danger to himself and his men. No one could rely on him. He's been off work ever since.

Confusion

Jeannie, Brendan's girlfriend, had finally had enough of his behavior and his temper. He kept making vague promises that he would do something, although that something was never made clear. She made an appointment with the union welfare officer and dragged Brendan to the appointment.

"The more she told Carol, the welfare person, the more upset I got. I could feel the tears flooding up from within and I couldn't stop crying. I could feel all that pain that I'd been pushing away for months and months."

Brendan broke down in Carol's office, sobbing and sobbing some more. He felt fragmented and distorted and couldn't seem to make sense out of what the two of them were saying. Later, much later, he realized that his breakdown was inevitable, given his depleted state. When he regained some composure, he left there to drive home.

"I remember Carol saying, 'Are you all right to drive home? Should I get you a taxi?' Jeannie had to go to work in her car and she offered to drive me home, but I insisted on driving.

"I don't remember the drive home. I couldn't work out where I was; nothing seemed familiar to me. I asked a young kid on a bike for directions, but I couldn't remember what my street was called.

"Eventually I arrived home. I tried to take my car for a service later that day, but I ended up in a totally different suburb five kilometers in the wrong direction. I turned the car around and drove home. I was lucky I didn't kill anyone on the way. I had no idea what I was doing. It felt like I was doing everything for the first time. I remember thinking that I was on a main bus route that went past the local hospital if I couldn't go on."

Brendan lost his ability to cope with daily activities almost completely. He stopped eating, he spent hours wandering the streets, frequently losing himself, and burst into tears in public with almost no provocation.

Later, during his recovery, he remembered little about this phase, which lasted for several months. He has vague snatches of memory: watching a neighbor's playful cat for hour after hour; listening to his accountant but failing to comprehend anything that he said.

"Jeannie used to leave me notes. She'd write them very large and put a few of them around the place. They'd say things like "bring in the washing" and I'd read them, but they didn't seem to register and I'd forget, or I'd do a few things and I'd forget the rest."

Brendan's confused state slowly improved over nine months. His doctor was worried that his symptoms suggested he might have a brain tumor, but all the test results were normal. Then his doctor thought that he may have been abusing drugs. Jeannie's response was to treat him like a young child at first, but as his confusion receded, he was able to do a little more around the house, like pick up his clothing and wash a few dishes, and she adjusted her attitude towards him.

Brendan returned to work 18 months after his breakdown, but was still slower than he had been and lacked stamina. He worked in the head office of his old department, in a computing job. He found this work much easier; he was pleased to be back.

Deadness

Margaret felt as if everything was dying around her; her vitality, warmth, love, all seemed to wither and die. For some time she lost interest in her surroundings and her mind seemed to live in a distant country.

"I felt dead for weeks. I didn't feel good, I didn't feel bad, I didn't feel anything. It was a sort of numbness. My own theory now is that I had taken so much I just couldn't take any more and my system just shut down.

"It was like someone had pulled the plug and I'd gone into hibernation. I didn't care. I didn't want to care. I could feel Andrew and the kids pulling me back and I didn't want to go back. If I did that I would have to start feeling terrible again."

The sense of deadness can last for many months. People who break down lose their sense of vitality and joy. They feel as if they are going through the motions and playing at being human when, inside, they feel a void, an inability to love or be loved.

Despair

Many people think that if you burst into tears you are breaking down and for many people, floods of tears do signal the beginning of a breakdown. The barrier is cracking and all those feelings of pain and anguish are flooding out.

Jennifer, a farmer's wife, the mother of five children, was an infant teacher at the consolidated school in a nearby town. She was an overweight, bubbly woman who loved teaching and who managed to juggle the competing demands on her time from her own children, her husband and her work.

She had been teaching at the school for six years and although her husband Brian resented the time she spent on school work, he knew how much she enjoyed her work and she provided a stable source of income when the farm economy slumped, as it did every few years.

The stress that led to her breakdown occurred over 11 weeks. She had begun the school year with her usual vigor. She loved seeing the new children and her warmth and patience always won over even the shyest child.

"I had a normal-sized class of 22 kids. Some of them were pretty scared at first but you get used to that and most of them settled down quickly.

"There were three children who didn't settle; they cried and cried. They cried in the morning when they came in, they cried during the day, at lunch time they cried, at sleep-time they cried. They cried all day and nothing I did seemed to make any difference.

"I spoke to their parents and that didn't help. Then I spoke to the principal and he made some suggestions, but they didn't help either. Meanwhile, they had been crying now for five weeks. I realized it was starting to get to me.

"One of the other teachers took one of the three, a little girl, for half a day but then he brought her back; he couldn't stand it either. By that stage nobody in the school wanted to know about it, and I was getting desperate.

"I kept hearing their bloody crying in my head even when I wasn't at school. I wasn't sleeping and I was exhausted. I was getting crabby with the other kids in the grade, I was dreading going to school in the morning and I was getting a tension headache like a tight band around my head."

After 11 weeks of this, Jennifer's patience and resources had run out. She had tried everything she knew; nothing made any difference.

"I was dreading Monday, I'd had a terrible weekend, my own kids were driving me mad, and the idea of going back to those three was making me feel sick.

"I stuck it out until lunch and those three hung onto my skirt and wouldn't let go. They were all bawling their eyes out. I became furiously angry and pushed them out of the room, locked the door and started howling. I couldn't stop.

"The other teachers heard the commotion and were knocking on the door trying to get in, but I wanted them all to go away. The principal got the spare key and came in. Then, when it was all too late, he drove me home, and my husband put me to bed.

"I think I cried for days, I felt so hopeless and so filled with despair. Even now, my confidence is very shaky. I keep wondering what else I could have done. It sounds so silly, so petty, to break down because of three crying children, but it was really terrible."

Despair is one of the most common ways in which a breakdown is experienced. Sometimes it is diagnosed as depression and anti-depressant medication is prescribed. These tablets can help reduce the intensity of the despair, but the other symptoms of a breakdown continue unchanged. Despair is a powerful motivator in making people get help.

Exhaustion

Overwhelming fatigue can occur as a climax to months of battling stress. Some find that their breakdown appears as a sudden total loss of energy; they feel as if all their stamina has seeped away. Tom felt like a helpless baby when he finally stopped his frenetic search for a cure and another job. He thought his heart must be giving out he felt so tired.

"I've never known anything like it. My body seemed to come to a dead halt. I felt like I had nothing left, I really mean *nothing* left. I can't tell you how that filled me with despair, some days I couldn't even lift my head off the pillow."

Tom's fatigue faded quite rapidly, although he never forgot the feeling and, long after his breakdown had resolved, his stamina never really returned.

Resolution

Recovering from a breakdown is a long drawn-out process with four main stages leading to a full recovery, although some people get stuck in one stage for a long time. It is useful to be aware of the stages because it is easy to get discouraged when you seem to be stuck.

Stages of a breakdown

People vary in their ability to recognize that they have had a breakdown. Some find their body just refuses to "go" any more. Others are told by their family, doctor, or someone closely involved, that they're not managing, and they're forced to face that unpalatable fact. A few, like Tom, struggle on for as long as they can, knowing they are fighting a losing battle.

Once you realize that you've had a breakdown, you may be dismayed that you don't start improving immediately. Recovery from a breakdown generally proceeds through four stages. These stages fade into each other and the times spent in each stage vary. The initial stage is one of **collapse**, followed by a stage of **recuperation**, then one of gradual **restitution**; the final stage is **return** to the mainstream of life.

The first stage: collapse

The moment of breakdown, which may extend over days, is the beginning of the first stage of recovery. It is the stage of collapse, when you can feel yourself really "falling apart." This process seems to continue for days and weeks until you wonder how much further you can fall. You will become alarmed because you are not well again after a few weeks. All the symptoms that have been mentioned before are there in full strength, and you feel buffeted and powerless.

It is common to feel even worse during this initial stage. You may have been struggling to keep going, using all your strength to get through, but all the time you are slipping and losing ground. Your resources are being depleted and, when you finally stop, there is nothing left, the well is empty. You have used the last reserves of your energy in the hope of getting through. Once that hope is extinguished, your fight has been for nothing. You feel exhausted and despairing.

By this time you are confronted with the extent of the changes in your life. You can't work, you can barely cope with family demands, and you are worried about money. You may have to lodge a workers' compensation claim and deal with lawyers and unions. You may have trouble finding a doctor who can help. You may get conflicting advice from well-meaning friends, family and professionals. This adds to your confusion.

After these trials are over, and they may last months, you will feel that your recovery is really beginning. At first you will feel so worried and frightened that it's hard to see any pattern, and it is difficult to distinguish between feeling bad and feeling worse. With continued rest, you will feel better more often, and the feeling will last longer.

Setbacks are common, and they can be disheartening if they are not understood as being part of the recovery process. As you are able to understand more of what is happening to you, your recovery can proceed more smoothly if you are content to trust your body's ability to repair itself and to avoid getting in the way.

Towards the end of this first stage you will start to feel that you are coping better with your life, you can go to a party, may even enjoy it a little, you can go shopping without feeling light-headed and exhausted. You may surprise yourself at what you are able to do. Although you feel frustrated with your slow progress, boredom is not an issue. Just getting through a day successfully is an achievement. Later you will probably look back on this time with amazement. As one person described it, "Those first six months are a blank to me. I don't really remember much about it at all. It seems like six months out of my life."

The second stage: recuperation

The middle stage of your recovery is a time of recuperation, a slow, partial return of some of your old skills, of better control of your life. By this stage you will have learned the benefits of pacing yourself, of living with a damaged body. This is also a time of testing. You are testing yourself to see what you can do. You might try a hobby, an adult education course or even some volunteer work. You may test yourself in more demanding situations, traveling to the city, going to social gatherings or meeting new people. You can start doing more at home to ease the burden of others in the family, cooking a meal or doing some washing.

You will find that you tire quickly and can only do two hours work in the morning and maybe an hour or so in the afternoon. The work you do has to fit the amount of energy you have. If you try to do too much, particularly if you feel under pressure, you will find that your old symptoms return - exhaustion, tension, irritability, sleeplessness, and so on.

What you are aiming to do during this stage is to become more aware of your body signals. One way to do this is to stop when you feel the first signs of exhaustion rather than over-doing it and paying for the folly for days. It is useful to keep a diary at this stage as it will help you to see the connection between what you do and how your body responds to what you do. You will be learning to overcome the fear that comes whenever you try something new.

Learning to care for yourself is difficult if you have never done it before because you will feel guilty when you begin to say no to other people's demands.

This stage of recuperation is frustrating because it seems to go on for so long, but you will find that your stamina gradually increases, and you will feel a little more settled emotionally. It is difficult to motivate yourself because you don't seem to be getting anywhere, and you don't seem to have any clear direction.

Your friends will have noticed that you are looking better and doing more, and they will assume that you are nearly well and may start to pressure you to do even more.

However, looks are deceptive; you may still have problems with concentration and memory, particularly short-term memory, and your anxiety levels are still high, especially when anything reminds you of your breakdown. Situations that make you anxious are still best avoided wherever possible.

Throughout the ups and downs of this stage, you need to focus on the ways in which you have improved. You are able to use the phone again, you can enjoy a chat with a neighbor, and you begin to take some pride in your appearance. These, and other changes, may seem like small steps to others but, to you, they are clear indications that you are recovering.

The third stage: restitution

By now, your days have become more tranquil and predictable; you feel much more stable, as long as you lead a quiet life and avoid disruptions and reduce pressure. Even when your routine is interrupted, you bounce back more quickly. Feeling good again makes you uneasy.

It feels so fragile, any little tempest may knock you over.

You may finally start to feel bored. This will spur you on to thinking about the future. Now is the time to assess what went wrong, so as to learn to avoid getting into those situations again. Are you still vulnerable? What do you have to change in yourself? In your work? What affect has your breakdown had on your family? And what can you do to make family life easier? These questions are difficult to answer but are vital if you are to avoid the same thing happening again.

The final stage: return

The final stage is one of return to normal living, to studies, to some other line of work-but the convalescence is over. You may feel you have rejoined the mainstream again, with some scars and some pain, but you are back into life again. Career plans develop, family life becomes enriched, and many people feel that they have gained a deep understanding of themselves and a sense of peace and patience that they had never experienced before.

4

The Experience - What It Feels Like

No matter what the cause or one's background, one thing is constant, the symptoms of those who have a stress breakdown are virtually identical.

It was this startling fact that first led us to become interested in breakdowns. For a long time we had been seeing people who, although otherwise totally dissimilar, had the same symptoms. It didn't seem to matter about factors such as age, sex or way of life. Even when the catalysts were different, the symptoms were the same.

Symptoms fell into four groups - emotional, mental, physical and social - and we will look at each of these later. In some people we find that one or other group of symptoms predominate. Others have such overwhelming exhaustion, for example, that every other symptom seems to fade by comparison. We will look at that later, too.

Symptoms are expressions of the ways in which our coping has failed, of the ways in which we are not able to handle ordinary, everyday pressures. When Tom first broke down he was not able to cope with going to school, his capacity to do all the tasks involved had failed; even such things as getting dressed, driving, finding his way there were beyond him.

No amount of logic could help him feel better. His sense of proportion had been lost. His capacity for coping with everyday demands and irritations had failed, and his body responded as if every pressure was overwhelming. His symptoms help us to see that his body was not coping emotionally; for example, he was experiencing high levels of anxiety. He was not coping mentally as he couldn't find his way to school, among other problems. He also was not coping physically; he was clumsy and felt exhausted. He was not coping socially; he was irritable with his family and avoided people.

Symptoms also help us understand the process of breakdown. The symptoms of a breakdown are similar in kind to those arising from stress, even from minor stress, but are much more severe. All of us are familiar with stress surrounding an examination. We can all remember a sense of dread, of tension, a change in appetite as well as bladder and bowel habits with frequent urination and, often, attacks of diarrhea;

sometimes we get the shakes. This state of tension usually settles when we start the examination.

Symptoms of a breakdown are so much more severe than this that, if they were present, doing the exam would be impossible: the level of tension would be too high, diarrhea may be explosive and memory and concentration would be lost. People shake, cry and are filled with shame and despair.

When we compare the symptoms of Helen with those of Margaret we see the differences readily. Helen was very stressed but had not reached the point of stress breakdown. Helen's symptoms resolved quickly after her supervisor returned and took charge. She was still tired but she was able to go back to work and felt optimistic that her situation was improving. By contrast, Margaret was unable to function normally for a long time.

Symptoms of breakdown are the best guide to recovery. Recovery is basically a process of trial and error in which symptoms indicate that too much has been attempted at that time and symptoms are the body's ways of saying "back off."

Tom used to go back to his old school at first to pick up his pay check. He found, though, that it was a terrible ordeal. He would worry about it for days beforehand and become sleepless and a "bundle of nerves."

Betty noticed how irritable he became when he had to pick up the check and she spoke to the principal and was able to arrange for his pay to be sent home. Almost immediately, Tom felt a lightening of his spirits.

"I couldn't believe the difference in me when they started sending the pay check home. I'd been going to the school every two weeks for ages to pick it up. I used to make myself do it because I thought it was good for me, I thought it would keep me in touch and I could get the feel of the place.

"I used to dread going; sometimes I'd have to vomit before I went. Looking back on it, it felt like I was going to an execution: my own. It seems crazy now that I kept it up as long as I did, but I was determined I wasn't going to be beaten. When Betty told me that she'd spoken to Cameron, the principal, I got really wild, but it was a good thing and it really taught me a lesson."

His symptoms made sense. They were body messages saying, "This is wrong for you, this is making you feel bad, don't do it." When he was able to respond to his symptoms by decoding the message, he was on the road to recovery.

Margaret was unable to visit her daughter's grave for a long time; even thinking about it made her shudder, and yet she felt guilty for not going. Eventually she decided that it was the right time for her to go. She was very sad at the grave and very apprehensive on her way to the cemetery, but she was surprised at the strength she felt within and the peace she gained from the visit.

Margaret had learned to pace herself and to listen to her body so she could pick up the subtle messages her body was transmitting.

Symptoms give us clues to the areas of most damage. We have noticed, for example, that people who do intensive brain work have particular problems with memory and concentration, teachers and senior administrators among others. Brendan, the social worker, for many months was unable to string two thoughts together; he used to joke in a black way that he had suffered from "brain death."

We have to cope with all the varying demands of life if we are to lead a fruitful existence, enjoying our work, our family, and our friends. Freud said that true maturity is loving well and working well. When we are coping well we feel an inner harmony, our life feels balanced.

We cope in four ways: emotionally, mentally, physically and socially. We cope best when we retain a balance between these parts of our life and are able to maintain an overall inner harmony and a sense of inner peace.

One cardinal feature of a breakdown is that people lose a sense of inner peace, which makes them appear grouchy, angry, ungrateful and sad.

Emotional turmoil

"Falling apart," "coming apart at the seams," "losing your marbles," "crashing." We use all these terms when we describe the affects of a breakdown, and they all illustrate graphically the intense emotional experience it causes. There is a loss of emotional control and a sensation of being flooded with feelings of depression, anxiety, despair and rage.

George, the fireman, was a person who prided himself on his emotional control. That vanished with his breakdown. He became irritable, sad, anxious and despairing.

Margaret felt a sense of deadness; all her feelings seemed to have been put on hold and she felt empty and flat. This "deadness" seemed to protect her from overwhelming anguish. It was as if her body knew that she could not cope with any more and, for a time, all her intensity of feeling was put into a "back room" of her mind. After some weeks, this sense of deadness faded and Margaret felt despair and intense sadness, which was accompanied by outbursts of crying.

Tom experienced all these emotions too and, like many men, felt a deep sense of shame and humiliation. He felt his crying and his sadness to be unmanly.

All who break down find that their self-confidence and self-esteem have plummeted. Jennifer, who had coped so well with her life as a farmer's wife, a mother of five children and an infant teacher, became faltering and fearful when dealing with the farm hands or even when doing her housework and cooking. She was frightened of cooking in case she made a silly mistake. One day she made a cake mix and put it in the refrigerator instead of the oven. She was mortified when she realized her mistake and her self-confidence dropped even further.

Despair is very strong during the first few months after a breakdown; people feel they will never get over it, they will never get better. Tom felt this keenly.

"Those first few months were a nightmare. I couldn't get rid of this terrible feeling of despair and hopelessness. Every day I used to wonder why I bothered going on. I used to think about suicide a lot; it seemed the only way out. I couldn't see anything ahead except more anguish and misery. I really wonder how I managed to survive."

Tom and Margaret both found that eating and sex became perfunctory exercises and gave them no pleasure. Tom used to feel that he was just "taking on fuel" when he was eating. Margaret, who had enjoyed gardening when she had the time, watched plants die through lack of watering, and her lawn become overgrown.

Tom didn't open the door of his workshop for two years. He ignored broken chairs, rocky tables and broken windows, and Betty had to hire a handyman.

Despite the pain and anguish of this emotional turmoil few people who suffer stress breakdown are actively suicidal, although most of them think that death would be preferable to the living hell they are in.

Accompanying the loss of peace we have described is anxiety. This anxiety is always present and becomes overwhelming at times, especially when you are under pressure. Tom used to talk about his "nameless dread."

"Even now, years later, I get nervous over trifles. Back then, I'd been twitchy all the time, an unexpected noise, like a door slamming, would have me jumping out of my skin.

"It was really bad when I was under pressure, when I had to go to see a doctor or when I met a fella I used to work with, I could feel that I was shaking inside; it took all my self-control to stop and avoid making a fool of myself. I used to feel that my nerves were as tight as violin strings."

Anxiety and tension are not only feelings, they also appear in your body as physical symptoms. Chronic tension in muscles leads to muscular tenderness with widespread aches and pains as well as tension headaches in the temples, forehead and back of the head.

Margaret was affected by muscular tension, and her body looked very tight. As she lost weight, her muscles and tendons stood out, giving her face and body a drawn, skeletal appearance.

"I shook and trembled a lot. After a while my friends got so used to it they didn't take much notice. I could feel myself on the edge of trembling all the time. My body ached so much; it was a dull throb all over. I used to feel really sorry for my muscles, they seemed to have to take the brunt of a lot of it. When I was really feeling tense, I would feel sick and felt like I was close to vomiting."

Irritability and occasional uncontrolled temper tantrums are common. George had been a very controlled person before he broke down. At the most, if he was angry, he would become quiet and withdrawn. After his breakdown, as we have seen, he became enraged and violent. He blames his rages for driving his family away.

Tom's children found his behavior hard to understand. He would fly off the handle over trifles - milk not put back in the refrigerator or the famous butter incident when he sulked and raged for two days because no one would confess to having left butter and bits of toast in the honey jar.

Anger of this intensity is hard to control and is exhausting to the individual and his or her family. Some families feel they are living with a "caged tiger." Many people are aware of making enormous efforts to avoid raging, but it always seems to burst out when they least expect it. Betty could always tell when Tom was ready to blow. There would be a brooding silence for days and then a tiny spark would set him off.

Jennifer reached a point where she started having panic attacks. These were so devastating to her that she would do anything to avoid them happening: she began to avoid people, driving, or even leaving the house, and her panic attacks seemed to take over the rest of her symptoms. She had panicky feelings in her dreams, too.

"The panic attacks I had were far worse than the anxiety I felt at the start of it all. Those panic attacks were terrible. I could feel myself spinning out all the time. I used to try to force myself to drive, but I felt like I'd get tunnel vision and I was frightened of killing someone.

"I had psychotherapy for a while, but it didn't do a thing. Then

I started on some new drugs and the panic attacks more or less disappeared. After they were gone I had to go back to really dealing with all my other symptoms. I felt much stronger then because I thought that if I could survive those panic attacks I could survive anything."

These turbulent feelings are associated with an enhanced sensitivity to others' feelings and to other intense experiences. Margaret used to feel as if her "filter" had broken down.

"I'd always been a reasonably sensitive person before, but after I broke down it was really terrible. I seemed to pick up on everything, and it felt really painful. I think we have a filter that protects us from too much stimulation. Before it all happened I noticed that when I went to the city all the noise and bustle used to exhaust me and yet people living in the city didn't seem to notice. Their filter was able to shield out all that stuff. After I broke down, it seemed like my filter got big holes in it and everything used to really frighten me. Going into a supermarket or being with a crowd, it all used to terrify me." Margaret found that being with friends who were tense or upset was almost unbearable for her because she seemed to pick up on their pain. Tom noticed that watching television news upset him.

"Some stories would really get to me and I would find myself blubbing away. It was usually something really trivial, like a cat stuck up a tree, but it would make me very upset. I used to get horribly embarrassed, I used to avoid the news and try to stick with programs that wouldn't get to me."

As well as feeling very sensitive, people also feel more vulnerable. They feel very easily wounded and often find it difficult to defend themselves or to exert any authority because they feel so puny and weak.

Tom found this a problem because he had always prided himself on his ability to stand up for himself and defend a principle. He would rage inwardly at himself when he let someone "walk over" him. He had to walk away from confrontations. Once, he had to get Betty to tell their son that they couldn't afford to lend him money for a car. Tom was frightened that there would be an argument and he didn't think he could control himself. He was afraid that he might hurt his son, or burst out crying.

These feelings of powerlessness and dependency on others are harder for most people to accept than any other symptoms. George said, "I'm used to being in control of my kids and my men, and now I can't even control myself." These are the same sorts of feelings experienced by people who have been "brainwashed."

Recovery is a patchy business. Some days are better than others and this erratic progress makes people worry more. Will there ever be an end to it? Fear, anguish, loss of confidence and loss of peace make it hard to keep interested in the world or to enjoy anything.

The emotional symptoms wax and wane as recovery occurs. Some of the sadness comes from the recognition of the losses the breakdown has brought in its wake: the loss of a career or job, the loss of economic security, the loss of loved ones through marriage break-ups and estrangement of children. At times there is regret as people begin to understand how much they have contributed to their breakdown, to their loss of health.

Even when full recovery seems to have occurred, there is an awareness of a vulnerability to re-experiencing some of those turbulent times.

Mental exhaustion

When we talk about thinking, about mental function, we usually refer to intelligence, but thinking involves a great deal more than that. Mental activity is involved with organizing all the information that comes into our brains every day. This information has to be sorted into what we can discard and what we need to retain. This then has to be stored for later use, and it has to be stored so as to be easily accessible. Our brain functions like a computer, mostly under automatic control.

These complicated mental processes are so central to our daily activities that we take them for granted. Simple things, like getting dressed, involve a good deal of thought. What should we wear given the weather and what we expect to be doing during the day? Where are all the clothes we will need? What is the right way to put them on?

If you think back to when you were a child, you will remember how hard it was to get dressed. How did you work out how to put pants on the right way? Do you remember how hard it was to tie your shoelaces? We take this complicated activity for granted now. But if we've had a breakdown, these apparently simple, everyday tasks become very complicated. We have to consciously work out how to do simple tasks like getting dressed or even making a bed. Sometimes we can't even remember what we're doing when we're in the midst of it.

A breakdown leads to fragmentation of these activities. This is shown by poor concentration, constant forgetfulness, chronic indecision, an inability to think logically or to sort out the relevant from the irrelevant. These problems become much worse when you are under pressure. Then you find you lose thoughts or stammer and can't seem to speak a coherent sentence.

Brendan used to talk about his "brain death:"

"The only way I could make sense out of it was to think of my brain like a giant filing cabinet. When I broke down it was like someone had opened all the drawers and chucked the files into a big pile on the ground and kicked them around.

"If I needed to get access to something on file, like 'how to drive the car' my brain would go to a drawer in the cabinet, I couldn't be certain it was the right drawer, but even if it was it would be empty. Then my brain would scramble about with the files on the ground, occasionally finding the right one, but half the stuff inside was missing. So I took forever to work out how to do things and even then I'd get them wrong.

"Information I normally expected to have at my fingertips just wasn't there. It was much worse if I was under any pressure, then I was really hopeless."

Brendan found that his memory and concentration took a long time to improve. Even years later his memory was notoriously bad according to his friends.

Many people who break down have been high achievers and have prided themselves on their mental dexterity. When this has gone they feel humiliated and ashamed.

Margaret found herself in a chronic state of indecision.

"I couldn't decide whether to hang out the washing first or do the dishes. I couldn't decide what to cook for dinner. I remember trying to buy a bed spread, it took me four days. I couldn't make up my mind. I kept going back to the shop and looking at it, then going back home and worrying. I've never worn the clothing I bought then because it's all wrong, some of it doesn't even fit."

Margaret felt like a zombie. She couldn't hold a conversation or watch television because she couldn't follow what was said. When she tried to read, she would read the same paragraph three or four times and then throw down the book in disgust.

Some people find that their mind is racing even while their body feels exhausted, so when they are trying to sleep their mind feels in a ferment of activity. Much of this activity involves ruminations and repetitive thoughts that are unpleasant and boring but seem impossible to stop. The mind seems to settle on a thought that repeats and repeats like a needle stuck in a groove.

Tom found that he would seem to be talking quite rationally to a friend or to Betty but at the same time would have a torrent of thoughts going on in his mind that used to make him feel crazy.

"If the weather was bad, I'd think about it all day and I'd worry about it. I used to worry about kids coming home from school. Then I'd think about Betty driving on slippery roads and something happening to her, what I would do if she was hurt, and I wouldn't know where to get the car fixed because you can't trust mechanics.

"I used to think about bloody drivel like this all day, and I'd tell poor Betty and she would try and reassure me. It didn't do a scrap of good. I'd keep on thinking all those stupid thoughts. I still get them now sometimes, but I don't take much notice any more."

When Margaret was exhausted she would have two or three repetitive thoughts that used to really bother her. She would worry about philosophical issues that at other times seemed nonsense. Margaret also noticed that she had to check everything and would agonize that she'd forgotten to turn off the gas or lock the doors.

"I'd go out the door and I'd walk to the car, I'd stop and think, did I turn off the gas? I'd go back and check again, then worry that I'd forgotten to lock the door. I'd drive down the street and I'd have to come back and check the door. One day it took me an hour to leave! It was all so silly because we've never locked the door before; it's not that sort of town."

These mental symptoms take a long time to improve. Even when your emotions are settled and your physical health has improved, they continue to cause trouble.

Physical fatigue

Tom felt as if he had been turned into an old man overnight. He had always prided himself on his strong body but, after he broke down, his body seemed to crumble.

"I never seemed to have any energy, and my body ached all the time. I couldn't sleep even though I felt exhausted, and I was eating junk food. Sometimes I'd stuff myself with potato chips or ice cream. The other funny thing I noticed is that I was really clumsy. I know I'm a big guy, but I'm pretty agile. Well, I was banging into doors and dropping plates and I'd trip on steps. I think it was because I was away with the fairies a lot of the time and I didn't seem to be noticing what I was doing."

Tom's experiences are shared by most. The overwhelming physical sensation is exhaustion. This is very different from the fatigue you feel after a hard, physical workout; it seems to be more mental fatigue and is much worse when people are under pressure. Brendan fell asleep when he was under pressure.

"A few times I'd been talking to my doctor and I just crashed, I was fast asleep for a little while. It happened once when I was having a tense talk with Jennie, she got really angry and kicked me to wake me up."

As Margaret began to recover, she was able to do a little more. One day she was really pleased because she had been able to wash the kitchen floor and cook a meal without any trouble.

Betty found it difficult to understand how Tom could be home all day and yet nothing was done: breakfast dishes were left stacked in the sink, beds were unmade, he even left the bath water in the bath. Sometimes she wondered if he was just being lazy. Tom had the time, but not the energy.

Drug abuse can occur before people break down. They use drugs and alcohol to try and feel better and to get some sleep. Often this is done surreptitiously by borrowing tablets from their friends or partners.

Alcohol use may increase dramatically, to the point where they are drinking throughout the day. Sometimes problems caused by alcohol or drug abuse can precipitate or even mask a breakdown. It may only be after they have "dried out" from alcohol that it becomes clear that they have suffered a breakdown. Ironically, after a breakdown, most people find their alcohol tolerance has dropped a good deal.

Most find that sleep is difficult. They are exhausted and crave sleep, but it doesn't seem to come easily, and when it does it is often restless sleep with nightmares. It is common to wake in the early hours and be unable to go back to sleep, this time is the darkest of all, the mind is filled with despair and fears.

Margaret lost her libido almost totally. She felt repelled by Andrew's advances to her. She lost interest in sex, even touching or cuddling.

"I don't know why he kept seeing me; I had nothing for him at all. I didn't feel any warmth or love towards him or the kids or anyone. I just wanted to be left alone. Even when he tried to reassure me I felt like I couldn't breathe when he held me. It was the same with everything. I lost interest in everything I used to enjoy: food, wine, sex, company, the whole lot of it left me cold."

People who have broken down find that their interest and enjoyment in life seems to disappear. Hobbies, business, family life all seem a chore and a burden. Many find they were having some problems in these areas before they broke down and in that way their symptoms were warning signals.

We find that mothers with several children under the age of five get exhausted and are vulnerable to breakdown. Before they reach this point, however, they may complain of losing interest in their children and feeling indifferent to their husbands. In these situations it is amazing how a two week break from the children restores their energy and their spirits. With breakdowns, of course, the damage is done and this remedy no longer works.

General levels of health also seem to decline. People find they are more vulnerable to coughs and colds, they develop rashes and hidden health problems may show themselves. Diabetes, hypertension, arthritis, colitis and migraines can occur as part of a stress breakdown.

There are many other physical conditions that are aggravated by severe stress. Those most commonly identified include skin conditions, asthma, allergies and hay fever, headaches and muscular pain, nausea and diarrhea, backache, rheumatoid arthritis, recurrent infections, hypertension, strokes, heart attacks, ulcers and cancer.

Some families show a tendency to develop particular health problems. Asthma is a common condition, and there may be an inherited tendency to develop this disorder among family members. The first attack of asthma can occur at a time of stress and may persist even when the precipitating stress has passed.

It seems that any physical vulnerability or weakness we have shows up especially when we are under pressure. For some, the recurrence of an old problem can be an early warning that they are heading for a breakdown. A sudden attack of dermatitis, for example, can mean that you are very rundown and need a break, but if this warning is ignored, a breakdown may follow.

Ironically, health problems may prevent a breakdown. One policeman told us that his heart attack had stopped him from having a breakdown because it had given him a reason to get away from the job without losing face.

Physical symptoms are an excellent guide during the recovery phase. If the thought of going to a party triggers off sleepless nights, exhaustion and a skin rash, it is easy to see that you are not yet ready for that activity.

As people improve, they find that their physical symptoms improve quickly, although they may continue to fluctuate. Sleep returns, appetite control improves and coordination is better. Even so, levels of energy never seem to return fully. Years after his breakdown, Tom looks fit and strong, but he knows he still has to be careful and pace himself, he can still get exhausted easily.

Social withdrawal

Social interest and social competence fall away when a breakdown occurs. Within the family, people who have broken down are self-absorbed, withdrawn and irritable; with friends and strangers they are uneasy, anxious and tongue-tied. They hate social occasions where they feel trapped and isolated. They are unable to make conversation and sometimes can't follow what is being said. They find the exposure to noise, activity and people distressing and frightening. They feel they want to run away and hide.

Margaret had a wide circle of friends. All of them wanted to help her, but she found their attempts to show her how they cared were intrusive and exhausting.

"I wanted them all to leave me alone and yet when I was alone I felt desolate. I didn't know what I wanted. When the door bell rang, I'd hide and hope they would go away. The kids would answer the door at first, and I'd hear these cheery voices saying, 'Is Marg in? We just thought we'd drop off this pot of jam and see how she is.'

"I'd feel like I was going to scream inside, but I'd grit my teeth and put on that horrible grimace they thought was a smile, and I'd go out to be sociable, and all the time I'd be saying under my breath, 'Go away, just go away, I don't want your bloody jam.' I'd just smile and smile and occasionally burst into tears, which threw some of them off a bit."

Visitors appearing at the front door or the ring of a telephone can set your nerves jangling. They demand a response, an expenditure of energy when there seems to be so little available. Tom used to dread the questions people would ask him: "How are you?" "When are you going back to work?"

"I could tell the ones who were going to ask all those questions. The questions would make me question myself. What was wrong with me, why couldn't I cope? These doubts just made me feel worse. It seemed easier staying away from people, but then when I had to go out it made it that much harder because I seemed to have gotten out of practice."

When people do have to go to social functions, most put on a facade of coping so that no one suspects what a mess they feel inside. The effort of keeping up this front, as well as going out, leaves them drained and exhausted for days.

Family life becomes difficult for everyone. Living with someone who has broken down is like living with a time bomb. Jennifer had always been a very active mother. With five children she had little choice.

But looking after her children eventually became difficult for her.

"I couldn't cope with their noise. They always seemed to be screaming at the tops of their voices, or they'd have the television set on full blast. The kids would come and want me to help them with homework problems and I'd want to scream at them. But it was no good; I didn't have the patience. I had to leave all that to my husband and go to bed."

People who have suffered a breakdown find social interaction difficult even when they are with friends. It is harder with strangers and particularly hard when they meet a person who is hostile. Tom had several unpleasant experiences with fellow teachers.

"Betty had arranged for me to go to a dinner dance put on by the graduate association because a lot of my old students were going to be there and quite a few were doing well in the film and television world.

"A teacher sitting at a table next to me began making cracks at me because I was off work. The first time he said anything I couldn't believe it. Then an old student of mine was kneeling down next to me with his hand on my shoulder having a chat and the smart guy next door said, 'Don't touch him or you'll get stress.'

"I felt terrible. I wasn't going to give him the satisfaction of crying so I tried to ignore him, but he kept on going. Betty could see what was happening and got us away early. It took me weeks getting over that. Even now when I talk about it I feel all choked up."

There is a gradual return of social competence as recovery occurs. People are able to go out a little more. They can be with friends without anxiety, they can tolerate family functions and parties. Some experience a wonderful sense of freedom and a return to normality when they can browse in a supermarket and not feel scared. One man said he knew he was getting better when he could go shopping in K-mart.

Styles of breakdown

So far we have looked at the range of experiences of those who have suffered a breakdown. Some people experience breaking down in a different way. Instead of having the range of symptoms we have described, one particular symptom predominates and overwhelms the rest.

We have already seen how Jennifer's panic attacks took over her life. Because of them she was unable to leave her home and had to give up driving completely. After her panic attacks were successfully treated, she had to deal with the other symptoms of her breakdown.

These very focused breakdowns involve the same symptoms we

have already described. The difference is that one symptom is so "loud" that the other symptoms become a whisper.

We can look at these specific breakdowns using the same four categories we used before-emotional, mental, physical and social. But here we will focus on the ones that are most common.

"Feeling" breakdown

Some people find that their despair and sense of loss is so great that they are in tears, or close to it, all the time. This is usually a transient state, but it is very hard to endure because it is disturbing to others and exhausting to the person involved. This black despair may require specialist psychiatric treatment.

Many men suffer from this problem. Their anger effectively masks all their other symptoms, obliterates their distress and pain. Raging, angry people are also extremely wearing to be with, the added difficulty being that the people close to them become the butt of their anger. Some use alcohol as a way of trying to dissolve their inner turmoil.

Fear and anxiety commonly predominate. This is especially so in the first few weeks after a breakdown. Anxiety is pervasive. People become fearful of meeting anybody new or meeting old friends, they are frightened of leaving home, driving; they are frightened of everything. They need a good deal of support and encouragement.

"Brain" breakdown

Confusion is very hard to live with. Even the most menial task can seem too difficult as people struggle to get through the day. These people seem to have lost any mental acuteness; they operate in a fog. They are vague, easily confused and forgetful. They feel as if they are "wading through molasses." They are often investigated for brain disease.

Obsessional thinking is one symptom, in particular, that makes people think they are going mad. A thought gets into their mind and it may go around and around for days. It might be very trivial, such as remembering the name of an old movie, or it might be frightening thoughts about knives. The thoughts seem to take on a life of their own. The obsessional thought may just fade away, there is a feeling of tremendous relief, and then a new one starts.

These people go over and over and over the experiences that led to their breakdown. They drive their family to a screaming point and just can't seem to let it go. They can become terribly boring, not only to their friends and families, but also to themselves. They are often oblivious to the destructive influence they have on their relationships.

Sometimes the job of the therapist is to kindly tell them to shut up!

Suspicion and mistrust are features of some people's breakdowns. They seem to have lost the ability to trust anyone. Unfortunately their attitude towards others often leads them to being rejected in turn. These experiences of repeated rejection confirm their suspicions that no one is to be trusted. They become increasingly isolated and withdrawn.

"Body" breakdown

Overpowering fatigue is the predominant symptom for many people suffering stress breakdown. If there was a bank balance for energy, they would be in the "red" all the time. Occasional brief bursts of energy are quickly depleted by small tasks. People with this level of exhaustion may not be particularly depressed or anxious, angry or whatever, but their exhaustion overwhelms their lives.

Some people find they are plagued by chronic infections, muscular aches and pains, headaches, eye strain or diarrhea; they feel as if their body is cracking up. They lurch from sore throats to eye trouble to skin infections. Their capacity for warding off infection seems to be damaged.

Stress breakdowns are often associated with increased use of drugs or alcohol. This may have been a pattern that developed before the breakdown occurred and may have precipitated the breakdown.

Some people deal with their breakdown by seeking oblivion in a needle or a glass. This, of course, leads to all sorts of other problems that are social, physical, financial and mental. The task of actually dealing with the breakdown is never really attempted.

"Social" breakdown

Some people respond to their breakdown by withdrawing completely from work, family, friends and, it seems, life. They become reclusive and fearful of any contact and their isolation from others further aggravates their fear of contact.

Larry, a policeman who had been retired because of his breakdown, stayed in a caravan at the back of his family home, his wife and children saw less and less of him. He would avoid the family by coming into the house in the middle of the night to cook and shower. His wife understandably found this very difficult.

One day he hitched up the caravan to the family car and towed it to a country block he had bought unbeknownst to his wife. He returned the car and somehow got back to his block; she saw little of him after that. Soon he refused to see his wife or the children and would literally run away and hide if anybody tried to visit him. He was murdered by a vagrant for a few dollars. His decomposed body was found months later.

It is important to see these sorts of breakdowns as part of a larger picture. Unfortunately, these more specific presentations are often treated in isolation and the larger picture is ignored.

Specialist help will be sought for such problems as anxiety, panic attacks, phobic states, depression, anger, obsessions, paranoia, alcohol and drug abuse, eating disorders, hair loss, infertility, gynecological and marital problems and the various other symptoms we have already described.

Although these problems do require treatment in themselves, they are often part of a larger picture. Our aim has been to show the totality of the experience of stress breakdown and to illustrate how all these symptoms interact with each other, and with the world, to produce the person we see, the person with a stress breakdown.

5

The Features - Stress Versus Breakdown

What is the difference between being severely stressed and having a breakdown? Most people can tell you whether they have had a breakdown or not, sometimes immediately, sometimes several months after the event.

Tom and Margaret were both immediately aware that they had been damaged, that at the time of their breakdown they felt crippled in every aspect of their lives. George, who wrecked his room, and Brendan, who felt such confusion that he couldn't find his own house, both took a day or two to realize what had happened to them. Stan wanted to hide from himself, and anyone else, the fact that he had become so desperate he had attempted suicide. Like Jennifer, it was to be many months before Stan accepted that he had had a breakdown. Recognition came when they realized they weren't going to get better in a few months. The fear that they would never be the same again, that some permanent damage had occurred, was terrifying.

Those who have been aware of being stressed before their breakdown see the differences between stress and breakdown clearly. It is expressed in different ways but basically their capacity for coping has been reduced. Before their breakdown, even though it was very hard, they could push themselves to do something; after their breakdown, they couldn't. Margaret described her embarrassment and fear of losing control again.

"Even on my good days, the possibility of losing control always worried me. I remember writing down the wrong account number at the bank, feeling hot and shaky and then bursting into tears. The humiliation of having to leave the bank in that state is still with me. The fact that this was likely to happen over any little thing that went wrong in the beginning was very distressing and so you withdrew because you didn't like to be thought of as a fool or weak."

Dependency on others immediately after a breakdown varies from one person to another. Some people become so helpless that they either have to be admitted to a hospital or be looked after by a friend or relative. This acute phase usually only lasts a few weeks, but for those admitted to a psychiatric hospital, the stigma and possible inappropriate treatment may leave a life-long scar.

Although dependency lasts a short time, it tends to recur when the person is under further stress. Loss of confidence resulting from dependency takes a long time to overcome.

We can also see that the symptoms of a breakdown are more widespread and more intense than those experienced by someone like Helen who was severely stressed. When Helen and others like her get relief from the stress they are experiencing, they can expect to recover within a few months. Tom and Margaret will only be a little improved; it will take them much longer to achieve a normal life again.

Some of the symptoms of a breakdown are more long-lasting than others. Both fatigue and problems with concentration continue long after other symptoms have receded.

Someone who was very stressed can expect that, in the future, if they are under stress, they will get the same warning signs again, but they will be able to cope if they stop and do something about them. A person who has had a breakdown has to deliberately avoid pressure. Tom's wife Betty described it in this way:

"Tom is all right when he is able to do things at his own pace and when he feels up to the task. But, if something has to be done by a certain time, or if he feels under an obligation to do something rather than by choice, his symptoms return. He's good when he's doing physical work - he can do that for hours - but anything mentally demanding exhausts him and he becomes very uptight. I don't think he will ever be able to work in a pressured job again."

What does seem to be permanent after a breakdown is a vulnerability to stress. As we shall see later, although people do recover from a breakdown, the rate at which they improve varies depending on their age, the severity of their symptoms at the point of breakdown, the length of the build-up to their breakdown, the severity of the triggering event, and the frequency of re-exposure to the initial trauma. The degree of continuing vulnerability seems to be linked to this recovery rate. Someone who is able to lead a normal life two years after a breakdown will be less vulnerable than someone who doesn't feel in control again for five years or so.

Am I going mad?

Tom and Margaret have both had stress breakdowns, and yet Helen has not. Helen was severely stressed but she did not reach that irreversible point of breakdown. The essential question is what makes people break down?

Before we explore this question further it is useful to examine some misconceptions about breakdown. We are commonly asked such questions as: "Am I going mad?" "Does breaking down mean I'm neurotic or psycho?" "Am I weak to have broken down?" The answer is usually no. The misconceptions arise because of the many conditions that the word "breakdown" describes.

Breakdown is used by people because it is such a good description of how people feel at the time. They have stopped functioning temporarily in many important aspects of their lives. They cannot sustain normal relationships, activities or work.

"Breakdown" is also often used to describe an acute episode of a mental disorder like a psychosis or an unresolved grief reaction. These people often need hospitalization and certainly need urgent treatment for their underlying condition, but they are not the subject of this book. These acute episodes are also temporarily incapacitating but have different causes, symptoms and treatment from stress breakdown.

It seems to us that these two conditions of mental disorder and breakdown differ markedly but that they can, in some circumstances, occur together.

We can illustrate this point best by telling you about Phillip. He was a heavy set, shaggy haired, bear-like man with a crumpled grease-stained suit. He was obese and awkward in his movements. His major concern was some work stress that had led to a severe attack of dermatitis. This had taken over a year to improve. His story was unusual and the first clue to this was his comment that he was a "fitness fanatic." This odd statement, which contrasted sharply with his appearance, led to further disclosures.

He was an accountant who was unmarried and he'd lived in the same house all his life with his mother. He had done accountancy at the university, after which he'd worked with the same company for 12 years. He mentioned, in passing, that he'd thought he had developed cancer, or maybe heart disease, eight years before and he'd gone to hospital to have this investigated.

He was surprised and annoyed to be sent instead to a psychiatric hospital, where he stayed for only two days. His concerns about cancer and so forth have never been investigated. He has never been back and has never had any further psychiatric treatment, if indeed he had had any at all. He still believed he had cancer or heart disease but was not so worried about it. He mentioned that he was hearing voices, two voices, a man and a woman, who were talking about him to each other; they were being rude, obscene and threatening. He had been scared at first but had become used to them.

As well as the voices he believed there was a machine inside him that was going to kill him and there was a conspiracy afoot to push him off "the edge." He thought his mother was involved in some way. Even when traveling to work on the train, he was frightened that the other passengers might try to push him out of the carriage. He had become used to the conspiracy and, although it upset him, he tried not to worry too much about it. He had never told anyone of his strange experiences. He knew that there was something wrong with him, but he was frightened of what might happen if he sought help: he might be put back into the psychiatric hospital.

Phillip had a major psychiatric illness. He was suffering from chronic paranoid schizophrenia, and yet he had never lost a day's work. He lived a restricted life, but in his own way, he was content. The stress which had led to dermatitis had occurred at work. A number of people in the finance department were retrenched, and Philip's workload doubled. At that time a new computer system was installed, and he felt harassed and exhausted. He developed a widespread irritating rash that took some time to improve. His dermatologist wrote to his company suggesting that his workload be reduced. This was done and he felt better, not so pressured and his health returned.

Phill ip has never had a stress breakdown despite the presence of a major psychiatric illness. He is vulnerable to having a stress breakdown because his illness has been a long-term stressor, but until now, one could say he has coped remarkably well. He has worked out a number of different ways of reducing the stress associated with his condition. He has avoided stigma by not telling anyone about it, he ignores it as much as he can, he has a job to which he is well suited because it does not involve too much socializing with his colleagues and he has the security of living at home with his mother.

Major psychiatric illnesses and a stress breakdown are separate conditions. The stress associated with an illness such as schizophrenia or manic-depression is only one of many stresses that makes someone vulnerable to a stress breakdown.

Contrast Philip's story with that of Jennifer's, whose story has already been told. She had been a strong woman from a stable background, an experienced and competent teacher who was brought down by three crying children. Despite her warmth, competence and experience, she had been powerless to stop their continual crying. She reached a point where she began crying herself and couldn't stop. She was unable to go back to the school and has never returned.

Jennifer now avoids people as much as she can. She cries easily, and has difficulty coping at home with her own family, although she used to be able to do that and work full time as well. Jennifer has all the same symptoms as Tom and Margaret. She cannot go anywhere near the school and is terrified of meeting anyone associated with the place. Any such chance meeting reawakens the events surrounding her breakdown. Her capacity for coping has failed. She does not have, and never did have, a major psychiatric illness, although she did experience panic attacks for a short time. She has had a stress breakdown due to the intolerable pressures of the incessantly crying children and her inability to do anything about it. She has lost confidence, not only as a teacher but also in every other aspect of her life and it will take some time to build up this confidence again. She will almost certainly never be able to return to teaching.

6

The Causes

We return to the central question: what causes people to have breakdowns? We know that most people who break down have experienced high levels of stress, often for some time. There are, however, exceptions. People caught up in cataclysmic events, cyclones, bushfires and other natural disasters show a much higher rate of breakdown.

On 16 February 1983, Ash Wednesday, a series of fires started simultaneously in the tinder dry landscapes of southern Australia. Fueled by a hot, dry wind, the fire spread at great speed and generated temperatures of up to 1,000 degrees C. Seventy-two people were killed and an estimated 2,000 homes were destroyed.

The devastation did not stop when the fires went out. Many people's lives were to be changed forever. Over the following months a number of the survivors developed severe illnesses, some of which were difficult to diagnose. A large number received counseling after the fires and a few continue to do so. Five years later, local doctors find that they are still seeing people with symptoms that are clearly related to the fire. Some people cannot leave home without checking many times to see that all appliances are switched off. Many have great difficulty leaving their homes on hot, windy days. There seems to have been an increased rate of marriage breakdown owing to the stress associated with the fires and its after-effects. An observed high cancer rate in the areas affected is being investigated. It is difficult to know the full extent of the long-term impact of the fires because a high percentage of families have left their homes. Although most people have learned to cope in their own way, it seems that a small number have been severely incapacitated by the event because they have had stress breakdown.

Many such disasters have been analyzed and the few long-term studies carried out indicate that a significant percentage of people have not recovered from the event some years later.

The stress of war has also been investigated. One study showed that 17 years after the end of the Second World War, 70 per cent of soldiers who had suffered an acute traumatic reaction were still experiencing many of their old symptoms.

In these events, the stress level is so high and so acute that it overwhelms ordinary coping strategies. It's as if the disaster was so huge and so swift it caught people unprepared; it slipped under their guard. We know that any major disaster has serious after-effects on the long-term health of some of the survivors. But what of the others? Why is it that some are so badly affected while others seem to be unscathed by the experience?

Part of the answer emerges when we compare the two groups: those who survived unscathed and those who didn't. We can compare what they endured during the trauma, what had been happening in their lives in the months or years before the event, and whether or not they had previously shown some vulnerability.

In December 1987, an armed man entered the city offices of Australia Post and roamed through the building, gunning people down, before jumping to his death from the twelfth floor. Most of the eight deaths occurred on the fifth, eleventh and twelfth floors. Many others were wounded. At least one person escaped death when the gun jammed as it was fired at him. Many saw their colleagues killed or wounded and were spattered with their blood. Several hundred people working within the building received a brief warning over the intercom system that a gunman was loose in the building before the intercom ceased to function. They prepared to barricade themselves on their floor and remained hidden under desks or in cupboards in a state of fear until they were released about one and a half hours later.

There was an almost universal post-traumatic stress disorder among survivors, who showed symptoms of stress in varying degrees for some time after the event. By July 1988, most had recovered, but a significant percentage were still severely affected by their symptoms.

There were three main groups who were at risk. The first and most significant group were those who were most closely exposed to the trauma, those who felt that "it could have been me." The second group were those experiencing other major life problems at the time. Australia Post was going through massive organizational change at the time of the massacre, and this had been a cause of serious concern for some. The third group of people at risk were those who had some history of minor mental health problems. This last group was interesting, however, because they were more likely to seek counseling early; for them it was "the thing to do." As time went on their condition improved and six months later, the first group, those who were exposed to the greatest trauma, were most at risk.

It seems that the more traumatic an event and the more other stresses there are in a person's life, the greater the likelihood of a stress breakdown. Those who have a pre-existing condition may be more at risk of a stress breakdown, or they may be more likely to seek treatment.

Although most of us can easily understand why someone would break down after being intimately involved in an event as traumatic as Ash Wednesday or the Australia Post massacre, we do not find it so easy to understand why someone breaks down as a result of long-term stress. It requires us to try to put ourselves in that person's position, to try to understand what it must have been like for them. The issue is not, "what I would have done in the same circumstances to avoid a breakdown" - we can all be wise after the event - but we have to walk in their shoes, by understanding the forces that molded them, and the meaning of the pressures that finally overwhelmed them.

For most, high levels of stress are a pre-condition to breakdown. Tom and Margaret certainly experienced high levels of stress for some time. So did Helen, however, and yet she did not have a stress breakdown.

Tom's breakdown was almost inevitable; he knew that he was heading downhill fast. For him the stresses were multiple and accumulated to a point where he broke.

Margaret, on the other hand, had survived great strain with considerable success. The turning point was an act of malice, of evil. For her this was an experience beyond her understanding, a stab wound to her innermost self. She found it unbelievable that her daughter's murderer was not only known to her but that she had unknowingly attempted to give him some comfort. This realization broke her spirit. Yet, Helen survived, she was also under considerable pressure, she was also the victim of some malice.

In Helen's case a breakdown was avoided because her sense of powerlessness was altered by Vincent's intervention. Previously she had felt trapped. There seemed to be no solution, until Vincent dramatically changed the balance of power by coming in on her side. She experienced immediate relief from a chronically stressful situation.

In order to understand the question of what causes a breakdown we need to go back a step and look at the causes of stress.

Stress is both a feeling of tension and a body response that arises in us as we interact with our world. The feelings of tension can develop from a number of sources, some of which are outside and others which are within ourselves. Essentially, stress arises out of a lack of fit between our own or other's expectations of ourselves and the tools we have available to do the job.

We have described stress as both a feeling and a body response. We are all familiar with the feeling of tension - tightness, anxiety, restlessness and irritability - but we are not so familiar with our body's response which produces these reactions.

The body's response is designed to equip us better to deal with this unexpected challenge by either fighting or running away, the well-known "flight or fight" response. This response is triggered by the brain and involves both the nervous system and the endocrine glands that produce chemical messages for the rest of the body. The combined affect of these messages leads to a number of changes that make the body ready for action.

Blood is diverted from less essential areas like the gut and skin and directed towards the muscles, heart, brain and the facial area where the major sense organs are located. The muscles are tightened ready for action; there have been many recorded examples of extreme strength in a crisis as a result. The brain becomes very active and seems to be able to work at great speed. To keep the muscles and brain going, energy stores in the fat begin to be moved into the blood stream. If this process occurs over too long a time, however, a poisonous by-product starts to reduce the effectiveness of the immune system - the "fight or flight" response is only intended to last for a short time. Blood pressure increases to make sure that blood reaches the areas where it is needed, and blood-clotting time is reduced to minimize bleeding in case of wounds. Pain killers are simultaneously released into the body.

The sense organs, especially the eyes and ears, become more acute: the eyes are more light sensitive, the ears more alert. The skin becomes very responsive to touch, and it perspires more freely to cool the underlying muscles. Breathing rate increases to supply the lungs with more oxygen. Sex hormones are reduced so that procreation is less likely at a time when the species is more vulnerable, besides which the sex drive is not very useful at a time like this.

Basically what is happening is that all non-essential functions slow down or shut off, while the rest of the body and mind are made ready to work at a super-effective level in order to cope with a crisis or challenge.

The sense organs are ready to give the first warnings of danger. The brain is ready to respond to these and make the right moves, and the muscles are coiled, ready to be unleashed. The body is primed and ready to act. But if there is nowhere to run or nothing to fight, this is wasted, the priming is useless. All it leaves is a state of tension and anticipation. Our body is simply not intended to operate at this super-effective level for very extended periods. It's like a car engine revving up ready to move the car, but prolonged revving with no load on the engine will damage it. Similarly prolonged strain and pressure on the human body leads to a state of prolonged stress, which has many damaging affects. The process of mobilizing energy and delivering it rapidly via the blood stream can lead to increased fat levels in the blood and high blood pressure, both of which make people more prone to strokes and heart attacks.

The demands on the pancreas to increase insulin production can lead to exhaustion of those cells and diabetes. The continuing muscle tension is painful and tiring and may lead to joint diseases.

All of us are born with particular physical vulnerabilities, and when we are under prolonged stress our most vulnerable areas tend to show the effects first. Thus Margaret's skin reacted to the repeatedly altered blood supply and increased perspiration and sensitivity. Many people find that they get cold hands and feet when they are under severe stress. Stan later developed mild rheumatoid arthritis and was amazed to see how rapidly it became inflamed when he was under pressure.

Tom and Margaret were physically, mentally and emotionally exhausted. The overall affects of prolonged stress can be seen clearly in the symptoms described by them. Margaret ached all over. The pain in her neck and shoulders was real and largely resulted from constant muscle tension. She felt it more than normal though because her body's natural pain suppression had been depleted over a long time.

One of the most disturbing symptoms for both Tom and Margaret was that they couldn't remember, concentrate, or make decisions. For Tom, it felt as though "my brain has run a marathon." Margaret's brain was so exhausted that it seemed to get stuck in a groove and replay the same thoughts endlessly. Tom couldn't get out of the pattern of endless ruminations about little things that happened at his school. Faced with their inability to do almost anything, mental fatigue had aggravated their deep feelings of loss.

Why a breakdown?

So far we have described what a breakdown feels like, both during the event and afterwards. We have described the symptoms and explained how a stress breakdown is different from an acute phase of a major psychiatric condition.

We have looked at the two most usual ways in which the stage is set for a breakdown. One group of people experience very severe trauma over a short time; the other group are worn down by one trauma after another, so that they begin to develop a whole range of stress symptoms. Some experience both prolonged stress and then a crisis.

The fact remains, however, that most people who experience trauma do not break down; nor do most people who have significant symptoms of stress. A stress breakdown, even under either of these conditions, is a relatively rare event. What then are the extra factors or the particular combination of factors that cause someone to break down?

A stress breakdown is commonly avoided in people who develop severe physical illness. The illness may be such that it provides temporary or sometimes even permanent relief from a stressful situation. One woman described how she avoided a breakdown:

"I never thought that I would see the day when I would describe my asthma, my bronchitis and my tendency to be allergic to all sorts of foods as a blessing, but I can now see that they were. Every time things got really bad at work I became very ill and would need anywhere between a week and a month off. My condition finally became so bad that my doctor said I would just have to retire because of my ill-health. How right she was. I can actually see now that if I had been physically healthy I would probably have had a breakdown instead."

Heart attacks, repeated severe chest pain, palpitations, chronic skin conditions, back problems, arthritis and a host of other physical conditions can, quite by chance, remove someone from a stressful situation. Age retirement comes just in time for others.

There are still others who, either acting on instinct, deliberate intent, or again by chance, transfer, resign, become pregnant (only available to some!) or take some other form of leave.

In the five years following Ash Wednesday many families have chosen to leave the area as a way of leaving behind the constant reminders of the trauma. They are still leaving. Six months after the Australia Post shootings, staff turnover within the building doubled.

Some take the further step of rethinking their life direction and assessing long-term priorities. The relatively common phenomenon of a mid-life crisis often occurs after a period of prolonged stress and acts as the catalyst for a major review of how people are living their lives.

Sometimes other people intervene. This happened with Helen. Fortunately, she took notice of Vincent, stopped working, and got some rest. But this does not always happen. Some people are in such a confused and exhausted state that they do not respond, or are unable to respond, to the warnings of their colleagues or family.

We return then to our original question. What is it that turns trauma or a series of mini-traumas over a long period into a breakdown?

What finally happens for those who have a breakdown is that a combination of fear, fatigue and frustration develops. Each symptom reinforcing the other, creating a vicious cycle of fatigue, begetting fear and frustration, frustration causing more fatigue and more fear, and so the wheel revolves.

What significance did the event or series of events have for that person at the time? What meaning did it have for them? The issue of real threat or real danger is irrelevant; what matters most is whether the person involved saw it as a threat or danger. Did it threaten their life? Did it make them aware of their own mortality? Did it threaten their career? Did it shake their confidence in other human beings? Did it threaten, at its very heart, their sense of well-being and self worth? If the answer to any of these questions is yes then the fear element of the cycle is initiated. Let us look at some of the people whose breakdowns we have already described and listen to their impressions of what happened to them.

Fear

George the fireman said, "After the roof fell on me, I lost my nerve. I couldn't face that, and I think that working, while all the time I was so scared, is what led to me falling apart."

What happened was that George became terrified. He suddenly realized that his job was dangerous and that he could be killed. The fact that he wasn't was irrelevant to him; it was what might have happened that shook his confidence.

Harry was another whose breakdown was initiated by fear. Like George, he was not seriously injured, but he became terrified at the thought of being hurt, and for good reason. Harry worked with the railways, as did his father and brother. Harry was illiterate, but he was strong, and he had commonsense.

"I was in the bridging gang for 17 years. Then I was put in the bogie exchange. There were six of us in the gang, and Ken was the ganger. We were all good friends, until Ken's accident. I used to drive the tractor, and I'd push the rail truck over the jacks. I'd press the lever for the jacks to work, and the tray of the truck would lift up, and we'd push the wheels out and bring a new set so we could change the gauge."

Harry enjoyed his job. Although it was hard physical work, going to work was like leaving one family and going to another. He felt a sense of belonging. At this point there was nothing in his life that could be remotely seen as pressure or stress.

"About six months ago, Ken was under the truck loosening the brake rod when an engine hit the line of trucks too hard. I yelled at Ken to get out, but he was too slow. He was halfway out when a three to four ton jack toppled over and fell on him. He was squashed but was still conscious. I got the crane to lift the jack off, and we took him to a hospital. He was a real mess; he'd been crushed. I came back and cleaned bits of flesh off the jack and swept up the blood. It made me sick."

Although this incident really shook Harry and he was to have nightmares about it for a long time afterwards, it was not the ultimate cause of his breakdown. The accident had happened to someone else. He did, however, become more tense and nervous although he tried to push these feelings aside. He couldn't avoid the daily reminders of Ken's accident, he had to keep going to work, but he did avoid facing the danger in the person of Ken.

"Ken's never been the same. He used to be a great big fat guy, laughing all the time, loved a beer. Now he's skinny and quiet and he can't get around very well. I don't think I can go back and see him because it upsets me too much.

"I went back to work and an inspector came the next day. He told us the job was really dangerous, but nothing was done. I kept doing it, but I was very scared and then, in the one day, a rail truck fell off a jack twice while I was under it. I got the shock of my life - it's so loud - I couldn't get out and I thought I was finished. When it happened the second time, I'd had enough. I broke down in the supervisor's office and I've never been back to work."

Fear, after a six-month period of increased anxiety, had ultimately destroyed his capacity for coping. There was a large element of fear in Tom's breakdown too, although his was of a different nature. What was under threat in Tom's case was his professional competence as a teacher. It didn't matter that previously he'd had an excellent reputation or that other teachers had experienced hassles with these kids too. What was significant for Tom was that his self-confidence and his belief in his own abilities were being rapidly undermined.

For Margaret, the element of fear was different again. She had been a believer in the innate goodness of other people. Coming face to face with evil in someone she knew was enough to make her question her belief system. It not only undermined her confidence in other people, but also undermined her confidence in herself.

Support

Another factor in determining whether a person has a breakdown is the degree of support they have when they encounter trouble. For many people this is the turning point. If they get constructive help at this stage, a breakdown can still be avoided. If they experience frustration, if they blame themselves and don't seek support, or worse still, are blamed for their inability to handle a situation, feelings of shame, guilt, and helplessness escalate rapidly.

After a major disaster there is usually a great deal of formal and informal support. Counselors experienced in post-trauma work, emphasize to people that all the stress symptoms they are experiencing are perfectly normal. Contact with others who have been through the same experience confirms this. An Ash Wednesday survivor said, "Even though the fire directly affected each of us in different ways there was, and still is, five years later, a strong support network that is probably almost imperceptible to outsiders. You can fall apart now and then and others know why without asking.

"The ones I feel most sorry for are those who left the town, and there were many of them. We don't have contact with them and I often wonder what private hell they must be going through on their own. There is an immediate understanding on a hot windy day. We know that we are all thinking the same thing and it helps."

Support may or may not be available when the stresses are not so obvious, are cumulative, and build up over time.

Jennifer found herself in this predicament. No matter where she turned or who she asked, help was not forthcoming. Even worse than that, lack of support made her feel that it must be her fault. To this day she does not really understand why she had a breakdown and blames herself.

A work environment, where people pride themselves on the ability to cope and where there is subtle or not so subtle pressure on them to talk with pride about successes rather than to seek help when they are not coping may do a lot for morale, but it makes a breakdown more likely.

George felt too ashamed to ask for help. He told himself, "Everyone else copes, so there must be something wrong with me if I can't." The frustration that he experienced was partly of his own making and partly resulted from the prevailing "macho" climate he was working in. He was too ashamed to ask for help until it was too late, until he had broken down.

Stan, working in a similar environment, as a policeman, so successfully blocked off his feelings of inadequacy that he was unaware of them himself. Checking into the motel and attempting suicide seemed the only way out.

Boredom

We all need some stimulation in our lives. We all need some activity and, although we all hate to be bored, we don't think of boredom as being a significant cause of stress. We equate stress with disasters, trauma, overwork and conflict, or in other words, excessive stimulation, but of course lack of stimulation is also extremely stressful. Solitary confinement and brain-washing rely on sensory deprivation for their affect on our behavior. M uch of our entertainment industry is a recognition of the importance in our lives of the need to escape from boredom.

Boredom is the daily lot of many people: factory workers, inmates of large institutions, people stuck at home, the elderly, the impoverished, and housewives. Lack of stimulation as a cause of stress has been recognized and studied for a long time now and the solutions are readily at hand, primarily requiring new initiatives and money for their implementation. The groups who miss out on this activity are people who are not part of a large institution, usually people stuck at home - invalids, the elderly, or most commonly, housewives with young children.

Housewives are at a particular disadvantage because their work is so undervalued and it's hard to build up self-esteem as the mother of young children. Many mothers have been in the workforce and have left a successful career to raise their children. They have swapped the hurly-burly of the workplace for the solitude of motherhood and they are often isolated in outer suburbs. Young parents have had little opportunity to acquire assets and they may not have their own transportation. They have the constant responsibility and care for their children.

As a general rule mothers with two or more pre-school children are exhausted by years of broken sleep, cleaning up after children, changing diapers, cooking meals, tidying the house and mothering lively, young children.

An old Russian proverb sums it up very well: "You can't pay someone to do what a mother does for free."

Many women feel cheated. They feel they have become a drudge. They are burdened in unexpected ways, lacking physical and emotional support from their husbands and deprived of any fun and excitement.

Fatigue

The role of fatigue in the cycle that creates a breakdown is a crucial one, as we have seen with Dawn, the housewife. Helen's primary problem was also fatigue. It arose from the demands of her family and the extra workload placed on her once Vincent, her supervisor, went on leave. Out of her fatigue arose more frustration and then fear. Her fear was of the loss of her job, of her family falling apart and of the loss of her health. Vincent's actions on his return from leave interrupted the cycle by removing her sense of frustration and by dealing with her fatigue, with rest.

The others were not so fortunate. As their fatigue worsened, Tom, Jennifer, George and Brendan found themselves less able to cope. When they most needed stamina, a clear head and the strength to take a stand and ultimately defend themselves, they became locked into a downward spiral of exhaustion, frustration and powerlessness, and then fear. And yet they kept going. These people were not quitters. They pushed themselves until something gave way. Again they were showing assets that had become liabilities. Their commitment, pride, strength, and determination had kept them going long after they should have seen the need to stop.

There is a final fear component which, for some, is the trigger for their breakdown. For others, it is another of the fears that prolongs recovery. It is the terror and uncertainty of not knowing what is wrong, or worse still, the fear of going mad.

Those who have been through major and obvious trauma can at least partly understand their own condition. It doesn't seem to make sense to those who have endured slow-motion trauma. Often it doesn't make sense to their doctors either because they don't see the basic cause. The investigations and "treatment" that follow only add to the person's confusion and fear.

Margaret, George, Tom, Brendan, Jennifer and Stan all had treatment that made them worse, as we will see later.

Sometimes the treatment seemed to confirm their fear of going mad; mostly it just felt irrelevant. Each time they left the doctor's they felt more helpless and scared.

This cycle of breakdown with its three components of fear, fatigue and frustration has implications for both prevention and treatment of breakdown. If one of these elements can be removed before the cycle becomes established, a breakdown can be avoided. Thus someone who is afraid and experiencing frustration is less likely to have a breakdown if they are not so emotionally, physically and mentally tired. Similarly, even if fatigue and frustration are pronounced, but the person does not become fearful, a breakdown can be avoided. Fear was just starting to become a factor in Helen's situation when Vincent's actions prompted the amelioration of her frustration and fatigue.

Treatment of someone who has had a breakdown similarly needs to address all three elements of the breakdown cycle. It is not enough to deal just with fatigue, for instance, by resting, if fear and frustration are not also considered. Tom was able to rest physically when he stopped work, but he became more frightened. He wondered if he would ever work again, and he was frightened of going broke and of the change in his relationship with his wife and children. He didn't know what was wrong with him and the more people he went to for help the more bewildered he became. His fear of seeing a psychologist had to be reduced. He was enormously frustrated by having nothing to do. Whenever he tried some new project he found himself frustrated by his own symptoms and eventually had to learn how to adjust to his new state. He felt like a great engine that was running at full speed but had no work to do. Even the slightest exertion would render the engine immobile.

Once the point of breakdown has been reached, you must cope with an altered life, a changed reality and all the dislocations these changes bring in their wake.

The next section of the book will explore these changes, their influence on you, your family and your work, and ways of coping.

PART TWO

GATHERING THE PIECES

7

Coping With Not Coping

A breakdown is a shattering experience for most people. If you have been through a breakdown yourself, you know that it was one of the most difficult periods of your life. You couldn't work, you couldn't play, you had no love to give and your family inevitably suffered.

Yet most people do recover, most are able to pick up the threads of their life again. Some even find renewed strength and hope and say later that this has been the most productive time of their life. The pain and anguish has forced them to change the patterns of a lifetime, and that change may bring a serenity and harmony that is new.

This section of the book is written to help you get better, to help you get your life back together again. In this chapter we will try to answer a number of questions. How do people get better? How do I get well? Will I be able to work again?

Although the ideas presented are very specific, they are not intended to be dogmatic. These ideas are suggestions; a distillation of all the many strategies and tricks that others have used to help them recover. If a specific strategy doesn't work for you, doesn't apply to you, or causes too much disruption to the family, then modify it, or don't use it. There is no single answer, no single way. You must use these suggestions to suit you, your circumstances and your personality.

Most of us take for granted such everyday events as going for a walk, ringing a friend or cooking a meal. We drive to work and never notice the effort involved in steering, changing gears and driving through traffic.

We scarcely remember any of the decisions we make once we're there, or the chit-chat during the day with work mates. Our days have a familiar pattern and most of the time our ordinary, everyday activities are on "semi-automatic." If you are stressed, you will find these familiar, routine tasks become more difficult and require more concentration. If you have suffered a breakdown, these everyday chores may seem impossible, yet you could once handle them with ease.

Will stress management help?

  Tom's experiences in a stress management course can help us to see why stress management may not help someone who is on the verge of a breakdown. Tom attended a stress management course organized by the student counselor at the school. The leader of the course was experienced and enthusiastic and his suggestions were very sensible, but the timing for Tom was all wrong. It was almost two years later before he did another stress course, and this time he was ready, and he could act on the suggestions that were made.

  "At the first course I went to before I stopped working, the course leader suggested that we should build up our stamina by exercising for about 20 minutes, three times a week. He said it would help with sleep too. It made sense, but I couldn't do it. I was so exhausted after I got home from work that it was just too much effort. I tried it a few times but it just made me worse and then I thought I was being pathetic."

  Tom struggled with the course. He was feeling more and more desperate, and he clung to the leader's suggestions like a drowning man hanging onto a life-raft. The program followed the usual sequence of such courses. There was a talk on stress and its affects, an examination of the various pressures and strains the people in the course were experiencing and a demonstration of various techniques that help to reduce stress levels. Tom was shown how to relax, how to manage his time more efficiently and encouraged to try and think logically when dealing with stress.

  "He taught us various ways of relaxing, but I couldn't even do them in the classes, let alone at home. One technique was to imagine I was in a very peaceful place, so I thought about the farm. When I was a kid, I used to go off to the old watering hole to be alone, and to think. I tried to put myself back there, but it was no good, my mind kept sliding away. I had a stream of different thoughts jostling through my mind. I'd think of something Betty said, or those two rotten kids in the afternoon class, or my doctor's appointment. My mind wouldn't stop. The harder I tried to do what he said, the more difficult it became to turn off those thoughts. It made me feel really stupid and a failure. I mean I couldn't even do a simple thing like that!"

  Tom found the stress management course made him feel more stressed. By the time he began the course, he was too far gone to be able to benefit from it. Tom said later, "It was really a case of rearranging the deck chairs on the Titanic."

The importance of timing

It is much easier to deal with stress than it is to deal with a breakdown. The earlier you realize this and take action, the quicker you are back to normal. Recovery from stress is usually quite rapid, but recovery from breakdown is much more drawn out.

There are a range of options available for dealing with stress: taking a few days off, changing your job, developing a new hobby, cutting back your workload and getting fitter. If you are much more highly stressed, these "first aid" approaches won't work, and you may need professional advice quickly. Once you have broken down, your range of options becomes much more restricted. Techniques that work with stress do not necessarily work with breakdown and may even make the situation worse, as occurred with Tom.

The first and most important step is to recognize that there is a problem.

Recognition and understanding are the first steps towards recovery from a breakdown. Once Margaret and Tom knew what was wrong with them, they were able to make sense of what was happening. Their symptoms, and behavior, were understandable and certainly did not mean they were stupid, weak or pathetic, as they had imagined. Until they began to understand some of this, they felt they were operating in the dark. Margaret thought most of the "experts" were in the dark too. "It really was the blind leading the blind," she said.

Although this understanding may sound easy to attain in practice, it is not so easy to get and it's certainly not easy to put into operation.

The natural reaction of many is to fight back, or to deny that anything is wrong. Some people have done this throughout their lives when they have been faced with trouble and have often been very successful. This quality of resistance has become an integral part of their personality. It is ironic that this very quality may contribute to a breakdown, because they keep pushing, fighting and denying that they are in trouble long after a wiser soul would have given up. As one man said, "I thought, at first, that I was either incredibly strong, or incredibly stupid, now I know I was both!"

A basic theme that underlies all the suggestions and comments that are made here is that of knowing yourself, of listening to your body, of listening to all those body messages we have trained ourselves to ignore. We pride ourselves on keeping our feelings under wraps, in keeping cool when all around is chaos. This is admirable, to a degree, but you pay a price for this sort of control.

People who break down have a tendency to ignore their body

signals. In doing so, you do yourself harm, and over time this harm to your resilience, to your coping capacity is cumulative. The essential task in recovery from a breakdown is to learn to listen to those forgotten, and often ignored messages. You must learn to act on them and avoid the vicious circle that has been established, where you push and push to the point where your whole system is screaming at you to stop.

8

Getting Help

Finding the right person to help you recover from your breakdown may not be easy and unfortunately you have to do this at a time when you have no energy, when you're not thinking very clearly and when you feel extremely sensitive and vulnerable. This is someone you'll need to trust and have confidence in over a long time so it is necessary to choose that person carefully.

Although you will probably have one primary person who is involved in helping you to deal with the main elements of your recovery, you will possibly need to see other people at various times for specialized help. Some people regularly see both their family doctor and a psychiatrist or psychologist.

Later you might need to see other medical specialists, a careers advisor, a marriage guidance counselor or a lawyer. Depending on how intimately involved they are in helping you, you will need to apply the same criterion to each of these people. You will want to find someone who listens to you, who tries to understand your predicament and who can offer you professional advice based not only on their own training but also on an understanding of how your breakdown has affected you. The first task you will confront is to find the right person to help you get over your breakdown.

Both Tom and Margaret found that getting the right treatment was not easy. Tom saw a number of doctors and was given conflicting advice and went through a number of "treatment" programs. Fortunately these did not seem to make him worse, which is more than Margaret could say. Her local doctor had been an old family friend. He thought she was being "dramatic" and although he seemed sympathetic at first, his manner changed quite abruptly.

"I called him one night because I was feeling so terrible. He took ages coming to the phone, and he seemed very peeved. I began crying. I sensed his hostility, and it made me feel worse than before I called. He told me that I should be ashamed of myself, that I was letting everyone down and that if I didn't pull myself together he could have me certified. I hung up on him and stumbled away from the phone; I think I really reached rock bottom then. It took me a long, long time to trust anyone after that. I still can't speak to him. I feel so angry at him that I could kill him. I heard from a friend that he had told several people that I had needed a good talking to. She said he was quite smug and seemed to think he was responsible for my improvement.

"Looking back on it, the funny thing was that I had really known he was no good for me even when I was well, but I couldn't trust my instincts. He'd always been superficially nice, but he'd get a glazed look in his face if I spoke to him about anything important. I've seen a few more people since then and I was very happy with two of them in particular.

"Both of them gave me lots of time. They weren't particularly sympathetic, but they seemed to know what I meant. I felt like they understood me.

"The most important thing was that I left the appointments feeling better, and I think now that's the most important thing to have; it's the best guide of all."

George, the fireman, had an equally dismal experience with his doctors.

"I knew I wasn't coping and it was only a matter of time before I had to give work away. I'd seen my local doctor and he'd given me some pills but they weren't much good. I wasn't sure what they were meant to do. I probably didn't tell him very much so he didn't know how bad I really was, so I can't really blame him for what happened.

"I was using booze as a sedative. I was really getting into it at home, mainly liquor, but I reckon it was the only way to fall asleep. I was drinking a bit at work, too. I'd keep a bottle of vodka in my locker. I figured you couldn't smell vodka as much, and I'd go to my locker a few times during the day and have a quick snort. I think the other guys knew because they'd nod at each other and smile when I went to the locker room. When I stopped work, I was feeling terrible. I was too scared to do the job, my wife had left me, and my kids thought I was a drunk.

"I was sent to see a psychiatrist and put into the hospital to dry out. I stopped drinking all right, and he gave me something to calm me down. I think the pain of it all hit me there, and I began crying and really feeling terrible. I think that's when I really hit rock bottom, but I'd been delaying the inevitable."

George started crying in the group therapy session and his psychiatrist arranged for him to have a course of electric shock treatment. The treatment didn't lift his mood or help him to cope with the breakdown.

"When I eventually got out of that place I still felt pretty confused by that shock treatment, and I felt that I was a nut, a "psycho." I saw the psychiatrist a few more times, but I'd always feel a bit scared. Maybe it was me, but I never thought he was interested. He'd keep me waiting for up to an hour, and then he'd see me for only a few minutes. He'd give me some more "happy pills," and if I started talking about how I was feeling he'd put his head down and write notes - he never seemed to look at you. You'd sit in front of this big desk and the phone would ring or his secretary would come in. It was a damned circus.

"I was none the wiser. I didn't know what was wrong, I didn't know how to make it better.

"A friend of mine came to visit me after I'd been off work for a year. My place was a mess. I wasn't drinking, but I felt damned close to wiping myself out again. This friend of mine, Ted, had had stress problems and he got me to see his psychiatrist. Well! It was like chalk and cheese comparing the fellow I'd been seeing and this new fellow. The new guy was human; he'd listen to you. He didn't just listen though, he'd answer my questions. He didn't make me feel like I was a specimen in a jar, he made me feel like a person."

George's experience shows how important it is to find someone who really tries to put themselves in your position. The first psychiatrist had successfully worked on what he saw as George's main problem, his drinking, but George knew there was much more to it. Being treated with respect, and as a person with a number of legitimate concerns, was much more helpful than being treated as another problem drinker. George's new psychiatrist was also able to give him an explanation about what had happened to him.

"After I told him what had happened, he asked me if I thought I'd had a breakdown. That was the first time anyone had mentioned a breakdown. I'm no doctor, so I don't really know what a breakdown is, but I'd always thought I'd had one. He asked me when I thought it had happened, and I told him about the two girls in the car with only one resuscitator and that I reckoned it happened then.

"He listened some more and then told me about breakdowns, what causes them, what they're like and what you can do about it. He was the first person I'd seen who made any sense, he seemed to know all about it. Later on, after I got to know him a bit better, I asked him if he'd had a breakdown himself. He hadn't, but he'd listened to so many stories that he felt like he was very familiar with it.

"It made a lot of difference talking about me having a breakdown. I'd read the hospital notes about me. They'd called me a manic-depressive with an alcohol-dependent personality, whatever all that means, but I know it made me feel like a real nut case. They seemed to think I'd always been a bit of a nut, and I know I was a bit off for a while, but I'd done a good job for a long time, what about that!

"My new psychiatrist has been a lot of help. He talks to me in language I can understand, and he gives me advice about little things that bug me - like the phone, which sends shudders through me, and driving, which makes me shake sometimes. He's got a lot of patience and he's stuck by me.

"He has given me hope, and encouraged me to do more with my life. I've stopped all my tablets and I'm not drinking. I've started some jogging, and I go to an aerobics class. I've been seeing my wife again, once or twice a week, and there is a chance we could get back together. I've been working in the local plant nursery on a part-time basis. I love it, and I'm really enjoying working with plants rather than people."

George was fortunate to have a friend who could recommend someone who was reliable, who knew what he was doing and who didn't overcharge.

Tom was not so lucky. He went from one doctor to another and finally, in desperation, became involved with a number of alternative treatments, most of which did little for him. Each new person he saw thought they had the answer to his problems. Tom would initially be enthusiastic, but each time he became more disillusioned and more desperate when the hoped-for cure did not help.

Betty watched with a mixture of frustration, pity and anger. She felt that most of them were quacks, and she was worried about the expense. Sometimes it seemed the less they knew, the more they charged. She was reluctant to broach the subject with Tom because he was so touchy, besides which, she didn't know who else to recommend. Tom was embarrassed as he told of his search for treatment.

"Although I was feeling awful when I stopped work, I was still very restless and not ready to give in to it. I felt I had to fight my breakdown before it swallowed me; in those first few months I had to beat it. I'd do anything, because I knew there was something terribly wrong. I wore out my welcome with my local doctor.

"Next I was off to see a naturopath. She was a lovely woman, but I really don't think she had a clue, and then to a herbalist, next an iridologist. All useless as far as my breakdown was concerned.

"Then someone suggested I try orthomolecular medicine. This guy I saw was convinced he could help me. He did all these tests which showed I was being poisoned by mercury leaking out of my fillings! He gave me lots of vitamins, and I went off to the dentist to have my fillings fixed. Needless to say it all cost piles of money and nothing improved.

"The last person I saw before I landed on my feet was a doctor who reckoned everyone had some terrible fungal disease everywhere and it gave you all those symptoms. Fool that I was, I got really excited. I remember telling Betty that I thought I'd found the answer. I took the tablets - but nothing happened.

"When Betty told me that she would leave if I didn't stop, I knew she was right. Deep down I knew I was fooling myself and fighting against the inevitable.

"None of those people had much idea about what I was going through at all and they didn't have an answer any more than I did. I was just stupid to think that I could even think about another job at that stage.

"Later I started seeing someone who knew what they were talking about and things started to slowly improve and I've gone on from there."

Jerry, the bank manager who lived in the country town, saw a psychiatrist. He told him he was depressed and put him on a course of anti-depressants. Jerry put on 10 kilos in three months. Three years later he is still struggling to lose weight. He stopped taking the anti-depressant long ago because it didn't help.

Jennifer, the teacher with crying students, saw a psychotherapist. He seemed uninterested in the trouble she'd had at school and kept focusing on some hidden resentment she'd had towards her mother because her father was away in the war for three years. Jennifer was unsure what the therapist meant, but he seemed to know what he was talking about. Jennifer felt that it was irrelevant to her school experience and she stopped going.

Brendan, the social worker, who was so confused after his breakdown, had an even more bizarre experience. He fell into the hands of a religious zealot, a general practitioner who believed in devil possession. This doctor told Brendan that his breakdown was caused by his living in sin with Jeannie. He told Brendan to get up at two every morning and read the bible for two hours. Then he had to tell his parents that he'd sinned by sleeping with his girlfriend. His parents sensibly thought he was being silly because, after all, they already knew. Brendan decided he'd had enough of this. He was getting worse rather than better, and Jeannie thought it was absolutely ridiculous. She urged him to go back to the union welfare officer who seemed to be a bit stunned when Brendan told her what the doctor had recommended. She suggested a psychologist who was much more help.

Other people can tell similar stories of dealing with therapists who are ignorant, unwise, rude, confusing, even cruel. So what do people who have broken down need? What are those who have broken down looking for? And how do they go about getting it?

Margaret and Tom have learned to look for someone who is caring, understanding, consistent, willing to help and to listen. Both had seen therapists who had ignored or dismissed their feelings of having "broken down". But they felt they needed more, they needed a therapist who could trust them and help them to trust themselves. Margaret and Tom had both found therapists who asked them directly if they thought they'd had a breakdown.

Everyone who has had a breakdown knows it. Others, like Helen, who have come close but have not reached the breaking point are just as aware that they have not broken down.

Margaret said, "Being asked about my breakdown was wonderful. He just took it all in. We seemed to be working together. He encouraged me to trust that my body knew how to heal itself. His job, he told me, was to help me stop interfering with my body and let it get on with its job. He helped me learn ways of getting through the day. He was like a coach to me. He helped me to trust my body. I found it much easier to feel bad then because I could see it was part of the healing process. All that gave me so much help."

Tom's therapist seemed to have similar aims. Both of them felt it could be a long search finding the right person, but it was worth the time. It didn't seem to matter whether this person was a psychiatrist, a psychologist, a counselor or a social worker.

Margaret developed her own strategy for finding good health care professionals: "My general rule was that if I saw someone new I had to feel comfortable with them, and if I was no better after four visits I had to tell the person I was seeing that they weren't helping, and if they couldn't handle that I gave them the flick. I realized that there are a lot of people out there who are making tons of money out of us. Even the good ones can cost a bit."

Workers' compensation paid for Tom's treatment, but Margaret had to pay for herself, and she found it was cheaper to see a psychiatrist because her health fund refunded more money. At times it was handy to see a doctor because sometimes she needed medication to help her sleep.

Tom's psychologist worked closely with a psychiatrist and both of them collaborated in Tom's treatment.

Tom said: "After I got over the first bit of my breakdown, I got a bit restless and wanted to do a bit more. My psychologist helped me sort out what I wanted to do. It was terrific because I was settled enough to be able to sit quietly without feeling terrible. It was totally different from the time I tried it before I left work. The timing seemed right, and I could get the most out of it. It was the same with the other things I did - the timing had to be right for me to get something out of them. I joined an early retirement group, and I'm still a member. The group has been a terrific support because we are all at the same place in recovering from our breakdowns. We've become good friends and socialize quite a bit."

Margaret said: "I don't think I could have got through it without my doctor. I'd talk about my crazy thoughts or about my feeling that nothing was helping and he'd listen. He didn't get angry or upset. I looked for someone who was empathic and who knew what it was all about. Both were necessary: empathy and knowledge."

These qualities are not only needed by those providing your main treatment. You will probably need to see other professionals to get advice about the different dilemmas arising from your breakdown. They may be therapists, financial advisers, lawyers and accountants but their advice will be of much more use to you if they are familiar with the limitations that a breakdown puts on you.

Brendan found such a person when he was thinking about leaving social work and trying a new career.

"At one stage, when I was getting a lot better, I wanted to investigate other careers, and I arranged to see a vocational psychologist who was used to advising people who'd had a breakdown. He understood straight away what I wanted. He knew I couldn't go back to a pressured job involving contact with other people and that I didn't want a laboring job either. He had a few ideas about what other work I could do, and investigated the retraining courses that might be suitable. He sent me to a computer programmers' introductory course. It was after talking to him that I asked my boss if the department could organize different duties for me. They gave me part time administrative work and some study leave to do the computer work.

Like Margaret, Tom and Brendan, you will find that it is just as important to find someone with the right personality for you as it is to find someone with the right knowledge and expertise.

Presenting your story

During your recuperation you will be surprised at how many people you will have to tell the story to. It will start to sound like a broken record as it is told to yet another doctor, counselor or lawyer. As time passes, you might worry about forgetting important details and be bothered about these omissions later.

Invariably, someone who has had a breakdown is shocked by how intense their feelings are when they are asked to recall what happened. Even more disturbing is the realization that the memory has not been very well buried. Any small reminders of the trauma are bad enough but having to explain it to someone new is like being right back there, re-experiencing it. The more successful you think you have been in forgetting it, the more distressing it is to find it all emerging again. It can feel as though all this time has passed and yet you are no better, although actually you have recovered much more than you imagine.

Perceived or actual insensitivity, or even hostility, on the part of the interviewer will add to your feelings of rage and impotence. Tom described his frustration:

"Everyone I saw made me go through the whole thing again. It was no good saying I'd told everyone else. The trouble was that every time I went through it again I'd start feeling terrible and I'd cry and I'd make a fool of myself. It's no good saying I didn't, because I did.

"I told the welfare officer at the union that I couldn't go through any more of these torture sessions. I'd get really scared, even days beforehand. I wasn't sleeping, and I'd go into the session feeling awful and expecting some aggravation. I think I must have given off those angry vibes because some of the doctors who saw me were unbelievable. I reckon they were unethical in the way they talked to me. One doctor told me to my face that I was a liar. God, I nearly whacked him.

"Then, for days afterwards, I'd be reliving it all again. I felt like they were really making me pay for my money in blood. I began wondering myself if I was putting some of it on."

Tom started to work out some ways of making these sessions less upsetting.

"The welfare officer helped me sort it out. She helped me write a statement; it was a biography. It gave some of my family background, my early career and other interests, and it related, in some detail, the events leading up to my breakdown and afterwards. She made me keep it quite short, about three to four pages, I think. She told me to bring a copy to each new doctor. It helped a lot."

Tom also began to realize that he was better off if he told his interviewer how hard it was for him to go through it all again. That seemed to bring about a much better response than when he tried to tough it out or skim over details because he didn't want to get upset again.

The welfare officer gave him a few ideas about managing the interviewer's hostility.

"She also told me how to deal with rudeness. We even practiced a couple of times. She told me to leave immediately I began feeling upset and to keep a record of all that happened in the interview by writing it down or using a tape recorder and sending a letter to the insurance company or whoever had sent me there, with a copy to the doctor. I did that twice. It was terrific. I felt like I had some control of my life again. I even got a response. I began to think I was dealing with people and not just them."

Other health problems

The physical affects of a breakdown vary from one person to another depending on their biological predisposition to various illnesses. While being under severe stress for a prolonged period is not the sole cause of these health problems, they may be aggravated or accelerated by such pressures. All three, Margaret, Helen and Tom, found that their general level of health declined. Their physical symptoms were different, but all of them reflected the same underlying aggravation.

Tom's doctor was treating him for high blood pressure and his arthritis, which had suddenly flared up; Margaret developed menstrual problems; and Helen couldn't get rid of her constant headaches.

Margaret commented, "I felt like my body was breaking up; bits of me seemed to be going on strike." Others find that they have developed multiple allergies, various aches and pains, or skin problems.

Many such conditions require active treatment, although the success of treatment may be limited by the person's ability to reduce their stress levels.

Margaret explained to her gynecologist that she had been experiencing stress problems. He found it helpful in understanding her unusual symptoms, and he was more comfortable in allowing her symptoms to settle gradually. Margaret resisted the impulse to pour out her heart to him because she had learnt from experience that it was best not to say too much. She'd had enough of well-meaning but unwanted or ill-informed advice about stress breakdown, so she told him the bare facts, all he needed to know to treat her gynecological condition.

It can seem as if your whole life revolves around your "breakdown." Some doctors will try to ascribe every health problem to stress. There may be a connection, but it can be misleading and confusing to ascribe everything to stress, especially if it means that your doctor fails to treat a condition adequately that has little to do with your stressed state.

Brendan developed kidney stones, and his kidney symptoms

were first thought to be caused by "stress." He knew these symptoms were different, and he insisted that he have proper investigations. The X-ray showed some small kidney stones that, fortunately, didn't require an operation.

After Jennifer had been off work for a few months, she became troubled by severe stomach pains and an inability to digest certain foods. At first she thought this was just another nervous reaction but, unlike her other symptoms, there was no pattern to them. They occurred whether she was rested or tired, tense or relaxed. Her doctor finally referred her to a gastroenterologist who diagnosed gall bladder disease. After the operation to remove her gall bladder she was surprised at how much better she felt physically. The symptoms of her breakdown remained and she began to get a better idea of how to manage them

Drug therapy

For some people, medication is a really useful tool to help them recover from a breakdown. For others, having to resort to medication would be the ultimate in loss of independence. Most people do use drugs at some point during their recovery and, although they do not provide a cure, they can make some of your symptoms easier to endure.

The main question for you to answer will be whether the relief you experience outweighs the personal and chemical side-effects of using drugs. Your doctor can be useful in helping you learn the proper use of drugs. Everyone has heard horror stories of people being "bombed out" on medication, and these stories can make people uneasy. The key to making medication work for you is intelligent self-education under the guidance of your doctor.

Helen had a short course of a tranquilizer and this helped her to sleep and to lose some of her tensions.

Margaret had a bad reaction to an anti-depressant: "I felt unreal and sluggish. I was stumbling and felt really dopey, but I was still feeling terrible. He told me I wasn't taking enough! I threw them away, of course. In a way, I was relieved they hadn't worked. I really wanted to do it myself. A long time later, my current psychiatrist suggested I take Valium tablets occasionally to help fatigue. He knew how scared I was of drugs, and he didn't push it at all. I took a Valium occasionally, and it helped, but I always felt like I was being sinful. Silly, I suppose."

Tom had a course of anti-depressants, and he found them very useful. He thought the difference was that his doctor advised him to increase the dose gradually to a level that seemed to work for him without making him feel dopey.

"I checked my dose each morning. If I was feeling drowsy, I'd keep the same dose that night. If I was feeling clear-headed, I would increase the dose by one tablet. That way I found that I could take five tablets at night. The doctor told me how to take it and what side-effects to expect. I knew I'd have a dry mouth and sometimes feel dizzy. He respected me enough to know I'd behave responsibly and sensibly. He'd also told me not to expect any miracle cures. So my experiences with drugs were quite positive."

Tranquilizers can be very useful. Sometimes your level of anxiety and agitation can be so high that it is hard to endure, and because you feel too awful it is impossible to do anything like meditation or relaxation. Tranquilizers help a good deal to reduce your anxiety to manageable levels. The drug can't get rid of your anxiety altogether but it helps you at times when you are likely to be overwhelmed by your tension.

Tranquilizers such as Valium or Serepax are also useful in helping you to sleep better. Short courses of a month or two and then a break can avoid dependency. Take the dose about an hour before you want to sleep.

The hypnotics, like Mogadon or Dalmane, and some of the anti-depressants, Tryptanol, Tolvon and Sinequan among others, can also help if you are not getting enough sleep.

Tranquilizers can also help you to manage that "bone-weary" exhaustion that many people experience in stress breakdown. This profound lethargy is very disabling. Valium seems to be effective in reducing this because the weariness is not just muscular fatigue, but also seems to be closely connected to tension. Normally, taking half a five-milligram tablet before a stressful event or every hour or so afterwards for three or four half tablets seems to work best. It is useful to keep a record of how much you take and when you are taking it.

There are some people who develop very specific psychiatric illnesses arising out of a stress breakdown. There may be a vulnerability in their families or they may have had a similar illness before. Whatever the reason, they will need specific treatment for that condition.

The three major psychiatric conditions that can be triggered by stress are schizophrenia, severe depression and panic attacks. They all require expert psychiatric diagnosis and treatment. Improvement, or even resolution of these conditions may not have much influence on the underlying stress breakdown that triggered off these illnesses.

A final word of caution about medication. It can be extremely dangerous to suddenly stop taking some drugs. When you get to the stage where you want to try managing without medication seek professional advice about the best way of doing so, because there are some which you need to reduce gradually over a period of weeks.

9

Handling Work

Angelo was pleased when his old boss, Harry, gave him a job back in the furniture department at Monroe's, the department store where he had worked as a young man. He had been operating his own furniture business with his brother-in-law, Roy Kelly. They had called the store "Kelly and Madonia." The business never quite met Angelo's expectations, but he made a reasonable living until Roy's heart attack and then the fire a few months later which burned the poorly insured building to the ground.

Angelo was out of a job, with big debts, and a sense of failure. He remained unemployed until weeks later when he happened to meet Harry in the street and was offered the job at Monroe's. He was to be responsible for the whole furniture department: ordering, pricing, sales and advertising. He had something to prove and threw himself into the work.

Within a year he had boosted sales by 30 per cent, but unwittingly he had made a rod for his own back. He was expected to produce the same percentage increase every year or be fired. He wasn't going to fail again, so he set to the task, cut his suppliers' margins to the bone, drove his staff mercilessly, and worked even longer hours. He was successful that second year, but not so the third, and he was threatened with dismissal if the figures didn't improve.

Angelo felt trapped; he could see no way out. His suppliers were already bitter about their narrow margins, and the sales staff were disillusioned and were quitting. His health deteriorated rapidly. He was drinking and smoking too much, and not sleeping. He was tense, irritable, and frightened. His job was becoming a nightmare, but what could he do?

Angelo's dilemma is common enough. Work pressures were undermining his health. He felt trapped and powerless to change his situation. He knew that work was "killing" him, but the thought of leaving the job made him feel like a quitter, and what else was he to do? It had been difficult enough getting this job.

If you've had work problems and you're considering your options, you will know how tough it is to make the right decision.

Sometimes, as with Tom and Margaret, the decision is made for you. You can't continue; your health won't allow it. Most people, however, have the choice, certainly in the beginning, of staying at work or leaving. Stress, whether from the job or from elsewhere, will affect your ability to do your work effectively. How you feel about this will depend on the meaning work has for you. For some people, work is central to their life, for others, work has been a drudge, or a means to an end.

The decision about whether or not to stop work may be a difficult one to make. Some people find their work so unpleasant, however, that the decision to leave work is easy. If you are keen to stay at work, you must decide whether work is helping or hindering your recovery. If your work is causing you problems, these difficulties need to be identified quickly and, if possible, resolved. This may require the cooperation of the management and your co-workers. If this proves difficult, you should think about changing jobs or having a spell from work completely.

Colleagues and management can help by reducing your workload. This could involve dropping some responsibilities or working shorter hours. Often this help is too late, and you must take some time off work. This time off may vary from a few weeks to some years, a nd it will depend on your state of health, your job, your ability to do the job, and the cooperation you receive. Despite your reduced effectiveness at work, you may be very reluctant to leave, even if you're aware how poorly you're coping. Many simply don't recognize this, however, and can see no reason to leave, or even to get help.

You may try to stay at work, even if you're struggling, out of a sense of loyalty. If you have good work mates and a supportive boss, it may be difficult to leave them in the lurch. If the pressures on you arise away from work, then work may be your refuge. Whether or not work has been contributing to your difficulties, you may not be able to afford to stop work, even for a short time. Some of us get a sense of our status, our identity, at least in part, from our work. An impending, or actual breakdown, rocks our sense of identity, and the inability to work further knocks our self-esteem. You may be reluctant to leave because you fear that once you go, you may never be able to return. You will have fallen behind technologically, or in the promotions race, or you may simply lack the confidence to face your work mates again.

If you decide to try and stay at work, then fatigue may overwhelm you; it is one of the symptoms that can force you to stop. It's very difficult to work effectively if you can't think clearly, if concentration is poor, and memory unreliable, when things go in one ear and out the other. Similarly, it's hard to work when you feel irritable, anxious, despairing, and withdrawn. These symptoms make for impulsive decisions, poor judgment, and diminish your capacity to plan ahead.

In making decisions about work, you will need to consider your state of health; your ability to do the job; the affect your health problems are having on the people you work with; the nature of the work; and your commitment to it.

Work stress

Work itself is often a major source of stress as Angelo, the department manager, had found, but most stressors in themselves aren't enough to cause breakdowns. When we think of work pressures we think of such things as a heavy workload, long hours, an unpleasant office or factory to work in, low morale, inadequate pay, discrimination, excessive red tape, and danger in the job. These factors can all cause health problems, but the trigger to a breakdown, the final straw, is when you feel unappreciated and used.

Reducing work stress

If you're heading for a breakdown, cutting down your work pressures may be the answer. This may involve discussions with your boss directly, or through your union. You need to isolate what it is that's troubling you and suggest realistic changes.

Angelo contacted other department managers at the store and found they were experiencing similar problems. Angelo did some detective work and found that the store management was worried by the increased staff turnover because training new staff was proving very costly.

Angelo began meeting regularly other department heads to develop a plan to save their jobs and benefit the store. The store had become tired and rather stale.

The first inklings of the plan that saved Angelo's health occurred while he was on vacation. He hadn't wanted to go, but his wife insisted - she was at her wit's end. They stayed at an expensive resort, which irritated Angelo but, ironically, a chance remark by his wife in the resort boutique triggered off a chain of thought that culminated in the plan that saved his job. She had said that the quality of the clothing in the boutique was excellent and that she didn't bother shopping at Monroe's, even with their staff discount, because the range was so limited.

Angelo's plan called for moving the store upmarket, away from high-turnover, low-margin goods into high-quality, high-fashion items with an emphasis on service. The owners grabbed the plan with enthusiasm. Within a year the new strategy had proved to be extraordinarily successful. As a result, Angelo saved his job, his sanity, and his marriage. Morale among the other managers soared. Angelo was justly rewarded when he was offered promotion to a senior planning position.

Coping with work fatigue

The decision to leave work is heavily influenced by how tired you have become. The main reason many people stop work is because they're exhausted and they need to rest. This may be difficult to achieve if they keep working. Both Margaret and Tom knew in the end that they had to stop work. But the decision was really made for them because they couldn't continue. Both of them were exhausted, and they had to rest for a long time before their stamina improved. Some people force themselves to continue working despite their breakdown. It is an impossible task, and they soon have to admit defeat.

Patrick, an accountant, tried to stay at work as long as he could, despite his breakdown. He was a long-distance runner and was used to pushing himself. He was particularly concerned about leaving work at tax time. At the end of each day he would flop into bed as soon as he returned home, get up to eat, and then go back to bed again until morning. He couldn't sleep, but he was just too exhausted to do anything else. This regimen only lasted for a few weeks before he was forced to stop work altogether. Patrick realized later that pushing himself to stay at work had made his breakdown worse and had delayed his recovery.

It was more than 18 months after his breakdown before Tom realized that he had been fighting a losing battle at work for years. Some of his work mates had tried to talk to him about his health, but he refused to discuss it. Several of them told him later that they were relieved when he left because they were frightened that he might harm himself for he was looking so haggard and seemed so downhearted.

Work as a refuge

If the pressures on you are unrelated to work, your job may become a refuge, and you will try to stay there as long as you can. This is especially so if you have a good deal of support at work from your work mates, your boss or even from clients, customers, students or whoever else is there. Work can provide a haven from all your other pressures, and it can occupy your mind so that you don't have time to dwell on your troubles.

Pat's mother was dying of cancer. She took a few days' leave every few weeks from her secretarial job to take her mother for radiotherapy treatment and to care for her afterwards, but she was always glad to get back to work.

"Although I felt guilty being away from mom, I knew that I had to look after myself so that I could cope with what lay ahead. Being at work gave me a chance to forget for a little while and feel a bit normal. About a year after mom first got sick we got a telegram from Indonesia. My son Larry had been traveling overseas for two or three years and we'd not heard from him for some weeks but that wasn't too unusual.

"The telegram said that he was sick - nothing else. I was frantic. We couldn't get much information from the embassy in Jakarta except that he was in a small hospital on one of the outlying islands. We had to fly there and bring him back. I had to tell mom about his illness and she became very upset because Larry had always been her favorite grandchild.

"We eventually reached the island after a nightmare trip. We had to fly to Jakarta, get on a small plane that looked like it was held together with paper clips, and then take a small ferry to the outlying island. The last part of the trip was in the back of an old truck. When we got there, I was really beyond exhaustion. The 'hospital' was very primitive, we found Larry in a tin shed in a filthy bed tied to the bed frame. He was unrecognizable. He had lost so much weight and was dressed in rags. He didn't seem to know us at first and was very confused. We were helped by the locals and a man from one of the trade missions.

"God knows how we got him back home, but we did. The embassy people were wonderful. We had made arrangements in Indonesia for him to go into a hospital here. They told us that he had schizophrenia. We were devastated, although it had been our secret fear - he was so strange and withdrawn, in his own world. We arranged for him to see a psychiatrist, and he's on medication, which keeps him fairly stable. mom had a relapse, which was probably related to Larry's illness.

"A few days after we got back home, it all came tumbling in on me. I couldn't get out of bed, I cried all the time, I couldn't think straight. I knew I had to get back to work though, and I started again after four weeks away. My boss knew the whole story. He arranged for me to do some part-time work, and he got in a temporary to take over my job. I was probably not much good to anyone when I first went back, but it salvaged some of my pride."

Pat continued working part time. Her son's condition improved rapidly, but he remained very subdued for a long time and Pat's fears about him receded. Her mother died, quietly and peacefully, about a year after Pat's breakdown. Pat missed her mother very much but was glad that she had not suffered greatly. Pat and her husband left their home soon afterwards and had a leisurely holiday, taking a caravan trip around the country. She took six months' leave from her job to do the trip. She looked forward to going back to work on a full-time basis when she returned. She believed her job had saved her sanity. The attitude of her boss and her work mates had given her a haven from trouble and helped her to build up her self-esteem again.

On being indispensable

Staying at work, when you are not coping, may occur because you refuse to face up to the seriousness of the problem, you feel they couldn't survive without you. You feel a sense of loyalty to your fellow workers and to your employer. Unfortunately, if you stay at work for too long they will have to do some of your work and inevitably they will have to correct your mistakes and their workload can increase considerably under these circumstances. Their initial compassion and support can turn to resentment and antagonism. You become even more isolated and your self-esteem declines further. If this situation has occurred, it becomes much more difficult to come back to the job when you've recovered because your work mates will be more wary and less supportive.

The staff at the bank where Jerry was manager had been concerned for a long time by his behavior. He was angry, tense, irritable and explosive. The staff turnover had been high for at least a year and many had left because of Jerry's rudeness. The morale among those left was very low. Customers were upset with Jerry's abruptness and the long, unexplained delays in transacting their business.

The accountant at the branch had been an old friend of Jerry's and had tried to cover up for months. The older staff members had done the same, but Jerry was hostile about their efforts to help him, and he was suspicious of their motives. At first, they were very sympathetic to Jerry. The problems he was facing were real enough: a dying country town, a bust in the rural economy, farmers going broke and the bank pressuring him to foreclose on properties. Jerry was very much in the middle.

The State manager sent a curt memo to Jerry listing a series of complaints about the operation of the branch. The complaints were very petty but were too much for Jerry, who exploded with anger and "tore strips" off the accountant and the senior staff, blaming them for all his problems. He threatened to write a poor efficiency report about the accountant, which would have been a serious blow to his career and his impending promotion.

The threat lost Jerry his major ally; the accountant felt disillusioned and betrayed. He confronted Jerry the next day and demanded that he get help. Jerry was persuaded to see his doctor and broke down in the doctor's office.

Jerry was off work for several months and during his absence a relieving manager carried on in his place. During his time off work his work mates had little contact with him. They still felt resentment at his behavior, even though they knew he was sick. He returned to work on a part-time basis for a few weeks, but he was treated with suspicion by the bank staff. It was clear that he wasn't wanted, and they resented his return, especially on a part time basis, as it increased their workload, and he had used up any reserves of goodwill. He found the atmosphere at work oppressive, and he was advised to stop work again. His doctor suggested he approach the bank about a transfer, He reluctantly heeded this advice and was transferred to another country town.

The importance of work

We may not realize how important work is to our sense of identity until we have to stop. Then we may feel sadness, loss of purpose and a sense that life has lost its meaning. One of the first questions we ask when we meet someone new is, "What do you do?" Their answer helps us to assess them and give them a position on our own pecking order. How often do we hear people say, "I'm just a housewife," an answer that indicates the low status that seems inherent in that role nowadays, partly because it is seen as unskilled work and partly because it's essentially unpaid. By contrast, a stockbroker's chest may well swell out with pride as he announces his occupation.

Many of us define ourselves, to ourselves, as a teacher, a doctor or a journalist, or whatever, and if we have to give up that occupation we experience a loss, a kind of death of our self-image. Those people in our community, who have particularly low status are those with no money and no job. Being unemployed is not only financially difficult but also demeaning because of the lack of status. Similarly, people who are forced to leave work because of poor health often feel ashamed at their lack of occupation. They feel open to criticism, especially if their illness is not obvious. People feel particularly vulnerable if they have mixed feelings about it, and are secretly frightened that they maybe weak-they may just be trying to avoid work after all.

Jill was a nurse who worked in an intensive care ward. She

developed a golden staph infection and was shattered when she realized that it may stop her working as a nurse again.

"When the full implications of the staph infection hit me, I couldn't stop crying. I loved nursing. It's the only job I ever wanted to do. It felt so cruel that it was being snatched away.

"Mom and Dad have been great, but they have been trying to get me to think about something else. Mom comes into my room and says in that bright voice she uses, 'I just bumped into Mrs. Duncan. Her girl is doing pharmacy. She loves it. She can't talk about anything else; she's doing very well in her course, she enjoys helping people, and she loves the contact with doctors. Do you think that might suit you, dear?' I tell her, 'I don't want to do pharmacy, I don't want to operate bloody computers, I want to do nursing'!"

Can you afford to stop work?

For many, money is the most important consideration in deciding whether or not to stop work. You may not release that most people receive less money on sick leave or workers' compensation than when they are working. All of us have financial commitments and these are usually undertaken with the assumption that our income will continue unchanged. If we do think about sickness, we optimistically assume it will be for only a short time, a matter of weeks at the most.

Unfortunately, having to stay at work because you have used up your sick leave, or because you are self-employed, may create the extra pressures that lead inevitably to a breakdown. It is worth considering, at an early stage of your working life, what you would do if you couldn't work, and make plans accordingly.

It might involve selling your house and buying a smaller one to reduce mortgage payments, as Helen had considered in her darkest moments. You could buy disability insurance, sell your business, or you may survive on social security payments. Angelo's wife was worried about his health, and she began part-time work, anticipating that he would be off work for some time. As it turned out, he did not require any time off work after the pressures at work were reduced.

If you are not aware of your conditions of employment, you should talk to your employer or union about your options. Having an alternative plan of action takes some of the heat out of your situation.

Julie, a medical receptionist, worked for two plastic surgeons. After they had a falling out they would only communicate with each other through Julie. The strain affected her health. She asked for help from a psychologist to work out what she should do.

After some discussion, she decided her health was more important than money. If leaving her job to save her sanity led to the new car being sold and the family doing without the tropical vacation, then it was a price worth paying. She doubted that it would come to that, however, because she anticipated getting work again quite soon.

She had considered receiving workers' compensation payments if she left work. Certainly, her work was causing her poor health, but she was not "sick" and was planning to leave the job before that happened. She saw no point in waiting there until she became ill merely to go onto workers' compensation. She decided to resign from her position if the situation was not resolved in a month. As soon as she made this decision, she felt very relieved. Somehow the tension at work seemed more bearable.

Julie was in a better position than Heather whose husband was unemployed after his clothing store failed, leaving the family with heavy debts. These debts could have led to the family losing their home. Her job as an office manager for a large legal firm provided the sole income for the family and was needed to pay off his debts. She decided that if she had to stop work she had two alternatives: either they could file for bankruptcy, which she hated to do, or she would leave him and get by on social security payments. There was scant consolation in either option but at least she had a plan of action and would not be caught unawares again.

Losing touch with work

The fire service had been George's life, and he had been very happy with his own fire station. He was worried that if he was away from work for too long he would totally lose his nerve and may never be able to return. He was worried, too, that a prolonged absence would lead to his replacement at the station, and he would be sent back to the head office where he would be given a desk job. "They'd like to make me a trumped up clerk!" He outstayed his welcome with his men and with the department and ultimately lost the fire station and hope of any position in the fire service, including a "trumped up clerk's job."

People in career jobs or in jobs with rapid technological changes are reluctant to leave work, even for a short time, in case they miss out on an opportunity, or fall behind in maintaining their expertise. This can prove to be a very short-sighted decision. A brief spell away may be sufficient to deal with a minor health problem because if relief is delayed it's likely that the time away will be much longer. Some people want to stay at work and resolve the problems there before they take leave.

Sometimes this works - it certainly did for Angelo. Remember, though, that Angelo and others in his position have not had a breakdown. It is rare that someone with a breakdown is able to stay on the job. If they do stay at work, they will need a great deal of support because their work performance will have deteriorated markedly.

How long should you be away?

Jennifer hoped that a brief spell away from the class would restore her health. She was dismayed to see days stretching into weeks, weeks into months, and yet, she still felt unable to go back. It was to be a long time before she realized that she may never return to her old job. Helen found that four weeks was enough to let her rest a little and that, with other changes in her life, was sufficient to restore the balance.

Once you have decided to take time off work, the question arises, "how much?" You need to balance up the benefits of being off work for a time with the disadvantages. The benefits are that you get to rest, and the drawbacks are that you lose touch with the job and may jeopardize your prospects there. Of course, going back before your health has improved, no matter how short or how long a time you have been away, makes it likely that your condition will go downhill again rapidly, unless there are some drastic changes in your working conditions.

Once you have decided to leave work, the issue is not so much how long you will be away, but how you use the time. One reason for leaving work is to allow you time to regain energy. A secondary bonus is that you are away from the pressures at work that may have been worsening the situation. The amount of time off depends on the improvement in your health. This can be assessed by monitoring your symptoms as they are the best guide to progress. No matter how long you have off, your symptoms will reoccur very quickly if nothing has changed at work.

The therapy of leaving work

Kevin's doctor told him again, "If you don't slow down, you'll have a breakdown, or a heart attack!" Kevin had been a union organizer for 15 years. He was a committed unionist whose life was a whirl of meetings, driving and "hosing down" disputes. He worked 10-hour days routinely and saw little of his family. His territory extended over a third of the city and a quarter of the state, and he was on the road for two or three days of every week. Kevin was very active in the political life of the union and had been one of the leaders of a reform group that had taken over the running of the organization.

"Ironically, I reckon us union organizers have the worst pay and the worst conditions of just about any worker. It's common for me to work 50 or 60 hours a week with no overtime. I'm driving around all day, admittedly in a union car, but I'm dealing with problems all the time: demarcation disputes or unsafe working conditions or negotiating with management. I get to bed and I can't sleep because the events of the day run through my head. Karen told me she had to bring up the kids virtually by herself and she was sick of me hassling her, and them, over nothing. I kept getting chest pains. The doc did every test known to man, but they were all negative. He told me I had to slow down, or have a break, but I just didn't have time."

One Thursday morning, when Kevin was at a work site discussing a demarcation dispute with an organizer from another union, the talk became heated.

"Before I knew it I was rolling around on the ground with this guy, trying to rip his head off! We were pulled apart. I was still seeing red. My head was pounding and I had a massive pain in my chest. I went back to my car and started crying. God, did I feel stupid, fighting like that and in front of the men too. I waited for awhile until I settled down a bit, and I then drove straight to the doctor."

Kevin was put into the hospital for a few days. His boss, the union secretary, visited him in the hospital. He was not happy about the fight and told Kevin that he'd been concerned about him for some time. He advised him to take some time off and reassess his position. Kevin reluctantly agreed to do so. He took three months off. He did all the things he'd put off for so long: he got to know his wife and family again, he learned to enjoy a walk along the beach, a sleep in, a lazy afternoon with no phone calls, he pottered in the garden. He looked, and felt, 10 years younger, and during this time he thought about his life, and did some stock-taking.

He realized that he had been irritable with Karen and the children for a long time. He hadn't been sleeping well for months and he'd dropped all his interests and his friends. Generally, his work and personal life were out of balance.

"I forgot what was important to me, my family and myself, and I hadn't really looked after either. It's not that I'm selfish, it's just that I realized people were always telling me about their concerns. I'm a good listener, I suppose, and then I'd go home and worry about them. You know, I'd think, 'they're having a good night's sleep and I'm lying awake worrying about them!' When I do things for people now, it's because I choose to, not so much out of obligation."

Kevin was good at his work and had the support of the union management, so that taking three months off didn't risk his job. When his leave finished, he looked forward to trying out what he had learned.

"I knew the hardest part was going to be putting what I'd learned into practice at work. I'm still making mistakes, but I'm learning. I keep on asking myself, 'What am I being paid to do in this job?' I'm working for the benefit of our members, but I have to keep in mind what I can do, rather than what I should do. One of my biggest problems was that I used to get caught up after work, and I'd never get home. Now I stay on Friday night for half an hour, to have a drink, and then I'm off home. Three nights a week I pick Karen up from her part-time job and drive her home, so I have to leave work on time. We enjoy the drive home together. I don't talk about work much now. I don't worry about it like I used to. I know I've changed a lot. I guess I needed to. Having that time off was the best thing I ever did."

Most people who are severely stressed need a minimum of a month off work; anything less is a waste of time. Kevin said that it wasn't until he'd been off for a month that he was able to get an idea of what a bad state he had been in. Some show improvement in a shorter time, others, particularly those who have had a breakdown, take much longer.

During your time off, you should be monitoring your progress. Initially, rest is of prime importance, and as you improve you can give yourself more challenges and see how you cope with them. Eventually, you will find that you can deal with most situations quite well. Then you can begin to make plans to return to work, but try to be realistic about your work capacity. It is better for you to take too much time off work rather than too little if you want to stay at work. Time off work can be more than just time away from the job, it can be a very positive experience in which you actively work to regain your mental and physical health. You can reassess your priorities. If you learn nothing while off work, it is likely that the same situation will occur again and you will need even more time off.

Leaving work: what are your options?

Once you have made the decision to stop working, you have to work out how you are going to live and where your money is going to come from. You have the choice of workers' compensation, sick leave, ill-health retirement, disability insurance, sickness benefits, the invalid pension, leave with-out pay, or resignation. How do you decide which one is best for you?

Jill, the intensive care nurse with golden staph infection, had been shattered by her enforced departure from her job. The staph infection had made it impossible for her to continue to work with sick people. She was distraught about this and about the attitude shown towards her by the nursing administration. They had seen her as an embarrassment.

She had given little thought to her finances, but the union representative at the hospital advised her to apply for workers' compensation. Her infection had arisen while working in the hospital and her emotional state had come from the affects it had had on her life. Jill's application for workers' compensation was successful, although she found the process demeaning, frustrating and stressful.

"I'm used to dealing with doctors so I didn't feel worried when I saw the first insurance doctor. He was a psychiatrist, and he was pleasant, but I felt really uncomfortable. It took me a while to realize why he was making me feel so tense. It wasn't the questions he was asking, although I didn't like them. I couldn't see why he wanted to know about my family - he even asked about my grandparents - and I didn't like talking about my sex life or my boyfriends. He explained why he was asking all those questions. He said he was trying to build up a picture of my life to see if anything else could have caused me to become so upset.

"No, I didn't like any of that, but that's not what bothered me. What really got to me was that I realized he was not seeing me for me, he was seeing me for the insurance company. It wasn't that he didn't trust me so much as make me feel I had to justify my breakdown. I felt like a criminal and that I had to prove my innocence. I started crying in his office and he told me that people get upset quite often when they're talking to him. I can really believe it. Later on, after a few more experiences, I realized he was pretty nice compared to some doctors I had to see. One or two were really rude."

Jill became accustomed to the "system," although she never found it comfortable. Her claim was processed rapidly, and she was declared eligible for workers' compensation.

She had a number of other options that she discussed with the union representative. She could have stayed on sick leave or she could have resigned and found another job when her emotional state had improved.

You may find that you have several options available. They include all the ones that have already been mentioned, including workers' compensation, sick leave, ill-health retirement, private pension plans, sickness benefits and invalid pensions. There is also the option of taking leave without pay, if that is available and, of course, there is always the possibility of resignation.*

Each of these options have advantages and disadvantages and the details of each scheme vary according to the State or country in which you live and at times from employer to employer. It is most important that you speak to your union representative, your employer, or your lawyer before you make any final decisions.

It is useful to have an overview of each of these options so that you have more clarity in deciding between them. Although eight are listed, usually your choice is between two or three. Of course, the details of most of these will vary depending on where you live and who you work for.

Tom had initially applied for workers' compensation and had been accepted. He also found the experience unpleasant. Tom had been on workers' compensation for a year when he decided that he could not go back to teaching again. He discussed his decision with Betty and his psychologist. His union representative suggested he apply for ill-health retirement, as his pension plan had provided for this. Tom agreed to his suggestion. He could now look to the future rather than dwelling on the past.

He was asked to see yet another lot of doctors. This time he was more prepared, he had his statement ready, and he felt he had a more sympathetic hearing. The decision was made in his favor, but he remained on the payroll of the department until his sick leave and other accumulated leave had expired. He was told that he would be reviewed again regularly, that it was very unusual for people to be brought back to work who had been retired in this way. He was surprised by how mixed his feelings were on the day that he was officially retired.

"It was a relief, but it also felt like part of me had died. All those years of experience, and I couldn't do it anymore.

"I hated being on workers' compensation. I always used to think people on that were shirkers. Well, when I was on it, I always used to worry that people were looking at me like that. Now I feel better. I mean I contributed to this superannuation fund, and I don't feel such a parasite."

Betty was relieved when Tom decided to leave the department. She had to bear the brunt of Tom's anger and tension whenever the news came of yet another medical appointment.

"I was glad Tom could get workers' compensation because it

---

*Because this is an international edition, not all options can be included here. But it should be mentioned that, in the USA, various types of government as well as private disability insurance are available, and what is called an "invalid pension" in some countries is called Social Security Disability in the USA took a lot of worry out of the situation, but I sometimes used to wonder if they used all those medical appointments as a way of encouraging him to get off it. I learned to play the game a bit too. It was no good Tom going by himself because he'd get confused and upset, so I used to go with him.

"I made sure we got there really early because otherwise Tom would get more anxious. Although it was expensive, it was often better to go by cab so he didn't have to worry about navigating or parking. Tom would bring his Walkman radio and sometimes played relaxation tapes to settle himself down a little, as there was sometimes a long wait before he was seen. After it was over, we'd go and have a coffee so he could talk about it and unwind. I think that really helped a lot. It seemed like he could leave it all in the coffee shop."

Sometimes, these options aren't available, or the harassment involved isn't worthwhile, so whatever you finally choose to do, it is important to have a full understanding of your choices.

Workers' compensation

Workers' compensation has been available over the last 100 years and has expanded enormously, both in its scope and in the range of benefits provided.

Basically, workers' compensation is available for workers who have suffered an injury or illness related in some way to their employment. Workplace injuries or diseases can be either mental or physical and can occur at work or away from the workplace.

Workers' compensation also covers any illness or injury you might have which has been made worse by your job. George, the fireman, had a workers' compensation claim for a rash that broke out when he was exposed to toxic fumes. He had eczema and it was aggravated by the fumes.

It has only been over the last 40 years in some states that people with "nervous disorders" have been recognized as being eligible for workers' compensation. The requirements for this vary enormously. In some States the work may only need to be relatively minor, whereas elsewhere, work has to be a very major contributing factor for you to be eligible.

Some jurisdictions provide a lump-sum payment, and others provide a lump-sum payment only in very restricted terms. As well as these expenses most workers' compensation claims also pay for your medical and similar expenses. These include hospital costs, ambulance bills, chemist bills, nursing costs, traveling expenses, the cost of artificial aids, the cost of treatment by registered chiropractors, osteopaths and psychologists. Liability to pay these expenses continues whether or not you return to work.

Advantages
1. The weekly payment may be for a prolonged period, in some States, virtually until you are due to retire! In other regions, however, you are only eligible to receive payments for a certain period of time.
2. Workers' compensation pays all medical and like expenses including rehabilitation costs where this is obtainable.
3. If you have received workers' compensation payment and you are fit to return to work your medical expenses will be paid as long as they are related to the work injury.
4. Time off under workers' compensation does not jeopardize your sick leave entitlements.

Disadvantages
1. There may be considerable difficulty in getting workers' compensation for a stress claim.
2. Workers' compensation m ay only be available for a limited period of time.
3. There are a number of obstacles before a claim is successful. Medical assessments may be unpleasant and are intrusive. You will be expected to answer many questions that are unrelated to your work. You will also be required to submit to insurance investigations, both at your work and in your home. This procedure invariably causes a worsening of your condition.
4. The attitude of others can be negative if you are on workers' compensation. Both your fellow workers and the general public tend to look down on people who are on workers' compensation and regard them as shirkers.
5. If you are only partly disabled, you may be expected to obtain some kind of job. If you are unable to find suitable employment, you may be expected to give proof that you have looked for work.
6. If you are applying for a lump-sum payment, which is available under some jurisdictions, you will need to undergo further assessments, which will impose extra pressure.
7. People who are on workers' compensation often feel that they are obliged to stay sick so that payments will continue.

Sick leave

Many businesses and other organizations provide sick leave for workers. In most situations you are entitled to a certain number of days a year and in some instances this is allowed to accumulate so that over a period of time you can build up as much as eighteen months consecutive sick leave.

Sick leave is usually on full pay, although people who normally do out-of-hours' work or overtime will only be paid at their base rate; their income will effectively decline. In some places you are paid six months' full pay and six months' half pay. But while you are on sick pay, you may be sacked.

You must provide regular medical certificates if you are to remain on sick leave.

Advantages
1. Sick leave doesn't require the same intensive investigations as occurs with workers' compensation.
2. The attitude of your fellow workers and the general public is much more relaxed if you are on sick leave.
3. You generally receive a higher income on sick leave than when you are on workers' compensation.

Disadvantages
1. Sick leave does not pay for medical and other expenses.
2. Sick leave is significantly more limited in duration then workers' compensation.
3. It uses up sick leave entitlements that could be used for a catastrophic illness unrelated to employment.

Private pension schemes and superannuation

Most industries organize private pension schemes to which both you and your employer contribute. Some of these schemes have provision for ill-health retirement. But there are some strict limitations on whether this can be used if you have a stress-related condition. The criteria for retirement from work in most schemes is that you are totally and permanently disabled. Understandably, this involves investigations by medical representatives of the insurance company. If your claim is upheld, you will receive a percentage of your last salary scale; this is often indexed for salary rises but may not necessarily be so.

You may be recalled and re-examined medically, and it may be decided that you are fit to return to work, although this is unusual.

You are obliged to notify the insurance company if you take up employment of any sort and your payments will usually be reduced accordingly.

Advantages
1. Private pension schemes cover you until your death and can provide a continuing benefit to your spouse.
2. There is not the same stigma attached to private pension schemes as there is with workers' compensation.

Disadvantages
1. There may be a considerable time lapse between applying for a private pension and receiving it. Normally your outstanding leave entitlements will be discharged first.
2. There may be a delay of up to two years before some people become eligible for a private pension scheme or superannuation.
3. Some private pension schemes are not indexed and with inflation the income received can be minuscule.

Disability insurance

Margaret did not have a work-related problem and as a freelance writer she was not entitled to sick leave. Fortunately she had disability insurance. One of her work mates had strongly advised her to take it out and although it was a recurring cost to her, she was very pleased that she had the foresight to do so.

Margaret's scheme was planned for her. She elected to pay an extra amount so that any income she received was increased yearly to keep pace with inflation. The scheme had been in operation for some years to provide protection for her and her family. At times she regretted the cost, but she was pleased it was available when she was in trouble. When she became sick and could no longer work, Andrew applied for the disability payments on her behalf. At that stage, this was not in the forefront of her mind. She had two medical examinations at first and then another two with psychiatrists. The doctors' job was to determine whether or not she was disabled and to what degree she was disabled. Again there were some problems because her condition was a stress claim rather than any obvious physical problem. She was found to be totally disabled and her checks began arriving.

Disability insurance varies according to the amount of cover taken and to the exclusions within the insurance policy. Some policies, for example, exclude any disability arising out of certain sports. Some occupations also preclude you from obtaining disability insurance. Some provide indexed payments, hospital benefits and even rehabilitation payments. You are allowed to go back to work, either at your old job or some other line of work and you will receive an amount sufficient to bring your new income up to the level of your old.

Advantages
1. Disability insurance covers self-employed people and people who are not in any company run scheme.
2. You are a beneficiary until normal retiring age.
3. There is little stigma attached to disability insurance.

Disadvantages
1. It is a constant, significant cost to you. You may pay a rising premium, which entitles you to indexed monthly payments.
2. If you are insured for a fixed sum, this will become progressively less in value owing to inflation.
3. There may be strict exclusions that prevent a stress claim from being accepted. You must be careful to make sure you understand the insurance company's definition of disability.
4. Most have no coverage of any medical expenses.
5. You must submit to a number of initial medical examinations and further regular reviews.

Sickness benefits

Most governments provide a short-term pension for those suffering from an illness which has prevented them from working. To apply for sickness benefits you must be temporarily incapacitated for work because of sickness or accident and this incapacity must last for more than seven days. Payment of sickness benefits starts from the seventh day after you have become incapacitated.

If the incapacity is likely to last indefinitely then a claim for an invalid pension should be made. This is described later.

You must have suffered an actual loss of income because of the incapacity to qualify for sickness benefits.

You would also be eligible if you were receiving unemployment benefits, looking for work, or doing tertiary studies abandoned at the time you became sick. You must be in a position where, but for your illness, you would have received unemployment benefits.

The application must be supported by a medical certificate which certifies that you are temporarily incapacitated for work and indicates how long this will last.

The rate at which sickness benefits are paid varies according to your age and whether or not you have any dependents. In most jurisdictions the rate is the same as for unemployment benefits. Sickness benefits can't be paid for more than the amount of income lost because of the incapacity. The rate may be reduced if you have other income or have income which brings you under the benefits income test.

Advantage
1. Sickness benefits are readily obtainable on production of a medical certificate.

Disadvantages
1. The amount of money received is considerably less than would be received with either workers' compensation or sick leave.
2. The benefit is subject to an income test.
3. There is no cover of medical or similar expenses.

Invalid Pension

An invalid pension is a permanent government pension for people who are found to be incapacitated for work.

Advantages
1. This is a long-term government pension that is indexed regularly and has other benefits attached to it.
2. Reviews are usually not particularly onerous.

Disadvantages
1. The income received is small and corresponds to the aged pension.
2. The income is reduced according to any other income.
3. Medical and other expenses are not paid.
4. There is sometimes some suspicion about an apparently middle-aged person receiving an invalid pension for "mental" conditions.

Leave without pay

A useful option, which is not always available, is leave without pay. This means that you can return to your original job, without prejudice, after an agreed period of time.

Advantages
1. Leave without pay involves no harassment.
2. It is not subject to any community stigma.
3. Leave without pay entitles you to return to work after the leave has expired.

Disadvantages
1. It does not provide you with any income or other benefits.
2. The time span allowed may be shorter than you would like.

3. You must be fit enough to do other work.
4. Your income will usually be less than to which you have become accustomed.
5. You may have a period of unemployment.

Resignation

Ultimately you have the choice of resigning from the job. It may be a difficult choice to make. If you recognize that you are heading downhill and you can see that it will be difficult to avoid breaking down, resignation may be the best option.

If you are going to resign, you must resign before you have developed any health problems and you must be able to obtain work elsewhere if you are to maintain your income. There is little point in resigning when you are ill, as you may be better off to use some of the options already described.

Resignation may be the best way of avoiding being trapped in a sickness cycle that seems to be perpetuated by workers' compensation, private pension schemes and invalid pensions.

Advantages
1. This is entirely under your control. It does not require any form of assessment and hence your privacy is preserved.
2. There is no negative attitude towards people who resign and there is no loss of face involved.
3. If you resign at the right time, your health has been preserved and you are fit to do other work.

Disadvantages
1. Resignation involves loss of income and other benefits.
2. It provides a situation of uncertainty at a time when you may feel uncomfortable about facing it.
3. The status and position that you had achieved in your work or profession may be jeopardized, and you may have to start at a more junior level in your next job.

All the options that have been described involve significant advantages and disadvantages. Before you choose any, it is useful to discuss them with an adviser. This may be your union representative, an employment counselor, a solicitor, or your doctor.

Bear in mind that it is important to maintain your health even at the cost of promotions and other benefits in your job. For many people, resignation or leave without pay are their best early options.

⑩

Dealing With Relationships

Tom, Margaret, and Helen to a lesser degree, found that relationships with family, friends, work mates, even shop keepers and trades people, had changed. They had become so sensitive to any criticism, they mistook curiosity for antagonism. At the same time, they became astute at recognizing those people who were genuine in their concerns, although, at times, they tested everyone's patience with their demands for reassurance. This astuteness came with practice, and not without a good deal of pain and upset on the way. Margaret and Tom had both lost 'close' friends who had let them down.

The question is often asked whether it is best to be part of a family when recovering from a breakdown. Those who recover by themselves feel sorry for those who have to deal with the inevitable demands and intrusions of family life; others, who live with their family, feel sorry for those who live alone. The inevitable fatigue, introspection and irritability after a breakdown can cause major problems in families; the isolation resulting from living alone can encourage people to become even more of a hermit, avoiding contact with others and becoming estranged from the community.

Partners

Living with someone heading for a breakdown is like driving in a car with no brakes heading for a cliff; the choice is between bad and worse. Partners in this situation feel helpless and frustrated. Once the breakdown has occurred, you are expected to pick up the pieces. If the marriage has already been in trouble, this extra pressure is too much, and the marriage is likely to fail. Even if the marriage was strong, a breakdown throws an enormous burden on the partner and can make you feel as if you are heading for a breakdown too. It is difficult to be in a relationship in which you are giving out and getting nothing back, certainly nothing pleasant.

Tom's wife, Betty, had known for months that something was wrong with Tom. She tried to talk about it with him, but he refused to discuss it. She would feel irritated by his stubbornness and ignore him for a time, but her concern for him would lead to her bringing up the subject again, with the same predictable response. She could never tell from one minute to the next what he was going to be like.

"The slightest thing would set him off. One day he tripped over a bike Dennis had left near the back door. I heard him yelling, and he charged into the house. I thought he was going to have a stroke. He was purple-faced and the veins on his neck were bulging. He caught Dennis, and slapped him hard. Dennis just stood there, tears in his eyes, and he said to Tom, 'I hate you' in the coldest voice. Tom looked like he'd been struck. He let Dennis go and walked away, his shoulders slumped. I found Tom in the bedroom, tears rolling down his face."

Betty also worried about him when he went off by himself. She thought that he might hurt himself. Dealing with his moods was like walking on egg shells. At one stage, she thought there must be another woman, but she comforted herself with the thought that no one else would want him the way he was.

"We didn't make love for months. He seemed to have lost interest. He didn't want me around him sometimes, but he always wanted to know where I was. If I went to the supermarket, he'd want to come with me. When I went to work, he'd ring every few minutes. If I got impatient, he would get hurt and hang up in a huff.

"I used to cringe sometimes when the phone rang in case it was him. Sometimes I got Judy in the office to answer it and tell him I was out. God knows how she put up with it too. Everywhere I went he'd come too, but sometimes, he'd say very suddenly, 'I have to go home' with a terrible urgency in his voice, and I'd have to stop shopping, or whatever I was doing, and go home too."

Betty found it impossible to plan ahead. She'd accept an invitation for them both but, at the last minute, he'd say he couldn't go and she'd have to phone and make excuses. At first, she thought that he was being difficult to get on with, and then she realized that he really couldn't go out when he was having a bad day. He wouldn't answer the phone, he wouldn't answer the door, or even get the mail out of the letterbox. If a friend called in, he'd flee to the garden, or the tool shed. For many months, Betty had to make all the decisions for the family alone.

"You don't realize how much you rely on someone else until they're not there, and it was like that in a way. I suppose that's what people who have separated or widowed go through but this was worse really because I had Tom to look after, too. I had to do everything: pay bills, organize repairs, buy things, organize trips, all the decisions concerning the kids - Tom couldn't do any of it. At times, I thought I was the one having the breakdown."

Betty's job saved her sanity. Tom had begged her to give it up, and he refused to hear Betty's reasons for keeping it. He accused her of being selfish and inconsiderate. He needed her to look after him, and that was all that counted as far as he was concerned. Her peace of mind, and the family's need for her income, were really secondary considerations for him. Later, Tom realized how wise Betty had been to resist his demands.

"I know that he felt ashamed that I was working and he couldn't, that added to his guilt and feelings of failure, but I had to have a regular break from him, even though it caused a few problems. I thought that while I was at work, he could do some of the household chores, like the washing and vacuuming, but some days, I'd come home and he'd done nothing. It took all my willpower to hold my tongue. Sometimes he'd spend the whole day doing some small repair job, and would be really hurt if I didn't notice."

Betty had come to realize that there was no point in pushing or nagging him. He had to do things in his own time, but she was often very frustrated.

"He's so much better now. He helps a lot at home, and gradually he's been able to take up some of his old interests. He doesn't need his afternoon sleep as much these days, and things are generally a lot smoother now that we've worked out a few simple rules."

People who've had a breakdown are usually very self-absorbed. They tend to be very focused on themselves and seem only dimly aware of other people's needs or feelings, and, at times, they seem thoughtlessly cruel. Margaret's children resented her despair over Melinda's death. They felt she was not interested in their grief and was expecting them to comfort her. They felt guilty about these feelings and, at first, were only able to talk openly with Margaret when her therapist had family meetings.

Sometimes, people who've suffered a breakdown can put on a front in public and may go to great lengths to keep their real feelings of misery and anger hidden. This can cause two problems for their family: it makes it harder for outsiders to understand the difficulties the family is experiencing, and the family have to bear the brunt of all their unpleasant feelings, which they keep hidden from the world.

If your relationship is to survive your breakdown, you need to talk about your feelings, and not just express them in behavior. Your partner will always know if you're angry, you have gone quiet or you might be raging, but your anger is apparent. If it is not discussed at some time, then your partner, who knows you're angry, is confused. Your partner is confused about what has made you angry, and whether or not he or she is responsible for it. They usually feel blamed, although they may not know what they have done. This sense of being blamed leads to resentment and withdrawal, which can trigger further hostility.

Speaking about your hostility or your other intense feelings at the time they are surging through you is very difficult. The message, the words, are overwhelmed by the feelings. It may be best to leave any discussion until later, when you are calmer. Even then it is often difficult and frightening. People worry that putting their angry feelings into words may be very destructive.

If you say that you feel irritation, hostility, or even hatred, then your partner will take offense, and may withdraw for a time, or even leave. Similarly, your partner may be apprehensive about expressing his or her negative feelings in case the words trigger a relapse, or push you to behave foolishly. You may need help from your therapist to coach you in expressing hostility in words. You may even ask your therapist to do it for you.

Betty experienced a great sense of relief when Tom arranged for her to meet his therapist. When Betty understood what was going on inside Tom, she felt much easier in her mind about Tom's behavior, and felt better equipped to deal with him, although there were still days when she felt tempted to walk out. When Tom was much further down the road to recovery, they became accustomed to talking more with one other. This experience deepened their relationship in a way they hadn't thought possible.

Margaret was given a book on the topic of "suffering," written many years before. She had put it aside for months, and happened to be cleaning up her bedroom when she saw it again. She read the introduction and was surprised to find that it made sense to her. As she read on, she found much that related to her experience. She showed it to Andrew and her children, who gained some more understanding about her.

Stan, the policeman who had checked into the motel and taken an overdose of drugs, was contacted by two of his old friends, who had also been forced to retire from the police force because of ill-health. They began meeting him regularly, and encouraged him to talk more openly about his experiences. It was hard going at first, but they persisted, and Stan began to unburden himself of the tension that had been imprisoning him for so long. Stan's wife encouraged him in this, and she met the wives of the other men. She found their support and understanding invaluable.

"I felt so isolated and alone with Stan. I felt this terrible sense of responsibility for him. Every time I left him I would worry that he would go off and do the same thing again. His two mates were guardian angels. They called around to see him and they, and their wives, helped me to cope. We had a barbecue at home about a year after Stan stopped work. The other couples were there, and Stan was doing the cooking. The dog grabbed a sausage off the grill. I felt sick, expecting Stan to explode, but he laughed. I couldn't believe it; I hadn't heard him laugh for such a long time."

Parental responsibilities

Parents who've had a breakdown worry a great deal about the effect they are having on their children. All parents know how irritable and intolerant they can be towards children when they are tired, or under pressure. Helen had seen it as a mother, shielding her children from Peter's anger, and, again, when she became exhausted and close to cracking.

"I used to say to Peter, 'Why can't you be nicer to them? You make them scared when you yell so loud.' I couldn't understand why he was so awful. One Sunday I was trying to get the two kids ready for church. They didn't want to go, but my mom and dad like to see us there so we go every week. This time I was screaming at them. Peter said to me what I'd been saying to him. I was just as bad as he was! I got really upset and I couldn't go, so no one went.

"Mom and Dad came around after church to see why we hadn't gone. They got excited and yelled at Peter, who yelled back. I came out of the bedroom, and they started yelling at me. It was terrible. I was crying, and then mom got upset and began crying, Michael and Sophie began crying, and my Dad and Peter were yelling at each other, it was a mess."

If you've had a breakdown, you will know how difficult it is to avoid over-reacting. Even with full knowledge of the effects your behavior has on the family, you will have found it almost impossible to avoid angry feelings surfacing and causing disruption in the family, or with friends. You will know, only too well, that the family is only seeing the tip of the iceberg, that most of your emotions stay bottled up.

You can keep control for a while, but something always triggers off an outburst. It may be of rage, or of tears, but you feel you have lost control. Noise is especially irritating. Some noises, such as dogs barking, loud music, and fighting in the family, can make you explode with fury. The intrusive noise can feel like a deliberate attempt to upset you, a direct assault on you. As one man explained:

"It's like nails going into my head. When the children play up I just have to walk away; I can't handle it. If I stay there, I'm frightened about what might happen. When you get to punching holes in the wall, or cutting yourself because you've punched out a window, you know you're on dangerous ground."

Your partner may have been worried for a long time by your isolation from family life. As one teenager said to his mother, "Mom, we knew for about a year before you stopped work, that we had to keep out of your way on Sundays -you were getting tense about going back to the office."

Your children may find it difficult to get used to a parent who is no longer working, and who seems to be doing little. They may become offhanded, even critical in their dealings with you, and this further lowers your fragile self-esteem.

Your first priority is to recover. The first few months are especially difficult - it is as much as you can do to survive, you have nothing left over for the family. "I don't know how Betty did it," said Tom, "I was only vaguely aware how bad I was at the time. It all seems like a haze to me now." As Tom improved, he felt very guilty about his behavior to the family. His intense sense of guilt gave him his blackest moments, and he often thought the family would be better off without him.

"Betty must have sensed that I was feeling like knocking myself off. She talked to me about it, and I cried for hours, but it was a turning point for me. I could only go up from there. I'd reached the bottom. We worked out some ideas for me to deal with my feelings, so they weren't so upsetting for everyone. I talked them over with my therapist, who suggested a few more ideas.

"I knew I couldn't deal with the kids, as far as discipline or any confrontations. It's part of that business of not being able to defend yourself, or stand up for your rights, without feeling like you're going to make a fool of yourself. Rather than become involved, it was easier if I went off to the bedroom, or even outside, when it got too much for me."

It was to be a long time before Tom felt he could deal with family problems without getting upset and then making the situation worse. He found it was best for him to rest in the afternoons - he wasn't so cranky when the kids came home.

He found it easier to be with them one at a time. He went swimming with Dennis on Tuesday nights and played golf with Paul once a week, although he found that he could take both fishing.

"It was so quiet, just bobbing up and down in the boat, and they seemed to like it. It gave me a chance to talk to them about what they were doing. It helped me to relax, too, and I could enjoy their company. Occasionally they would hassle each other, but I didn't seem to mind. I told them once that I didn't think I could go back to teaching. They seemed to understand - there was a teacher at their old school who was hopeless with discipline and who went off sick. I'm starting to feel that I'm making up a bit for all the bad times I gave them, although I still have to walk away sometimes."

Not long after Tom had that talk with Betty he went off camping by himself for a week - walking, fishing, doing as he pleased. It was as much a break for the family as for Tom.

Friends

Inevitably, your relationships with your friends alter in this situation. It can be difficult for both you and your friends to maintain contact. Most people learn by experience what to say to their friends. Brendan, the youth worker whose breakdown was so unexpected, had been hurt by friends who assumed that he was weak, or faking. Some acted as if he had a contagious disease and avoided him. A small number were genuinely interested and did not seem to have any preconceived ideas about his condition. Brendan eventually found a way of telling his friends that seemed to satisfy them, without having to go through the whole story.

He would say to them, "I've had a breakdown, I can't seem to cope with things now. My doctor tells me that it doesn't mean that I'm crazy or neurotic. The basic problem is that I seem to have run out of energy. I think the job wore me out. It's taking a while to get better, and I have to be very careful about what I do, but I feel optimistic."

Some of his friends wanted to know more; others just accepted what he had said. Brendan was philosophical: "I figure that the ones who are your real friends will stick by you and, anyway, most of them have seen how bad I can get. As for the others well, forget them, they weren't worth it."

Those who have the greatest difficulty with friends are the ones who feel a deep sense of shame and failure about their breakdown. One woman didn't tell her friends or family that she was off work for two years. She pretended she was still working! She avoided her friends and family as much as she could. She was living alone, which made the deception easier. It was actually a great relief to her when they found out. Her friends told her that they had been worried about her for some time but had known that she didn't want to discuss it.

Generally, it is better not to say too much. Neutral words like "rundown" and "exhausted" are better then "stress," "breakdown" or "depression." Keep your explanations short. Most people will be interested in what you say and are happy to leave it at that. They will respect your privacy, so there is no need to go into lengthy explanations - a brief account will do. Resist the temptation to tell the whole story, or you may make your friends feel uncomfortable, and your complaints may seem to be moaning. You'll get to know which friends remain interested in knowing more, and which friends will lose interest.

Margaret's experiences with her friends were fairly typical. Most of them were mildly interested. Some, like Ruth, were a great support. Others, like her friend Kerry, were very disappointing. Kerry had been a friend of Margaret's ever since she moved into the community. Kerry was a bright, chubby, red-haired woman who had used Margaret as her confidante. She was always having problems with her children, or her husband, and as soon as she ran into trouble, she'd be on the phone to Margaret. Margaret enjoyed Kerry's "giddiness" and didn't mind being used as a "social worker."

When Melinda was murdered, Kerry sent a sympathy card, but she didn't come to the funeral, she didn't call Margaret on the phone, and she stopped visiting the house when she was passing. She dropped Margaret like a "hot scone." Margaret called her in desperation one day, feeling suicidal. Kerry said she couldn't talk for long because she was cooking, and she didn't call back.

"I still can't get over the way Kerry behaved. I mean, she was my best friend. I know people say that you can't know what a breakdown is like unless you've had one, but she didn't even try. I know it's because she's weak and she didn't feel she could cope with me, but she didn't even try.

"I heard later, from another friend, that Kerry was telling people I was doing it to get attention. I couldn't believe she could be so cruel. I don't even acknowledge her presence now. I know she feels guilty, and I'm glad that she feels bad."

Margaret dreaded meeting people on social occasions. She couldn't do social chit-chat anymore; she felt vulnerable and exposed. She'd cling to Andrew and felt lost for words.

"I used to dread people saying to me, 'How are you?' I never knew what to say, and I would either say nothing, or think they were really interested and start giving them an explanation. I would get halfway through and then feel embarrassed because it had finally dawned on me that most of them really didn't want to know how I was, they were just saying hello. Now I just answer, "I'm okay" or "I have my good days and my bad days." If they want to know more, then they can ask."

Colleagues and contact with work

Your reactions to your colleagues will vary depending on the contribution of work to your breakdown and how you were coping when you left work. Although it seems to make sense to stay in touch if you can - a return to work will be easier if you do maintain good relations - many people find that contact with colleagues or anything associated with their work makes them feel terrible.

It is like going back to the scene of the crime and fear, shame and tension combine to produce a rapid return of their worst symptoms. Tom found that he couldn't handle seeing a group of school children on an excursion or a news item on television about education. He even changed where he voted because he didn't want to go into the school building that was being used as a polling booth.

"There is a certain smell that brings all the old feelings back: it's a combination of sweaty bodies, decaying food and even disinfectant. It's sad, but I've lost nearly all my teacher friends, and some of them were terrific people. The only one I still have contact with is my technician, and we always did have a lot in common - both of us have a trade background. He never talks about school to me. Occasionally I ask about this one or that one, but it's only a passing comment. He packed up all my things for me after I left and brought them home, too. I really appreciated that because I couldn't do it myself. He also had a word with the office staff and told them not to ring me, because he knew I found it hard to answer the phone. All that part of my life is finished; it's a painful process rebuilding a new identity and new friends."

Margaret's experience was quite the opposite: "So many of my work friends have been helpful and understanding; there when I needed them. You name it, they did it. Colleagues at the papers and magazines I've written for would ask me to come in for lunch or someone's farewell. I didn't stay long at first, just enough to keep in touch, but it's been their patience that has helped me to write again and feel that little spark of enthusiasm come back. It's so precious. I thought I'd lost it. There was just a black hole, but now I feel it growing. I get really worried when I lose it for a while."

Social functions

Being with people is demanding. One must listen, observe what the person is saying with tone and gesture, think about a response and watch how your response is interpreted. If other people are around, they are observed too; noise, light, movement all have an impact, and unless you can get onto "automatic," that is, do all these things without thinking about them, as most of us do, social occasions are exhausting.

The extreme emotional sensitivity of someone who has had a breakdown also means that careless comments or small slights are not ignored. The big occasions that can't be avoided are often the worst - weddings, engagements, birthday parties, Christmas day events, reunions. The general rule is to prepare an escape route beforehand. Margaret became good at it, particularly with Andrew and Ruth's help.

"I learned my lesson from my niece's wedding. Everything just crowded in on me, and I had to go. Then I was so embarrassed I couldn't go back.

"Now, I usually tell people beforehand that I will only stay a short while because I get tired and that I will just leave without a fuss. One friend arranged a room for me to go and lie down in for a while. I was there for about half an hour and then stayed at the party for another hour. I always take my own car or we go in Andrew's so that we don't have to wait for someone else. I find I'm better if I'm near a door or sitting at the end of a table.

"Andrew says he can tell by my eyes when I've had enough. He either stays with me or stands where he can see me. I feel safer that way. I still haven't got the knack of knowing when I've had enough myself, though. Sometimes I'm enjoying myself and stay too long. Then I've got to put up with a few bad days afterwards. Occasionally it's worth it."

Dealing with the unexpected

As we have seen, people who've had a breakdown are very vulnerable. This sensitivity makes social encounters frightening. You may be questioned, put on the spot or even be subjected to an unexpected verbal assault. These situations leave you feeling defenseless, upset and stupid. You maybe caught unawares by a request for help, or for advice, or you may simply be trapped with a bore. Often, people may be merely making conversation, yet you find their remarks or questions intrusive, even hostile. Sometimes your suspicion is warranted. You may find yourself taken aback by an attack, thinly veiled or otherwise. "You must be enjoying yourself at home with your creative talents," or "You should get off (or on) that medication, stop (or start) seeing that psychiatrist and get back to work (or pull yourself together)," or "Are you enjoying your holiday at the taxpayer's expense?"

This sort of behavior is encountered unexpectedly, often when you feel most vulnerable; in social situations, medical examinations or even with friends. People may leave themselves open to the unexpected by attempting to explain too much. It seems that the more you say, the deeper the hole you fall into. Gradually people work out some answers to suit them, usually the shorter the better.

"Why aren't you at work?" "I'm on leave." "I've left that and I'm looking around for something else." "I got very rundown and the doctor said I had to have a break."

"Why can't you help on the committee?" "I'd love to but it's a pity my health won't allow it." "I'll let you know when I can manage it but it won't be for a while." "What do you do with your time?" "I'm never bored."

Margaret had real problems saying "no." She had been so used to putting other people's needs first, her sensitivity to the feelings of others meant that she was reluctant to disappoint them. She also found, particularly in the early part of her recovery, that it was easier to say yes and not make a fuss rather than stand up for herself and say no. As her health improved and she became stronger emotionally, she started to practice a little.

"I learned a few little tricks like delaying a decision. I'd say, 'I'll have to let you know' or if I was on the phone, I'd say there was someone at the front door. That gave me time to think of an excuse. I had a list of excuses written under the phone to remind me, too. A friend of Ruth's and mine was very persistent about us doing a course together, but I think Ruth must have said something to her because she suddenly stopped saying it. The first time I said no, I couldn't believe how easy it was. I felt very guilty, but my mother just accepted it. I didn't realize how powerful I could feel. It's all been part of me taking control of my life again. Now when I do something for someone it's because I want to, not out of a feeling of duty or obligation."

Although coping with family and friends is difficult and often painful when you have had a breakdown, ultimately they can be your salvation with their support and love. At times this can mean taking the risk of opening your heart and showing yourself as you truly are; this is a risk that is always worth taking.

11

Living With Yourself

Living with yourself is something you have to do 24 hours a day. All other aspects of your life are peripheral. How do you live with yourself when so much has gone wrong? How do you live with feeling exhausted, frightened and terrible? For most this is uncharted territory. Living with yourself means living and coping with your shattered emotions, it means living with a fuzzy brain and with a body that feels broken down.

Living with shattered emotions

Your life may have become a roller-coaster ride of anger, remorse, irritability, despair, anguish and an overall feeling of loss of control. All of these symptoms progressively improve as your recovery takes place. This improvement is not steady.

Tom, for example, often felt as if he was taking two steps forward and one step back. Even when he had improved a good deal, many of his old feelings re-emerged when he was feeling tired or under pressure.

Loss of control

Both Tom and Margaret remember their feeling of loss of control as being more painful than anything else. Tom found that he couldn't seem to control anything. "I'd cry for no reason, I'd get crazy mad and all the time I felt this terrible feeling like I was going to explode. My body seemed to have taken on a life of its own. I'd gorge and then at other times I couldn't seem to eat anything. What was so painful was that I'd always prided myself as being so much in charge, of being cool and sensible and now I was anything but that.

"Well, I learned to cope. It was like everything else. I took it a day at a time, and I'd let myself feel terrible without getting too fussed about it. I learned how to let myself just feel bad without feeling bad about feeling bad."

Unstable mood

For people who are used to being in control, the seemingly unpredictable and dramatic lack of mental energy means that you find

136

it harder to dismiss small slights or rationalize things that go wrong. These mood swings are destabilizing. Relatively minor events become catastrophes, and you will feel your self-confidence evaporating.

For Margaret, this was an issue of central concern. "My roller-coaster emotions were so disruptive. I had periods of black despair, of rage and crying. I always seemed to be crying. They were hard for me to live with and almost impossible for my family and friends. With time, these changes became less frequent and less wrenching. That was all little consolation when I was in the thick of it. But, God knows, I tried to keep all my feelings hidden so as to preserve some tatters of my self-respect. I kept thinking that everyone must see me as pathetic or neurotic.

"As well as feeling all this stuff I also felt terribly pressured. Everything I did seemed to be mountainous, every relationship seemed to impose another expectation, there never seemed to be enough time to do everything that had to be done. For a while it seemed that everything had to be done."

Margaret learned to accept that these feelings come and go from hour to hour, and from day to day. Once she learned that, her fear became much less, although she had to be reminded of this from time to time by her therapist, her friends and family.

"It was terrific to have someone outside the family and my friends I could talk to about how I was feeling, who understood what I was saying and could reassure me that I wasn't going mad and that my feelings would get better. Sometimes I would stay in bed all day if I was feeling particularly bad.

"Looking back on it, I think feeling bad was necessary, it was part of the healing process, and it forced me to work at getting better."

Anxiety and fear

Sometimes fear can be a warning, one that must be heeded; at other times, it is a normal reaction to a new venture and you will need to overcome the fear so that you can move on.

Understanding the cause of your fears can be vital. Some people are frightened of going mad; others are frightened of never improving. Talking about your fears with your doctor or therapist will help you to understand them and reassure you. This is a time when you need a lot of support, and medication may be needed to bring your fear down to a manageable level. Helen needed her doctor's reassuring words.

"I had a feeling in the pit of my stomach like I was going to explode, something terrible was going to happen. I could feel it all the time. Everything I did, that feeling was there: when I was cleaning the offices or looking after my husband, it was there all the time. Occasionally, I would hyperventilate. I would breathe too hard and get very dizzy and a tingling around my mouth and in my hands and feet. He taught me how to stop it by breathing into a paper bag, but, boy, was it scary at first; I thought I was having a heart attack. He told me not to worry about it. It was simply 'nerves' and nothing serious was going to happen.

"When I first went off work, my doctor gave me Serepax, a tranquilizer, and this seemed to settle down that feeling. I was scared of becoming hooked, so I stopped them after a month. I could have used them for a while after that, but I didn't really need them. The feeling comes back at times. I know now that it usually means I've done too much and I try and rest; it seems to work."

Overcoming this sort of fear is often a matter of timing. The fears that may have led to your breakdown tend to diminish the longer you are away from the original situation, although you will be surprised at how long it takes for these fears to go and how swiftly they can affect you again.

Tom had a bad reaction whenever he met someone from his work. "I'm still really sick with nerves if I have any contact, no matter how remote, with the school, so even now when I meet colleagues or old students, I feel really tense. I feel like I want to run away. I think this anxiety and feeling of loss of control has really made it hard for me to just get through the day, but it's so much better now than it was."

Like Tom, you may find it best to avoid any reminders of what has upset you. He had as little contact with his work as possible for several years.

Anger

Anger has a bad effect on your relationships with other people. All your other feelings make people concerned and willing to help, but anger drives people away. Anger is often triggered by trivial events: dishes left unwashed in the sink, bikes left in the driveway, someone answering back, a barking dog that just won't stop, or a careless driver. There is often a point, just before the rage emerges, where it can be controlled, where it can be stopped. You'll gradually learn to see the warning signs. Tom has learned this painful lesson.

"Once I reached that point of exploding I was gone. I had to get away alone until I felt better, otherwise I'd rage at whoever was there - my wife, my kids, students. Once I even exploded at a shop assistant who seemed to be ignoring me when I tried to buy some perfume for my wife. I just hit the roof, and I could see she was really upset by it, but I couldn't stop myself.

"I learned to get away before I reached that point. I'd get away to another room, I'd go outside or get in the car and drive to the park and just think. Sometimes I'd scream and yell in the car. That made me feel much better. I made sure the car was parked away from anyone else though.

"Sometimes I'd lock myself in the bedroom and punch the pillow around. I felt really silly, but I felt like I was getting rid of something, like a poison inside me."

Other people may be able to tell when your anger is building up before you can and, at a time when you are calm, talk over with them how they can help. Betty would encourage Tom to go for a fast walk or go outside and chop wood if he looked very tense and was becoming withdrawn. Hard physical work is a good way of releasing your tension. Tom used other methods too.

"After a while, I could pick when I was going to explode, and I'd go off and try to get rid of the feeling. Sometimes I would let myself be triggered off by some small incident, and then I'd use that as an opportunity to blast some of the people I felt had let me down. I made sure they weren't there of course. I even wrote some abusive letters but, fortunately, I was smart enough not to send them.

"When I felt rational, I could tell the family how to handle me. That usually meant leaving me alone to work it out and to try and not feel hurt if I blasted them. Sometimes they could see that I was just making noise and there was nothing personal in it."

Coping with depression

Depression, melancholia or simply the "blues," it's all the same, a profound sadness that strikes many who have fallen apart. Naturally, everyone who has had a breakdown feels sad, regretful and unhappy. Sad for the losses that have occurred, regretful of what might have been and unhappy about the changes in their life. But many deny being depressed, often despite being given this label by their doctor. And they're right, they're not depressed, at least not in the way psychiatrists and psychologists describe depression.

Depression is a different matter. Anyone who has been depressed knows how different it is from just being unhappy. It's far more pervasive and profound. It's an inner anguish, a psychic pain that is disabling and exhausting.

The treatment of this type of depression first involves its

recognition. The commonest treatment modes are psychotherapy, or talking therapy, in its various forms, and medication. Electroconvulsive therapy (ECT) is rarely used nowadays and is hedged around with all sorts of safeguards and restrictions. Surprisingly, despite its terrible reputation, ECT can be very effective in a short period of time with very severe cases of depression.

Harry, the railway worker whose mate was crushed, fell into a severe depression some weeks after the second incident at work, which had finally broke his nerve.

"I've never known anything like it. I was crying all the time. I was feeling so totally hopeless and a failure that I thought about suicide almost all the time. And I couldn't eat or sleep. I felt like I had this terrible pain inside me, but I couldn't tell anybody where it was. I was losing weight and I was staying in bed all the time. I reckon I just about drove my wife crazy.

"My doctor had told me I was depressed when I first went off work and he wanted me to take some pills, but I knew I wasn't depressed and I wouldn't touch them. I didn't reckon I needed them. But after this depression hit me I'd have done anything to feel better. I took the tablets and they really helped although I put on a lot of weight. I still can't get it off."

Many people have a biochemical depression that may only be improved by the use of anti-depressants. Some have a family history of depression, or have a tendency to become depressed when they are under pressure.

Harry had a family history of depression. Most likely he had a tendency to become depressed, and this only became apparent with the extra pressure from his breakdown.

"My mom told me that she had a couple of depressions and she was in the psychiatric hospital once for a few weeks. My brother Johnny has always been a boozer, and I reckon he might have copped it too, so maybe it's in my blood."

Some people develop a manic-depressive disorder as part of their breakdown. This involves large, disorienting mood swings that may overwhelm all the other breakdown symptoms. This condition requires the use of Lithium tablets, which must be given under expert supervision. Once the disorder is controlled, many of the previously hidden symptoms of breakdown become apparent.

The misery and sadness that is an unavoidable accompaniment to a breakdown fluctuates according to how you feel. As you feel better, it lifts and, as you feel worse, it deepens. When you have over-reached your strength and fall into a heap, this sadness and sense of loss intensifies.

Jennifer had been offered anti-depressants by her doctor, but she turned them down: she was taking enough already.

"I wasn't depressed, I just felt terrible. I know I was crying and I looked depressed, but I really wasn't. When I got really down, I used to hibernate in the bedroom for a day or two and I wouldn't speak to anyone. My husband would bring meals in and he was really worried about me at first, but he could see how much better I was in my sanctuary. It was like having a rest in the hospital without all the fuss. The kids call it mom's time-out room, and I think they're right."

Jennifer still feels despair and sadness at times, but she is no longer frightened. She knows it's a feeling that will pass.

Crying

Your crying will seem like a release, although you will probably feel very ashamed if it happens in public.

Margaret still smiles when she thinks of Ruth's explanation to an embarrassed shopkeeper. "Take no notice of Margaret. She's had a hard time lately and she just cries a lot." In this situation, if you don't have such a quick-thinking friend with you, your best tactic will be to get away and cry in private. Just let the tears flow. Friends won't be so perturbed if you tell them that you feel better after a good cry.

Margaret did cry a lot. "Niagara Falls in action - that's how I felt. I cried when I got up in the morning. I cried when I went to bed. I woke up during the night crying. I cried watching television. I even cried in the butcher's shop. I'd be talking to my kids about school, and tears would be running down my face. I didn't mind so much with the kids, but I hated it with everyone else. I just wanted them to take no notice, but they would get embarrassed and try to make me feel better, and I'd feel stupid and pathetic. I began telling my friends to just ignore it. I told them that they didn't have to make me feel better. I even told some of them that it was good for me, and I think that's true.

"I think that my crying is a way of releasing some feelings I should have released years ago, because they're all coming out at once. I seemed to be crying all the time, but I think it was making up for all the crying I hadn't done before. When I saw it like that, I felt that, every time I cried, I was letting go of a bit more pain, and I was being healed just a bit more.

"After a while I didn't even try and stop. It was still embarrassing, of course, but it made sense to me. I had to cry. I stopped apologizing for it. I'd just excuse myself and go somewhere where I could fall apart safely, without feeling as if I had to pay too much of a price for displaying my emotions. In the shopping center there is a small parking area behind some of the shops with a big tree in the middle. If I started crying, I'd stand behind the tree. No one seemed to notice. It sounds absurd, I know, but one day I realized it was a weeping willow. I laughed and laughed, with tears running down my face. Sometimes I would stand in the shower and cry. It didn't matter a bit. I think the best way of dealing with crying is with a large box of tissues."

Like most men, Tom never did come to terms with crying in front of the insurance company doctors. It always felt like weakness to him and even though his therapist told him that it was better to show his true feelings to those doctors and that the crying might make him feel better, he still felt ashamed. Tom was relieved when his crying phase was over.

Panic

Panic is a horrible experience, and most people who have a panic attack will do anything to avoid it happening again. Panic attacks are unpredictable. They can occur unexpectedly, and they make you feel that you're going to die or go crazy. You might have a number of symptoms, including a feeling of choking, with chest pains, numbness and feelings of unreality, dizziness, sweating and shaking. Although the attack usually only lasts a few minutes, it seems like an eternity. If your panic attack occurred in a particular place, at work or in a supermarket, you may find it difficult to go back there. Similarly, if the attack was brought on by exercise or some other activity, you will probably avoid that too. So, as time passes and panic attacks continue, you become more and more restricted in your activities, eventually becoming almost totally house-bound.

People who suffer panic attacks need not have had a breakdown and, similarly, people who have had a breakdown may not have panic attacks, but there are a number of people with a breakdown who have severe panic attacks.

Harry, the railway man whose friend was crushed, subsequently developed severe panic attacks as a major part of his breakdown, as did Jennifer.

"I'd get these shakes, and I'd think I was going to drop dead. I thought I was having a heart attack the first time it happened, but the Doc checked me out with all those machines, and he reckoned it was just nerves. It's terrible. It comes on when I'm driving or when I'm feeling tired. Bang! It just hits me hard. It's a terrible feeling.

"I was sent to see a head doctor, and he gave me some tablets that helped a lot. It's almost totally gone. When it comes up now, I don't get frightened. I know my heart is okay. I try to distract myself until the feeling passes."

Others carry Claire Weekes' book *Simple Effective Treatment of Agoraphobia* with them (agoraphobia is fear of leaving the house). Weekes has an audio tape that some people find very helpful. The panic feeling always passes, and if you can get some medication to reduce its intensity and learn to distract yourself while the feeling passes, you will master it.

Frustration and disappointment

Accepting that you have had a breakdown and that you are no longer as capable as you once were sounds so easy, but it usually takes a long time to reach that point. Until you can stop comparing yourself with your old self or comparing yourself with other people, you will be continually frustrated. For Tom, acceptance was a slow process.

"I gradually learned to reduce my expectations of myself. I was rock bottom as far as self-esteem and self-confidence were concerned. I felt terribly inadequate and really frightened about my future. Basically I was feeling terrible. You can understand how frustrated I would get, mainly at myself, but also at some of the people I had to deal with.

"The man at the local service station used to drive me mad. He was so slow. He'd amble everywhere, and he never seemed to get the knack of opening the hood of my car. I used to get so wild at him. But it wasn't him, it was me."

Tom would meet a small setback, and it felt like the end of the world had come. After a while he began recognizing a pattern. Some small thing would go wrong, and he could feel his frustration swelling up. It happened all the time at first, and then he learned to accept it. Even when he was getting a lot better, some trifle thing would upset him. An encyclopedia salesman came to the door and wouldn't take no for an answer. He nearly throttled him.

"I learned not to worry about these setbacks, as I got used to them. I didn't get so upset about being back to square one. I realized that there was always a moment of choice. I could stay calm or I could blow up.

"Once I had blown up, I just had to wait for the feeling to go away. Afterwards, I'd sit down and try to work out what had happened and where I'd gone wrong. I tried to see if the situation was avoidable or if I could have anticipated getting frustrated. For example, I gave up going to the local service station because of the owner. I went to a self-serve place where I could do it at my pace; that helped. It sounds really petty, but each day is filled with hundreds of such incidents.

"Some days I was just no good. I was exhausted, or I'd had a blow up with Betty, and I knew that I just had to get away alone because I was like a time bomb waiting to explode."

There were other times when Tom knew he was vulnerable. If he tried to do too much or work for too long he'd feel like exploding. At social functions, like a family birthday, he felt tense, uneasy and trapped. It was the same if he had to do something quickly.

Contact with the school or colleagues really set him back, so did the end of the summer vacation when other teachers went back to work. Tom would be "cranky" for a week or so because he was reminded once again that they were doing something he couldn't do. Guilt was worse at these times too.

"I now know the things that upset me and I can plan for them a bit, have some rest beforehand, give myself an escape route and give myself a day or two to get over them.

"Of course, the most frustrating thing was being caught up in the workers' compensation process. All those doctors asking the same questions, never telling me anything. I'm glad I didn't have to go to court because I reckon I could have really let go there. I went to a factory once and watched little glass jars jolting along a process line. They were washed and dried and filled with pickles. The bottles were labeled, packed and then stacked. It was just how I felt: a little bottle on a production line. I felt sorry for those bottles."

Guilt and shame

Feelings of guilt and shame are present in almost every person who has a severe illness, but these feelings are profound in someone who has had a breakdown. Their shame comes from many sources. One of the first questions that people ask is, "Why me? Other people cope with all sorts of pressures and yet I didn't. Surely this means that I must be weaker then they are?" Very few people can understand their downfall may have been caused by a deadly combination of bad luck and their own obstinacy, which made them vulnerable. Other people's reactions, like those of Margaret's sister or some of Tom's colleagues, reinforce their sense of shame.

Tom felt better after his therapist introduced him to a group of teachers who'd had similar experiences.

"I don't know what I expected. I must have been thinking that they would all have two heads or be crazies or something. You could see that they all thought the same thing too, because I reckon they were as scared as me. It was amazing. They were all normal people and had been teaching for years. They'd been damn good teachers, too; you could tell by the way they talked, and some of them had been school principals. It made me feel sad afterwards to see such waste; all those people and not one of them could go back to the job they had loved. I felt a lot better knowing I wasn't the only one. We were all going through the same things, and as you heard each one talk, it was like listening to yourself. We all had the same problems, and some of them had worked out a few good ideas, which helped me a lot."

Meeting other people who shared the same experiences helped to dissolve some of Tom's shame and guilt, although he could still be very harsh towards himself. He needed to be a little kinder towards himself and not be so judgmental.

"The people in the group were all very special to me for a long time. They were the only ones who really understood what I was going through. When we met, it was one of the few times when I could really be myself. I often think about them and wonder what they are doing now."

Your therapist or doctor will probably spend some time talking to you about the causes of your breakdown and how you can avoid it happening again. Although this is one of the first things that people want to know, we generally find that people are able to take it in better when they are over the first stage of recovery and able to manage day-to-day routines.

Another cause of shame and guilt may be your inability to cope with even the simplest tasks. Margaret felt upset about being unable to do the most basic chores.

"There seemed to be so many things to be ashamed about. I couldn't seem to work or look after my family, I couldn't cope with friends, I was crying all the time. I felt so guilty at letting people down, family, friends, the world even."

Margaret often talked about these dilemmas with her doctor:

"All my life I've felt that I had to do things for others, care for my parents and friends. I had to put myself last otherwise I was being selfish, and yet I also wanted things for myself. But it was like I had to put everyone else first. When they were satisfied, then I could look after me. Of course, what happened is that no one was ever satisfied. It seemed like they wanted more and more.

"I used to think it was them, but now I realize it was me driving myself on. Even when I'd broken down that part of me was pushing me to do things, and if I didn't it would punish me - call me pathetic and stupid. I realized I was wasting a lot of energy trying to avoid feeling guilty over really trivial things.

"Some people, my sister for one, and one of the doctors I saw, would feed into all that and make me feel even more guilty. I've learned to keep good company, to only be with people who make me feel good, and I've learned to say no for the first time in my life. What freedom!"

Living with a fuzzy brain

Living with a fuzzy brain is difficult and yet a usual part of a breakdown. Brain function seems to take a long time to improve. You may find that you feel dulled, slow-witted and stupid, and this may trouble you on and off for a long time.

This seems to be a severe problem in those people who have been used to working with their intellect. Teachers, academics, managers and others report that this is a most difficult part of their breakdown.

There are a number of areas of brain function that are particularly disturbed, leading to problems with organization of thinking, repetitive thoughts and slowing of thought processes. In addition, memory and concentration are severely affected. It is handy to know what to look for and what you can do about it.

Organization of thought

We take our mental skills for granted until they let us down. Most of us can perform apparently simple but really quite complex functions like walking, eating and talking with ease, and we are able to do at least three tasks without even being aware of what we are doing.

People who are physically immobilized for many months have to relearn how to walk, and so it is with many of the automatic processes that are temporarily damaged by a breakdown. Your ability to deal with meeting new people is a case in point. When you are introduced to a stranger, you follow a ritual. You acknowledge the introduction with a word or two, a handshake or a nod, you make polite small talk, and you endeavor to match the name and face in the context of the meeting. All this appears automatic and effortless until you have experienced a breakdown. Once this point has been reached, all these automatic processes fail, and you have to remember how to do each step. The result is that you seem hesitant, uncomfortable and awkward. The mere process of listening seems to require more energy then you have. Making a sensible reply while, at the same time, being aware of being scrutinized, can be too much of an effort. The result is confusion, embarrassment and shame.

Making decisions becomes a painfully hesitant second-guessing process, and your judgment can be impulsive and unwise. If you are used to being decisive and clear, this hesitant groping for clarity, however small, is very painful.

George, the fireman, realized that he was never the same after the house fire. "After the roof fell on me, I couldn't seem to do the job; this was different from being scared although I was scared too. I couldn't remember how the pumps worked or where my helmet was. I'd waste precious moments checking to see if I'd brought all my gear. I'd prided myself on knowing the location of most of the hydrants in my area. I'd driven around and tried to memorize where they were - it was all gone - I'd have to ask one of the other blokes or look at our map. One time I had us driving around the block three times before I could find the bloody thing. When I got to the fire, I'd be in charge until a more senior officer arrived. I'd sweat blood waiting. I couldn't remember what to do. We have a set routine, and I just couldn't get it straight. Sometimes the other blokes would look at me with a strange expression. I knew they thought I was cracking up, and they were right.

"I'd get really flustered, and that would make it worse. Someone would say I should do one thing, and I'd agree, and then someone else would tell me to do something else, and I'd order that too. I didn't know if I was coming or going. I couldn't get my act together. I was so delighted when it was a big fire because someone senior would tell me what to do."

George and Tom both had to relearn these automatic skills, but they could only do so a step at a time. If they tried to do too much, they ran out of energy, felt exhausted and started to make mistakes. Tom noticed he would get words mixed-up, and would get confused when very tired.

"The last year at work I couldn't think myself out of a paper bag. It still happens - not as badly - but I've worked out what to do now. I couldn't even get my words out. I'd stammer and stutter, and I couldn't seem to put two words together. In the early days, I felt that way all the time. But now it's pretty rare. It usually means I'm doing too much and I should have a break, a rest or whatever I need. There are times when I know I will get flustered so I make some preparations. I carry a card with a couple of simple messages: IT'S ALL RIGHT, YOU'LL FEEL BETTER SOON and SLOW DOWN AND TAKE IT EASY.

"I plan things to do while I'm rational and I stick to it. I do one thing at a time and that's it. It makes me a bit rigid. My wife would like me to be more flexible, but I get rattled if we change our plans.

"I watch what I do each day because if I see too much or hear too much, for example, if I'm in a large department store with all that noise and activity, then I can feel my brain going.

"Now I know I will have times when my brain feels extra fuzzy. I know a lot of things that cause that to happen, and I avoid them. When I do feel that way, I try to let it happen and give myself time to get over it."

Tom was skeptical when Betty told him that she didn't think other people noticed his confusion and his half-finished sentences. He was surprised and relieved when a friend told him the same thing. Tom told his therapist, "I was so wound up in my own thoughts that I thought they must be able to tell what a mess I was. I occasionally notice it in other people who've had a breakdown, but I guess that's because I know what they're going through. Maybe they're right. Maybe other people don't notice all that much."

Memory and concentration

Loss of concentration and associated short-term memory lapses are frustrating, and the more agitated you become about them the worse they seem to get. The sooner you are able to make allowances for yourself, by accepting your memory problems rather than by fighting them, the better you feel. Use any aids you can: a weekly diary, lists, other people to remind you about important events. Avoid relying on your memory.

Margaret became adept at making allowance for herself. "My short-term memory was hopeless. I couldn't remember what I was doing from one moment to the next. I'd catch myself with a piece of toast in my hand in the bathroom, and I couldn't remember what I was doing there. I would forget the names of old friends, and I'd lose things. I'm still finding things I mislaid. I found a pile of cans I'd carefully put in the bottom of the freezer!

"At times my memory problems were a blessing because I couldn't get a clear picture in my mind of all those terrible things that lead to my breakdown. It was almost like they had happened to someone else. But at other times it all came back and hit me with a horrifying intensity. It felt like I was in the midst of it all again, and I could feel all the old anguish and misery as fresh as ever it was. That could go on for days at a time. I'd have horrifying nightmares, and I'd lose my appetite. It would always fade away, but each time it comes back, I still feel a bit shattered. I just let it pass now.

"I use all sorts of tricks to deal with my rotten memory. I've become a past master of talking to someone without using their names. I use a small book with phone numbers, names of friends and relatives. I use a weekly diary to plan my week. That's become invaluable."

Later in your recovery, you might find that you can train your memory and concentration by doing something that demands these skills. Jennifer went to bridge classes.

"I'd always been quite a good card player but in the beginning I don't think I could have even played Snap. Much later, my husband suggested to me that we go to some bridge classes at the church and I must say that at first I thought it was a ridiculous idea, but he persisted so I thought, 'Oh well, I'll give it a try.' The ritual beforehand helped. We started out with a glass of wine at home to settle me down a bit; we'd revise the previous week's lesson and then we'd go. The first few times were hopeless. I couldn't remember a thing the instructor said. Then one week I realized it was starting to make sense. Now I find my concentration is lasting a bit longer each time. I might make a bridge player yet."

Other people train their concentration by doing short courses. The main point to remember is not to get frustrated, angry or panicked when your concentration lapses again. Take a break and come back to your learning when you are ready, even if it means working in short bursts over a longer period of time. Jennifer used a glass of wine to reduce her tension and thereby improve her concentration, Tom did some of the exercises he had learned in his relaxation classes before he attempted tasks that needed concentration.

Lack of motivation

Because you have no energy, anything you used to enjoy has become a chore. George was particularly bothered by this. "I used to feel like I was wading through molasses I was so tired. It seemed such an enormous effort to think about anything, I seemed to have no interest in anything, and I didn't seem to care. I'd sit around for days at a time. I'd get a fleeting impulse to do something, but it all seemed too hard. And, of course, I was drinking a bit to settle my nerves."

There will be times when you have to push yourself to even do the essentials, eat, dress or even talk to your family. Jennifer worried that she had "lost" herself.

"I thought I'd become a different person, but I hadn't really. The old me slowly came out in bits and pieces, like small green islands appearing on a vast gray sea. It's nice when I'm on the islands, which seemed to have got bigger, and when I'm in the sea, I let myself bob around like a cork on the ocean."

Like Jennifer, you will be concerned about how long it takes for your motivation, drive and enthusiasm to return and, then, just when it seems to be coming back, it evaporates again as exhaustion seems to take over.

Repetitive thoughts and actions

Repetitive thoughts and actions can make you fear you're going mad. When these thoughts and actions are part of your breakdown, you will need a great deal of reassurance that they do pass and that you are not going mad. Talking about them to someone that you trust can help to make them lose their power, and diminish your fears.

Jill, the intensive care nurse, wrote in her diary: "I've had some more of those terrible thoughts again. Like what makes me who I am, or makes anybody who they are, when who you are is really your mind, and you're thinking about it with your mind? It seems to calm down when I talk about them to Dr. S. I think it's because he's not bothered by them. They're not so scary when you tell someone else."

Later extracts from her diary mirror her concerns. "Now I've got a lump in my groin, and all those thoughts have gone into the background. When I felt the lump, all those awful thoughts didn't seem to matter. They say it's not cancer.

"Even though this awful stuff is going on, and I'm tired, I want to go out and do things. I think I'm getting better. I miss old friends. I was really uptight worrying about this lump, worrying as much about that as about the things on my mind.

"It has been fading - a feeling now that I'm more of who I used to be. I felt stunned, felt like I wasn't there for a long time. Now I'm coming back. All these frightening thoughts are ones I've thought before but they never frightened me."

Jill felt she was going mad and required much reassurance that her experiences did not mean she was losing her mind. These repetitive thoughts continued to trouble her for months, but slowly they are fading. They are less intense and less frequent. She has learned to let the thoughts go and not be frightened by them to the same extent. She thinks now that the breakdown led to circuits in her brain being messed up so her thoughts seemed to reverberate.

Living with a battered body

How often do we remark on someone who has retired or been on holidays, "You look 10 years younger!" Similarly, a year after your breakdown you may be almost unrecognizable: your physical ailments are gone, your skin clearer, your gait and voice stronger, and you may start to take more pride in your physical appearance. As you improve, it is surprising how many physical problems get better or disappear altogether. Chest pains, palpitations, chronic infections, nausea and diarrhea, allergies, skin conditions, arthritis, diabetes, headaches, muscular pain, hypertension, premenstrual syndrome and hormonal imbalances come under control. This doesn't mean that you don't need to seek treatment for these conditions. Expert medical advice should always be sought, particularly for those conditions that are severe or life-threatening.

This improvement in your physical well-being can, paradoxically, cause further problems for you. Because you look so much better, other people assume that you have recovered and are ready to return to work. It is likely that only you, your family and your closest friends know that many of your unseen problems remain. The improvement in your physical well-being is usually only the first sign of recovery. Also, whenever you are under extra pressure or going through a difficult time, your own physical symptoms are likely to return to remind you how little strength you have in reserve.

Tom commented: "As I got better, my headaches, blood pressure and arthritis and even my clumsiness started improving; not all at once and not altogether, but I could see some light at the end of the tunnel. Like everything else in my life I had to learn patience, and I had to learn to recognize my body's response to pressure. All my old symptoms would come back if I tried to do too much. I used my symptoms as a guide of whether or not I was doing too much."

This is the time to build stamina. Tom found that golf was a way of gently exercising at his own pace. Often he would only do a few holes; at other times, 18 holes was no effort.

"I'd warn other golfers or anyone who has played a competitive sport that you have to change your attitude. Having to win or better your last score is disastrous. Whenever I tried to do that, my game would go off. I smile to myself now when I see the other fellas taking it so seriously. They're just like I used to be. Funny, that."

Two symptoms, in particular, were really difficult for Tom: his loss of libido and his exhaustion.

Loss of libido

The loss of libido is more than just not being interested in sex. Touching, caressing, even another person's presence, feels like a demand for performance, an expectation that you will respond.

"I didn't want to touch Betty or kiss her, and I'd feel irritated if she wanted any affection from me. She'd put her arm around me, and I'd feel really stiff. I didn't even want to sleep in the same room with her. I think that caused more trouble for us than anything else. A friend of mine who'd had a breakdown, became quite impotent. Even when he was a bit interested in sex, he couldn't perform, poor fellow."

Your partner will be very concerned about your behavior and is likely to misinterpret it as a sign that they are no longer desired or needed. Nothing could be further from the truth, and you will need to explain that this is another of the pervasive signs of your breakdown. Betty felt very hurt and rejected for a long time.

"It was funny really because I needed Betty more than ever, and I depended on her, and yet I kept pushing her away. As I got a bit better, I was able to explain to Betty that I felt totally depleted; it felt like my body had shut off my non-vital areas. Betty was able to see that I wasn't really rejecting her. It was a matter of survival. We had to talk about it a lot because she still felt really hurt at times. I knew I was really getting better when I could give her a heartfelt hug and a kiss, at the family birthday."

Like Tom, you will need to explain to your partner that your lack of interest comes from your breakdown and not from the relationship. It's chemical rather than emotional, and your libido will slowly improve as you recover.

During this time, your partner will have to be patient. On the infrequent occasions when you feel you have the energy to make love, your arousal is likely to be very slow and you may need all the help your partner can give you in reaching orgasm. What is important is your overall relationship, as the sexual side of it may not surface for weeks or months after your breakdown and during your recovery your lovemaking will still be infrequent. It can be a relief if you are not in a relationship, as you don't have to meet your own expectations or those of your partner.

Even if you don't experience a loss of libido, you may find that your partner does.

Jennifer's husband said: "I was so exhausted from doing all the shopping, cleaning, looking after the kids and so on, as well as my normal job, that I was the one who was always too tired!"

You know that you are getting better when you start to show interest in making new friends. Although Jill's parents were very perturbed that she showed no inclination to go out or have a boyfriend, it was the least of her worries.

"For so long, all I was really concerned about was getting through the next day or week. The only people I could have around me were, in the main, old friends. They knew me, and I knew them, and it was easier that way. It really wasn't until two years later that I started to feel I had enough self-confidence and enough energy to become involved with anyone new. Even then, it came in fits and starts. There were one or two men who I was really attracted to when I first met them, but they just exhausted me. Alan, who I'm seeing now, is different. He's very calm and quiet, yet he's a strong character - he doesn't take any nonsense from anyone. He seems to sense my moods so well and somehow he just knows when I want to be left alone. Our physical relationship is the same. I care more about him than any boyfriend I've ever had before because he really tries to understand and he cares about me."

Exhaustion

It took Margaret some months to workout how to deal with exhaustion. "Tiredness was another thing I had to learn to live with and accept. I tried everything to make it better but nothing really worked. It had to get better in its own good time.

"Plenty of things seemed to make it worse though. Most people told me that I was giving into it and that I should fight it. It was terrible advice and only made me worse. The irony of that advice is that I'd got into the situation I was in because I'd always pushed myself."

Your exhaustion will probably be most overwhelming when you first break down and this is usually the reason why people are put in the hospital. If you are concerned about the stigma of being admitted to a psychiatric hospital, your doctor may be able to arrange admission to a general hospital or even a health resort, provided you can afford the cost.

There are a few simple rules that you need to follow to cope with fatigue. Learn to pick when you are getting tired. Because this is different from normal physical weariness, the warning signals will come in other guises. Sometimes it is just a gut feeling that you shouldn't go out, at other times it may be a desire to eat more. It may be an increase in negative thinking, irritability, a headache, or uncontrollable crying.

Whatever your warning signal, stop and rest. Do essential things at the time of day when you have most energy. If you need a day in bed from time to time, take one. Experiment with the time you get out of bed. Some people advise getting up at the normal time so that you avoid those awful morning blues, but if you do this, you will probably need a longer rest time in the afternoon so that you have enough energy for the evening. If you have a family, they will make many demands on you at this time of the day.

Margaret concluded: "I'm much better at picking when I'm starting to get very tired and taking action rather than trying to recover after I've done too much. I've learned that I may never have the same energy as I had before, but I treasure what I have, and I think I husband it much more carefully than I ever used to before."

Physical exercise

Physical exercise is generally recommended as a strategy to help you get over your breakdown. It has been shown that exercise uses up many of the chemical by-products of the stress response. It helps to restore your body metabolism to normal, reduces the likelihood of weight gain and helps with sleep problems. Charles Darwin found that his regular afternoon walks around his estate developed his stamina and made him feel better.

But you will find, like Margaret, that it is a matter of timing and degree. Rigorous exercise during the first months of your breakdown will almost certainly be impossible.

"I felt so exhausted all the time at first and people were telling me I must get fit. Well, I tried. I went swimming, I tried aerobics and running, but it was no good at all. I'd feel even more exhausted. Sometimes I'd get dizzy and light-headed. I kept plugging away because people told me it was good for me, but it wasn't, it was terrible. I had to learn how to exercise properly; that meant doing what I could and no more."

It sounds simple, but it may take you some time to learn. You need to start with something gentle and then pace yourself. Only keep doing it if it makes you feel better and stop before you get tired.

Margaret described how she changed her approach: "I stopped doing all that other stuff and I began walking. I'd walk for a few minutes and then I'd come home. I wouldn't set any goals. I'd see how I felt. Some days I could walk further than others; other days I couldn't go at all. I began trying other activities too. I went back to swimming, but instead of setting myself 20 laps, I'd swim for maybe five minutes and then I'd stop and see how I felt. If I felt okay, I'd go on for a bit longer.

"I could always tell if I'd done too much. I wouldn't feel good. The other thing that changed as I began this light exercise program was that I was sleeping better and my bowels were working again - for a while they seemed to have gone on strike."

12

Getting Through The Day

Daily activities

We have already discussed our underlying philosophy for managing your breakdown. We talked of learning to be responsive to your body signals, and by doing this you give your body the time it needs to repair itself and avoid further damage. This is especially important in your daily activities. Many of the experiences we have already discussed occur infrequently. However, learning to cope with those ordinary, mundane matters gives us a base from which to tackle more difficult problems. Success in daily tasks boosts our confidence and the chances of success with weighty matters.

Rest

Rest is vital in your day. It doesn't necessarily mean lying down; it can mean watching a little television or pottering in the garden. Rest means a quiet time when you are most relaxed. It is important to rest as much as you can during recovering from your breakdown. At first, this may be most of the day. Helen, the cleaning lady, spent two weeks lying on the couch; she did virtually nothing else. Don't be concerned if you are resting all day and yet can't sleep at night - that should improve - but in the meantime rest, when required by your body, is vital.

Sleep

Sleep is a rare commodity for those who have broken down, but most people find their sleep pattern does improve. Tom still takes sleeping tablets occasionally, but his sleep pattern is better than before he broke down. Now, if he has a bad night, he resists the temptation to panic. He knows he can function during the day with only a small amount of sleep.

If you've broken down recently, you will feel exhausted and yet sleep seems to be impossible. You can't get off to sleep and when you eventually do, you may wake after two or three hours. This awakening in the early hours of the morning is the worst time of all. It is a time of desperation, of craving for sleep which seems to recede further and further the more it is desired. This is a time when the "night demons" crawl forth to spread their terror.

Sleep is a continuing difficulty for most for a longtime. The irony is that you have to be well rested to sleep well. Your pattern of sleep may be so disrupted that you feel very sleepy during the day but then can't sleep at night. It is useful to have regular rest times during the day, to allow you to sleep if you can. Take a break every four hours or so and rest. At night, plan that you may not sleep the full eight hours or so and make arrangements so you don't have to lie there waiting for sleep to come. You can keep occupied without disturbing your partner. Many TV sets have a plug for a headset or earphone. Keep a book in the lounge room. Explain the situation to your partner and get up when you wake rather than lying there, gritting your teeth and waiting for sleep to arrive.

You will find that your sleep is disrupted by extra stress: appointments, social engagements, and so forth. Sleeping tablets are useful in these situations on a short-term basis. There are a number of simple aids that you can use to help you sleep: avoid caffeine drinks, such as tea and coffee, before bedtime, try not to over stimulate yourself mentally or physically before bedtime, don't go to sleep hungry and don't try too hard to fall asleep.

Choosing what to wear

Margaret found that choosing what to wear caused her a great deal of anxiety at first, especially if she had to go out: "I could never decide what to wear, until I got into a routine. Now I have two outfits which I alternate for doctor's visits or business appointments and about four others I wear on other days. I notice they're all dark colors, so I don't look conspicuous, I suppose. Anyway, it beats staring at the wardrobe for half an hour or trying on one dress after another like I used to. That's the first decision of the day over with."

Diet

Eating patterns are usually disrupted in the time leading up to and after breakdowns. The only common theme is a change in diet and this can be so dramatic that it seems bizarre. Some eat almost nothing because food, like everything else, holds no pleasure; others find themselves gorging on cakes, sweets and chocolate. A few have major eating disorders, such as bulimia, repeated cycles of overeating and vomiting. These disorders can be triggered by stress and need specific treatment.

It may take some time for your natural eating rhythms to be restored so you will need to be more vigilant in the early stages. Check the side-effects of any medication you are taking so that you can keep weight gain under control if necessary by restricting your eating and going onto a light exercise program.

Helen almost stopped eating, and the weight seemed to fall off her. She is sure her weight loss contributed to her exhaustion. Tom found himself stopping at the shop on the way home to buy chocolate bars which he'd devour immediately. He drank more alcohol too, so his weight increased.

Many people find they have an altered tolerance to some foods. Margaret found that there were foods that she could not digest easily. Cheese made her feel very bloated, for example. A healthy diet had always been important to her.

"When I started improving - I mean when I could think about getting through each day - I experimented with my diet and after some trial and error I found those foods and style of cooking that worked for me and those that didn't. Fatty foods made me feel unpleasant, and I began using less and less meat. I began using a modified Pritikin diet. There were some good cook books for that sort of food. The meals were very tasty. I felt like I was pampering myself again."

Out of her experiences and those of many others we have developed some general guidelines.

Generally, it is best to have small, frequent meals, perhaps four or five a day. A vegetarian-based diet seems more useful than a high-meat diet. An adequate intake of vitamin B is important, use alcohol sparingly and try to cut down your cigarette consumption. Try to improve your physical efficiency. If you are overweight, reducing it will give you a good deal more energy and it will help your morale.

Alcohol

Alcohol should be used with great care after your breakdown. Even if you have only been a modest drinker, the temptation to use it as a way of reducing tension or even to go further, and try to block everything out, can be strong.

Tom had been drinking more heavily in the year before he broke down. His use of alcohol continued for some time afterwards but with much more damaging effects.

"I was feeling so tense and having so much trouble sleeping, I began drinking a few cans of beer at night to help me settle down. After a while I began to rely on those few drinks so I could sleep. I even found myself wanting a drink during the day. I got really drunk at one of our Friday night after-work sessions, not so much that anyone would notice, but I knew the next day all right. I don't think alcohol led to me breaking down, I think it helped me keep going and was really me giving myself a tranquilizer."

If you find yourself drinking too much, you may need to discuss it with your doctor or therapist who can either give you help, or refer you to a specialist.

Tom was lucky. After his breakdown, he couldn't tolerate alcohol at all because it made him physically ill. Others are less fortunate. In the process of avoiding a breakdown they have become very dependent on alcohol and have come to suffer the physical and emotional damage of alcoholism.

Alcohol tolerance is often very reduced when you breakdown, although a glass of beer or wine may be a pleasant daily ritual, especially when the pleasure outweighs any disadvantage.

The way to use alcohol is to keep listening to your body and drink only according to your capacity. This is the same philosophy that underlies recovering from all aspects of a breakdown.

Tobacco

As with alcohol, so with tobacco: use of tobacco generally increases in the period before a breakdown. Tobacco use reduces your body efficiency, and we discourage it. Nevertheless a breakdown is not a good time to break a tobacco dependency.

Try to reduce your intake and avoid the habitual use of cigarettes to give yourself something to do.

Reading

Reading becomes impossible in the immediate period after a breakdown, and you will be frustrated by your inability to read and comprehend even the back of your packet of breakfast cereal. This skill returns slowly and it is often years before you read without effort. Reader's Digest is a very useful means of returning to reading: it is upbeat and the stories are short and easy to read.

Radio, television and videos

Home entertainment machines can be a curse or a blessing. Heavy metal rock music can feel like a jackhammer pounding away in your head, but a "beautiful music" program played quietly can be very soothing. Similarly, television programs can be very jarring, especially news features, with their inevitable focus on accidents, disasters and bad economic news.

The trick to using your radio and television set is to monitor how they are effecting you, if you feel relaxed then you are doing well. As a general guide, when watching television, avoid news programs, movies involving excessive violence, rapid action sequences or heart-wrenching emotion.

Radio can be much less demanding, but again, it is useful to avoid news features, loud music and too much talking. The advantage of video is that it gives you much more control over the program you are watching and you can tailor the program to suit.

The problem comes when you are in a family with teenage children. It may be worthwhile buying or renting a television set for their own use so that you don't feel persecuted by their need for noise and action.

Diary

It is a good idea to keep a diary. It can be a simple one where you record your main activity and how you felt on that day or it can be more comprehensive and used as a way of expressing some of your inner life.

Recovery from a breakdown takes a long time, usually many months, and it is difficult to feel a sense that any change is occurring. A diary can be a useful record of all those small changes that progressively accumulate. Re-reading your diary periodically gives you a clearer view of your progress. A diary is also useful to pick up patterns of behavior. Tom noticed that every time he had a medical appointment he would go downhill for a few days beforehand and would take several days to recover. He could see the pattern clearly in his diary and began planning ways of coping better with this pressure.

Margaret began to use her diary to measure her improvement: "I couldn't remember anything, so I began keeping a rough diary. It was very patchy at first, but after a while I began using it to keep a record of how I was feeling and what I'd been doing. I didn't realize how important it would be at first. But later on I'd go back to it and although sometimes it was really painful seeing how bad I'd felt, it was also really encouraging to see how far I'd come. I think you forget how you were feeling even a few days ago and it was a good reminder of how far I'd come."

A diary doesn't have to be exhaustive, just enough to keep a record of your sleep patterns, your energy level during the day, any extra activities you have undertaken and alterations in your mood. Some find it useful to write in it once or twice a day and use a scale from 1 to 5 to grade their sleep, energy level or mood. Some partners keep a diary too, and comparing their diary with yours is interesting. It's surprising how unsuccessful you are at keeping your feelings hidden.

A diary can also be a good way of venting your feelings. Margaret found that when she described her anger or sadness on paper, her feelings seemed to lose their urgency and she was able to put them aside a little more. In this way she used her writing, in part, as a substitute for her therapist.

Again, this is something you need to experiment with to see if it works for you. If writing about your feelings in detail makes you sadder or angrier, don't do it.

Telephone

Accepting and making telephone calls is a common fear, and people are relieved when they discover that others find the telephone frightening too. The unexpected ring of the telephone has a similar effect to the ringing of the door bell: it produces tension and apprehension. Once you know who it is and what they want, you can feel more at ease, but when you hear the shrill bell sounding your heart sinks: a new demand, a new request, something else to face. A telephone call feels like an intrusion; your silences seem so much more deafening, your sighs and hesitations so much more obvious. It is hard to conceal your confusion with activity, and it seems so much harder to escape.

Tom hated the phone. "Even now, when I am so much better, the ringing of a phone sends cold shudders through me. I hate it. Another person, another demand. It seems such an invasion sometimes. I'd rip out the phone if we could do without it."

Tom and Betty worked out a number of ways of handling the telephone. Initially, he ignored the phone unless someone else was home to answer it. Betty and the boys would answer it when they were home and pretend to check to see if Tom was home before he accepted the call. That way, Tom was able to screen unwanted callers or ring back when he felt able to speak. If Betty or one of the children wanted to contact Tom, they would use a pre-arranged code: let the phone ring twice, hang up and ring again.

Tom found that it was best not to put off calls that had to be made. The longer he left the call, the more frightened and anxious he became. If he couldn't do it, Betty made the call for him. He also learned to prepare for calls, particularly those that could be awkward. He would write down what he was going to say so that if he got lost for words halfway through the conversation he would refer to his notes. He also had a list of stock phrases by the phone to deal with unexpected questions or demands: "Someone is at the door. I'll have to go." All these phrases gave him some breathing space.

As Tom said, "It probably all sounds ridiculous to someone who hasn't had a breakdown, but you wouldn't believe how much better I felt at home when we worked all that out." Recently Tom bought a telephone answering machine that enables him to ignore the phone, but the family can still get their messages. "It doesn't even ring, so I can totally forget that there is a phone in the place."

Driving

The loss of concentration and the self-absorption that is so much a part of a breakdown makes driving extremely hazardous, and it may be wise to stop driving altogether for a time. Driving for most of us has become an automatic process and you may find that you have to relearn those automatic skills. When you do start driving again, go on short trips at first and, if necessary, take someone with you.

Margaret found that driving had become a frightening experience: "I'd get flustered and crash the gears. I'd try to drive carefully, but I'd do stupid things. I banged into the back of a car at a traffic light. I thought I was going in the wrong direction. I got all panicky and I didn't notice the car in front had stopped. I'd get very nervous in peak-hour traffic and in the city. Sometimes I couldn't read the street signs."

Use public transport if you can, especially in the early stages. If you have to drive, cut down your speed and stay in the slow lane so that you can stop if you need to. It is worth checking with your doctor about potentially dangerous side-effects of any medication you are taking, such as blurred vision, slowed reaction time and interaction with alcohol. The main point to remember is that driving needs concentration and you may have to stop frequently to remain alert.

Margaret went further: "I sold my manual car and bought an automatic. If I was going far, I'd stop every 10 or 15 minutes and just sit quietly in the car. I'd check the route then too. I avoided peak-hour traffic. I tried not to push myself. If I didn't feel like going out, I'd just cancel my trip. My friends understood, although sometimes doctors or solicitors got annoyed about it. I didn't ever expect that I'd become a safer driver as a result of my breakdown, but I have!"

Shopping

When people who have had a breakdown get together, the discussion often turns to shopping. Dealing with noise and crowds, driving and finding a parking spot, and endless decision-making are common topics. Each person has worked out a way of dealing with what most of us find to be only minor irritants but have become major obstacles for those who have experienced a breakdown. It is best to shop for essential items only. Make a list to guide you, do your shopping in quiet times and in small bursts, and try not to search for presents or special items at the last minute.

If you plan a shopping trip, you might find it easier to go with a friend, particularly if you must travel to the city or if you feel under pressure to make decisions quickly. Margaret sometimes took her children and often went with Ruth.

"Ruth was a good shopping companion. We avoided peak-hour traffic, we never went to sales, and I even had all my Christmas shopping done before December. That was such a relief."

If you feel bad, cancel trips that are non-essential or go home as soon as possible. Starting to feel rattled usually means that you have stayed too long. Margaret learned to read the signals: "A few months ago I was trying on a dress in a big store. We'd come in by public transport, and I started feeling really uneasy. I just changed quickly, grabbed Ruth by the arm and told her I had to go. We walked onto the street and hailed a cab and went straight home. It was expensive but really worth it."

Meal preparation

Both Tom and Margaret had become convinced of the importance of a good diet, but for a long time, both of them lacked the energy or the initiative to prepare meals. Tom was fortunate, he had a wife. Margaret has often said that she would have found a wife very helpful too.

Margaret: "For quite some time I couldn't think about food. I was eating what was there. I couldn't seem to plan ahead. The children were upset about it and complained that I wasn't even getting their meals! I don't blame them, but I was a total mess, and all they could think about was their stomachs. They did help a bit, but they really couldn't cope with getting the food and preparing it and so forth."

You might like to do for yourself what Margaret's friend did for her; make a list of your simplest, favorite meals and rotate them.

"A good friend had helped me out. She'd let me have a cry on her shoulder and occasionally she'd bring over a meal. One day she sat down and drew up 10 menu cards. She made sure the food was easy to get and to cook, and that the kids liked the menus. She took me shopping to get the first week's supplies, and she helped me cook the first meal. It was a success, and I got such a boost. I followed those menu cards religiously. I didn't have to think and if I couldn't go shopping the kids knew exactly what to get. I still use them. They're getting a bit dog-eared now, but they work, and I guess I work better too."

Margaret also used to get her children to do some of the supermarket shopping. Sometimes she would push the cart and let them make most of the decisions; at other times she would send them in with a note and stay in the car. They would come out and get Margaret when it was time to pay. Margaret neatly summed it up: "I've learned a good general rule: if you don't have to do it, don't do it."

13

Spreading Your Wings

Leaving your house can be fraught with difficulty. But despite the effects of venturing into the world, you cannot avoid it. You must go shopping at times, deal with doctors, lawyers, family and friends. All these activities are difficult, but there are some solutions. If your trip is unhurried and planned, it becomes something to look forward to rather than to dread.

It is generally best to do only one thing each day and to go out at a time when you have the most energy. This is likely to be mid-morning. Leaving home then has the added advantage that you avoid the rush hour. If you are using public transport, workout the route and check the timetable beforehand. Similarly, if you are driving, take time before you leave to plan your trip if you are going somewhere unfamiliar.

Margaret followed some simple rules: "I found I had to plan my day and my week. I would work out what I had to do and spread that out over the week. I made sure I didn't do too much each day. I found I could only do one thing at a time. If I went to the supermarket, I couldn't go to the post office or the dry cleaners. If I tried to go there, I'd get exhausted and feel very shaky. It was a nuisance having to be so careful."

Make a list of the things you have to do on your trip and check that you have everything you need before you go. If you do forget something, and you will from time to time, try not to get caught in a cycle of self-blame and exasperation. You can always post the article or take it another time.

If Margaret had an appointment that day, she left early and went straight to the meeting place without taking detours. If she was going to a party or a social gathering, she found it better to arrive when people had gathered although not so late that she felt conspicuous when she arrived. She had a ritual for leaving home: "I have a few sets of keys scattered around the house with big labels. I didn't get so flustered about losing my keys then. I'd get my keys and my bag and then I'd go. I tried not to get flustered. Sometimes I used an audio tape in the car and that was very soothing and would settle me down. Occasionally, it was easier if I asked a friend to come with me, especially if it was a long distance or I was going somewhere new."

164

Interests and activities

Finding activities that give you pleasure and a sense of purpose after your breakdown will, at first, seem almost impossible. Lack of energy, low frustration tolerance, fear of failure and of socializing and an inability to enjoy yourself are all likely barriers. Although you will need to rest frequently, it is important to find some small interest so that you can take some small steps towards normal activity.

You might expect to start doing things when you feel better, but it seems to work the other way - even if you are still unwell, starting some activity will make you feel better. The danger is to try and do too much. Even in the unlikely event that you don't put pressure on yourself, your friends and family will, and it may take considerable effort on your part to resist their well-meaning advice. The challenge will be to find something that is satisfying but doesn't demand too much energy or too much contact with other people.

Interests that involve any sort of pressure or a lot of "brain work" are best avoided. Gentler interest that can be put down or taken up at will, such as craft work, gardening, cooking, woodworking, restoring furniture, lead lighting and photography, are ideal. Notice that all of these suggested activities produce something tangible.

George, the fireman hit by the falling roof, had been a keen pigeon racer until the months before his breakdown. He felt he'd lost any interest in his birds and in the racing club. His wife, Nancy, had looked after his birds at first until she left. Even then she persuaded George to begin taking a small interest in them; it was really a choice of looking after them or selling them.

"It was hard to be bothered at first and sometimes it still is. I still can't seem to enjoy things. I still feel like I'm going through the motions, but I plugged away with the birds. I could only do a few minutes a day at first. I'd clean out a cage or I'd bring some bird seed, but it's amazing how a few minutes a day adds up, and I look back, and I can see that I've done quite a bit. That's really helped my morale.

"So much of the time I seemed to be sitting around doing nothing. Some days I'd do a lot: other days only a little. If I was feeling better, I'd often finish up doing too much, and I'd feel terrible for days afterwards. I had to learn to pace myself. I even entered some birds in a few races, but I didn't care much about the result. Next year I might do some breeding."

As the months go by you will find that you can do more, but you need to be careful not to push yourself too hard.

As you pick up your interests, try and be aware of your body's response: ease off if you are becoming tired or frustrated. Work for a set time, say half an hour, and then stop.

Some people find it easier to take up an entirely new activity. That way, they are not comparing their performance today with how they used to be.

- Look for activities which give pleasure and do not have any pressure associated with them.
- Pace yourself with your interests. Stop when you start to feel tired.
- Gradually extend your activities, but only as you are able and keep monitoring your symptoms.

Handling finances

Many people find that their financial affairs fall into the same disarray as every other aspect of their life when they break down. As time goes on, finances can become such a mess that they don't even know where to start.

A breakdown can precipitate a financial crisis and you may need to take some action quite early in your recovery to prevent this occurring to you.

Margaret described what happened to her: "All my finances fell in a heap when I broke down. I didn't have the energy to even think about money, and I didn't pay a bill for three months. I couldn't even think about it. I had an old fruit bowl in the kitchen and anything that looked like a bill would be thrown in there unopened. When I felt like I should pay something, I'd look at that pile, and my heart would sink and I'd feel even more hopeless.

"When the bills started spilling out of the bowl, I put the bowl in a cupboard and just chucked them all in there - there were rate notices, electricity, phone and gas accounts, medical bills, charge cards and insurance payments. I didn't pay anything, not even my car registration. I drove an unregistered car for six months."

Many find that they can identify with Margaret. Although they may not have let their financial affairs fall into the state that she did, they can understand how it happens.

"The phone and power were cut off. At least with the phone off, I stopped getting calls about unpaid bills. But it was all such a hassle getting the phone back on and the electricity reconnected. It was the last thing I needed. I'd get visits at all hours from debt collectors. They'd really upset me; they'd even come late at night; it was scary. I'd shake and cry and make a fool of myself when they demanded payment."

When it gets to this stage, when basic things like energy bills are not being paid, when confusion, despair and loss of self-respect has resulted, the size of the task seems monumental and all these factors make it hard to know where to start picking up the pieces.

"Even when I tried to do something about it, I couldn't seem to get organized. I'd pay the first few bills, and I'd feel so bad I couldn't do the rest. So I'd pay bills that didn't matter. I remember one was for credit card insurance. What a waste - I couldn't even go into a shop so I wasn't using credit cards and I wasn't paying the essentials like the electricity bill."

There are a few simple things that you can do to avoid getting into the same mess as Margaret. Keep all your bills and receipts in the one place, use an expanding file to sort them alphabetically as they arrive, and try to set aside a time each week when you pay the most important ones. If the thought of sitting down for an hour or so to do that is just too daunting, do it for 10 minutes every few days until you have caught up. Get help from a family member or friend if necessary. Some people, like Tom, find it easier to give the responsibility to someone else.

"I don't know how we could have survived without Betty. She took over all our finances, paid all the bills and spoke to the bank about our mortgage, and so on. Although she'd never done it before, like everything she does, Betty was good at it. I was surprised and a bit ashamed at how resentful I was. It just showed me again how little I was able to do and I found myself snapping at her. I think she must have realized why I was carrying on because she started to do the bills when I wasn't around. She told me later that she tried not to hassle me about money and only discussed the important things with me when I was in a good mood!"

Margaret's finances were in a mess and yet, sporadically, she would be wildly extravagant. On impulse, one day she bought a full-length fur coat, a wild extravagance at a time when she was barely paying for her groceries.

"I call the fur coat my 'blues coat.' I still feel silly when I wear it because it was such a crazy thing to buy, but I really needed to give myself a present, and I'd always wanted one."

Having a breakdown plays havoc with your finances in other ways. Many of us are familiar with the pattern of impulse buying when we are feeling down, and someone who has had a breakdown may be even more susceptible to this sort of financial recklessness. Try to keep your impulse buying in check. If necessary, give yourself an allowance you can afford for sheer indulgences.

Margaret found that she had other expenses too. "I wasn't getting enough money coming in to pay the ordinary expenses and having a breakdown seemed to cost me more. I couldn't shop around so my food bills were larger because I'd grab the first thing I saw rather than looking for bargains. I'd give the kids money to get take-out food when I couldn't cook and that cost more. My medical expenses were very high, and I'd have to get taxis to get to appointments. I was lucky my house was paid off. I don't know how people could survive having to pay rent or mortgage payments when their income drops and they've had a breakdown."

Because of poor judgment and bad planning you may find yourself doing other things that cost money. Margaret's woes continued: "I did other things that cost me money unnecessarily. My car started making a funny noise, and I took it to the local service station. I shouldn't have done it because I've always thought he was a crook. He didn't fix it properly, and he said it needed new brakes and, stupidly, I told him to fix them. It was only later I remembered I'd got them done six months before and he'd just ripped me off. Another time I got a locksmith to fit two new locks, and he put them on the wrong doors. I was out and I'd told the kids to check that he'd done the right thing. I was really upset because I'd carefully told the locksmith what to do."

Like Margaret, you'll probably find it hard to assert your-self when you need to. Standing up for your rights takes a lot out of you and you'll find yourself tense and exhausted for hours or even days afterwards.

"I called the locksmith's shop, and they promised to fix their mistake, but nothing was done. I didn't pay the bill, and they sent me reminders, which I ignored. They went to court and got a judgment against me. I was so upset and rattled by it all that I paid it. All the extra costs made it double what it should have been otherwise. I paid it because I just wanted to have it over and done with."

When you're in this situation, you need to get outside help, like Margaret did.

"It all came out when I was talking to Andrew, and he arranged for me to see a credit counselor. She was terrific; she got me to bring every bill in, phoned all my creditors and told them I was sick and couldn't pay straight away. She drew up a list of the bills that I had to pay immediately and a list of ones that could wait, and helped me to get my finances organized.

"She was really good at persuading some of my creditors to wait for their money. For awhile I was seeing her every few weeks and she was helping me get through the backlog and stay abreast of it all."

Most creditors are reasonable if they know what is happening. They would generally much rather wait for their money than risk not being paid at all.

Although we've described some common financial problems associated with your breakdown, like everything else, people respond in different ways at different times. You may be too tired to go out and spend money, especially during the first few months and might even see your bank balance rising. Others become so insecure that they find themselves watching every cent and are overly cautious, causing quite different family problems.

Financial affairs are disrupted by breakdowns, and restoring financial order is as important as restoring all the other aspects of your life. Financial counseling can be as important as psychological counseling.

Requirements of a good financial counselor are similar to those of a good health counselor: patience, knowledge and a willingness to help.

If you live in a smaller town and do not have access to a financial counselor, your bank manager may be able to help. They maybe familiar with your affairs and have contacts with the local community.

In summary
- Keep all your bills and receipts in one place.
- Make a regular time each week or month to pay the most urgent accounts.
- If you have trouble managing your finances, get a family member or friend to help you.
- Try to resist impulse buying or at least limit it to what you can afford.
- If your financial affairs are in a mess, get help from a financial adviser or your bank manager about consolidating your debts and rationalizing payments.
- Keep your bank or any other creditors informed about your situation
- When making major purchases or decisions involving money, seek help from a trusted family member, friend or professional advisor.

Business appointments
Despite having had a breakdown, life goes on. Accounts have to be paid, food has to be bought, family matters have to be dealt with

and occasionally you have to see someone other than a doctor or therapist about your personal affairs. It may be an accountant about tax, a real estate agent about the sale of property, or an investment advisor.

These visits are all stressful, not only because of the need to get to the appointment on time, and possibly meet a new person, but also by their nature. Planning is the key to handling these situations well. It is good to bring adequate documentation, but it is useless if it is a mess, and if it is difficult to get information quickly in the meeting you will get rattled, embarrassed and possibly panic. Keep the documentation to a minimum and try to keep it in separate files. Many people find an expanding cardboard file with divisions very handy. You may need a friend's or relative's help to organize your documents and to remove the unnecessary ones. It is most important to make a list of questions that you want answered and bring them to the meeting. It may be useful to take a tape recorder so you have a record of what was said.

Avoid the impulse to apologize for your behavior or to relate the story of your breakdown. Most people will not be very interested and you will waste precious time.

Tom became something of an expert in dealing with these situations:

"The medical appointments were the worst, but some of those other ones weren't too good either. In the midst of all this my mother died, and I was appointed an executor of her will. I had to see her solicitor and accountant to work out what to do. They were pretty helpful really. I made sure my wife or a friend came with me each time for moral support, and we went by taxi so we'd get there on time and I wouldn't have to worry about parking. I made sure we got there really early so I wouldn't panic about being late.

"Even with those precautions I'd still get exhausted, and I'd take a day or two to recover. When I'd settled down, I'd go back and play the tape, and I'd keep a record of what had happened so I knew what was going on.

"I learned one really important thing. Sometimes I'd be really upset. I don't know why. Sometimes it was a rushed meeting or I'd had a bad week, or whatever, but I learned that I had to 'pull out.' I had to abandon the meeting and go home. If I didn't, the meeting was generally a disaster, and I'd make even more of a fool of myself, and it would knock me around for a long time afterwards."

Holidays

The instinct to flee, to get away after your breakdown can be strong and is best resisted. Think about what you are getting away from and what you will be coming back to. It is most likely that you want to get away from your turbulent emotions and that all your other concerns will still be present when you return. Post-holiday blues are common, and it might be possible to plan your holiday so that you have something to look forward to on your return, starting a course or a small project at home, for example.

Holidays are generally best postponed until you are able to benefit from them. You also need to take into consideration what sort of holiday is best for you. Holidays that are demanding because of tight schedules and contact with lots of other people won't be suitable for some time.

Tom and Margaret's contrasting experiences illustrate what we mean. Tom and Betty flew to Club Med. Betty had not wanted to go, but Tom insisted, and she had reluctantly gone along. He was tense in the few days before they left home, even though Betty had taken care of all the arrangements. He was irritable and anxious on the plane, and his mood became worse at the resort.

"I had this crazy idea that I needed sun and fun and adult company. Wrong, wrong and wrong! I tried to keep up with the frantic activity, but I hated it from the moment I arrived. I just wanted to crawl away and hide. Poor Betty had a rotten time. She was worried about me, and it wasn't her scene anyway. I tried to enjoy myself, but I couldn't seem to do it. I felt like a Rechabite in a pub. I reckon I needed a holiday to get over the holiday!"

By contrast, Margaret's friend Ruth arranged for Margaret to stay on a farm with some friends of hers. Margaret could do what she liked. She had a small cottage away from the farm, and she didn't see her hosts for days at a time: she had no demands or expectations made on her. She rested when she wanted to. She could go for quiet ambles, and sometimes, on balmy evenings, she would lie on a rug under the stars and stare at the moon. The holiday felt like a gentle healing, and she came home feeling more rested and refreshed. She returned several times and on each stay had the same quiet enriching experience.

"I knew instinctively it was the right place for me. I've learned to trust that instinct now. I think what you need is quiet, no demands, and a harmonious environment. Although I didn't see Jan and Todd for days at a time, I knew they were there. I didn't need to feel terribly isolated."

Travel

Travel sounds exciting but in reality it is rarely trouble free. Travel writers can give you many tips for anticipating and meeting travel problems; they offer suggestions about destinations, accommodation, money, and suggestions about clothing, travel and food. Some of the problems you may encounter can be anticipated. You may need to take extra care to reduce the inevitable pressures of travel by spending longer at each stop every time you change planes, for instance, or, if you are visiting several places on the same trip, avoid going too far in one day. Try to build flexibility into your plans, but basic arrangements such as tickets and accommodation should be arranged before you go. Some will find organized tours better because someone else takes care of most of the problems, but they don't suit everyone.

Tom had learned a great deal from the debacle of the Club Med experience. "After that holiday and a couple of long car trips, I began to see that I had to be careful about traveling too. I had to plan for this like I had to plan for everything else. If I didn't, I would pay the price."

Travel necessarily involves being exposed to rapid change. You will have all sorts of different experiences to contend with: new sights, noise and people. There will be lots of decisions to be made. Do you go here or there? Should you get a cab? What do you do with the luggage? What hotel to stay at? What to do tomorrow?

Traveling will be less demanding if you reduce sight-seeing and increase rest times even though your natural instinct, like Tom's, will be to cram in as much as possible.

"I got very tired, and my ability to cope, already pathetic, became even worse. I also felt under a lot of pressure because it was costing us so much and we wouldn't be this way again. I felt like I had to use the experience to the full.

"I thought we could try a bus tour. It would be easy because they would make all the decisions. Well, that was true, but I got driven mad by the other passengers. They all seemed so inquisitive and always talking. I felt like I was trapped and couldn't get away. Out of that I learned a few general rules which I use when I travel.

"For a start I expect traveling to be a hassle and not a pleasure. I found I have to get heaps of rest and be careful over my diet. I am really careful to do a small amount of sightseeing in the morning and then a little in the afternoon and rest in between. I break the journey as often as I can before I reach the stage of exhaustion. I use Valium tablets to settle me down if I'm starting to get really tense."

When Tom traveled a long distance from home, he carried a

brief explanatory note from his doctor in case he had to seek medical help while he was away.

"I wouldn't recommend travel to anyone in the early stages of a breakdown, it's a recipe for disaster. Now I travel a bit and sometimes I even enjoy it, and that's a plus."

Courses

Attending a short course is often a logical step in continuing the move away from the security of home. You might choose the class to learn new skills, to expand your interest or to help you with some aspect of your breakdown; aerobics, yoga, swimming, assertiveness training or courses in meditation might be suitable.

A course can be a way of gently exploring other possible job interests if you feel unable to return to your old job. Initially, the course content may not be as important as the side benefits: you will be involved with other people, you will be trying to extend your concentration and your week will become more structured; having to be at the course on time for every session is another small pressure for you to deal with.

Stan, the suicidal policeman, went to a course in furniture making. "I chose one that was being held a few kilometers away so I was less likely to meet anyone I knew. It was held once a week, three hours at a time for six weeks. I didn't believe how nervous I was before the first class, and I almost didn't go, but I knew this was one thing I'd have to push myself on; I had to start somewhere. The instructor told us what types of wood to bring each week, and I enjoyed going to the wood yard to choose it. The quiet chatter of people going about their business was very soothing.

"At the course I found myself getting irritated with the other people at times but, generally, I coped with them quite well. Some weeks I seemed to be all thumbs, but there were a few times when I was fired up and really got the knack of it. It certainly got easier each week and doing that course gave me confidence to try other things."

Various courses in stress management, yoga, meditation and relaxation training can be useful in the late phase of recovery. But before you launch into them, you must be able to get through most days without too much trouble and you should be able to endure sitting quietly for some time. Many of the courses on offer are useful, but you must be careful to monitor your response and make sure the course is giving you immediate benefits. A good course should make you feel better. If it doesn't, no matter how highly it has been rated, it is no good for you.

Retraining

The decision to retrain is a big one and is usually not possible for a long time after your breakdown. For most people, not being able to continue working in their chosen career is a loss that takes some time to come to terms with. A few people have in mind an alternative career right from the start of their breakdown, but it is usually a process of eliminating various possibilities. As you extend your interests and hobbies and attend short courses you will probably be developing ideas about what you might do.

Brendan found it useful to look back through his life to see what other interests he had had as a young boy and at school. He had always enjoyed mathematics and he decided to do computer training. At first he was horrified to discover how poor his concentration was and wondered whether he was doing the right thing.

"There were times during those first few months in the course when I had to fight a rising panic. It took me much longer to take in what the lecturer was saying, and it was only the support of my girlfriend, Jeannie, and my doctor that kept me going. I had to keep telling myself that the others probably didn't understand everything he was saying either. I'd go home and read over the notes, practice a lot in short bursts and then read through the notes for the next session. I felt much better if I knew what was coming up because then I wasn't panicked so easily."

Brendan was able to complete the course, and his rehabilitation advisor was able to negotiate a return to work doing administrative work on computers with his old department. He now had skills that were in demand.

If you think you might be ready to retrain, the main issue to focus on is whether you are ready to cope with the demands of using new skills. If you have been gradually extending your interests and involvement in other areas, this will be a useful guide for you.

14

How Family and Friends Can Help

George's wife, Nancy, has put into words what people in the family feel when someone has had a stress breakdown. The family suffers because family members bear this strain alone, usually with no support. They don't understand why the breakdown occurred, they don't know how to help and they are afraid of what might happen.

Ironically, the person who has broken down is only too aware of the effect they are having on the family. But with the best of intentions, they cannot help their behavior. Sometimes the family only sees what is on the surface. Silence is often a way of covering up fury, withdrawal may seem the only way of shielding the family from the full blast of a person's anguish and fear. Generally, people who have broken down are filled with remorse and guilt over the effects they are having on the people close to them. At times, well-meaning partners or parents shield them from full knowledge of their impact on the family.

Family life revolves around the wounded member. Everyone is expected to fit in with all the needs and demands of the one who has fallen apart. But this can be destructive. Everyone else needs to be looked after too, and if all the energies of the family seem to be going in one direction, the family as a group can be shattered.

Children vote with their feet. After a time they become jaded and irritated by the tension, the dependency and the anger from the parent who has broken down. They escape into their rooms, into reading or watching television, and many leave home, often after an angry outburst.

Partners have to bear the brunt of everything. If you are in this situation, you may feel expected to pick up the shattered pieces, cope with irritation, moodiness, depression and dependency. You are also expected to run the household unaided, cope with bills, with less money, and with all the daily chores. In the meantime, you are getting very little; no real help, support or affection maybe forthcoming. If you are a parent, much the same situation occurs, although it can be made more difficult by your child's anger at you taking on a parental role again. They do not realise how reluctant you are to play this part again.

You are often impelled to behave in this way by a sense of guilt.

Maybe you feel responsible for the situation that led to the breakdown; maybe you had your own interests and didn't notice how bad things were. You may also feel that it is your job to make your child or partner whole again.

What do you do? How are you meant to cope? What are your obligations? Is it fair for you to be selfish when your partner is' so needy? These questions go around and around in your mind and are difficult for you to answer.

The truth is that you are never responsible for another's breakdown; certainly you can never be as responsible as the person who has fallen apart. Similarly, you are never responsible for their recovery; this lies in your partner or child's hands. Your prime responsibility is to yourself. You must look after your own health and your own needs. This is more important at this time than at any other. If your health fails now, you are no good to yourself or anybody else.

The general rule in coping with this situation is "all care but no responsibility." If you look after yourself, you will not be resentful, and your caring can be much more consistent. In addition, you will set limits on their behavior. Your partner or child may resent this and see the limits you have placed as indicating that you are uncaring. This is not so and a simple statement such as, "I'm sorry you feel that way, it's not true," should suffice.

Brendan's girlfriend, Jeannie, had to be very firm with Brendan at night. "He couldn't bear me going off by myself to read. He wanted me to watch television with him. I'd stay with him a short while, and then I'd excuse myself to go and read in bed. Within 10 minutes or so, he'd feel lonely and come to bed himself. Then he'd complain that I was reading and he couldn't sleep with the light on. I'd get so frustrated with him; he seemed to resent me doing anything away from him, yet if he wanted to go off by himself he would think nothing about it. I told him that if he wanted me to stay up he would have to buy an earplug for the television set so I could read in peace and that if he didn't like me reading in bed he could sleep in the spare bedroom."

You must be vigilant in preserving your own peace of mind and cutting down on any unnecessary pressures arising from guilt. Living with stress breakdown is difficult enough without extra emotional burdens.

Kevin, the union organizer who was off for three months, did not have a breakdown, but he had certainly put his family through a difficult experience.

"I knew I was giving my family a hard time, but I was so bound up in my job that it didn't seem to matter. The major worry I had was that Karen would leave me. When I got scared about that, I would really make an effort to be home more often and to be less irritable. I can remember trying to smile at one of Karen's friends one day, but inside I was wishing she would get the hell out of the place. I could feel my smile was a grimace; I must have looked like smiling death.

"I would feel really hurt if I thought the kids were avoiding me, but, in a funny way, I didn't blame them because I would bite their heads off as soon as look at them. In fact, nothing made me angrier than the feeling that my kids were afraid of me. I would see red and really get unpleasant, although, thank God, I never actually hit them. But I was bloody close to it at times.

"One night Karen had a car accident. She didn't see a truck and the car was a write-off. She and the three children were unhurt, how, I don't know, but it made me realize how much I depended on them. I was really shaken up when I saw the wrecked car. Although she didn't say so, now I'm sure that Karen lost concentration because she had been so worried about me. It's the first crash she's ever had. It brought me up with a start at the time, but I didn't recognize the underlying problem straight away. It wasn't until I had the fight on the job site that I knew I had to get help for my nerves."

Kevin was able to get help before he had fallen apart. He had some time off work and used it to think through his attitudes to work and family. His wife, Karen, went to every appointment he had with his therapist, and they were able to work as a team in handling Kevin's behavior.

Margaret's behavior fluctuated markedly over a period of many months, and she knew that her family and her boyfriend, Andrew, were getting very little from her. When they talked about this time, years later, all agreed that it had really been a nightmare for all concerned.

"When I was stressed, I got tense and tired and didn't function too well but, after resting for a day or so I would be back on top again. But after my breakdown, I was simply incapable of doing anything, no matter what my mind told me I should be doing, my body couldn't respond. I was out of control. A wave of tiredness would come over me in an instant, and I would wilt. At those times I couldn't wash a dish, I couldn't talk, I couldn't go for a walk, I couldn't do anything. The whole burden fell on the kids and on Andrew. Although I hated myself for being so pathetic, I couldn't do anything about it."

Family and friends are afraid. They are afraid for the person who is sick and they are afraid for themselves. What on earth has happened? How do I deal with her? She's so upset. Is it because of something I did? Is it contagious or inherited? Is he insane, and will he ever get better?

These and many other questions come to mind and may never be properly answered, leaving confusion and mystery, long after the breakdown has resolved. Parents, partners and even children often carry a heavy burden of guilt and feel responsible. Some feel responsible for causing the whole thing; others feel they should have responded sooner. Some feel guilty about the strong emotions that they felt during the recovery process. Most people have times of feeling hatred towards a family member who has broken down. Some even wish they would die.

These concerns need to be answered in an honest way. Sometimes they are not put into words but are still causing worry. Sometimes questions are not asked because of fear of the answer. The truth is normally better than false hopes, and the truth is that all these fears and concerns are understandable, although not usually correct. Realistic optimism is the best way of approaching these thorny questions.

Until close friends and family understand about the breakdown, they may not be much help. They too have to learn how to cope, a process of trial and error. Some find the task too difficult - it is just beyond their experience - they feel scared and may even prefer to avoid having to deal with the problem, which can cause a great deal of hurt.

Even when people are very close to each other, the topic of stress breakdown may be avoided altogether because no one knows how to deal with it. In families where relationships have been under strain for some time, having to deal with a breakdown may be the final straw.

Brendan had never enjoyed a good relationship with his parents. He saw them as little as possible. He felt that he had never quite lived up to their expectations. He lacked for nothing, as far as money and material possessions but had felt deprived of love and attention. Brendan felt that his parents favored his younger brother Ken, who had become a doctor. Their favoritism showed even in such small ways as remembering the birthdays of Ken and his wife and forgetting his own or Jeannie's. His mother's cold gaze, when he tried to explain why he had left his job, was effectively the end of their relationship.

"I kept in touch with them for a few months afterwards, but it went from bad to worse. Little things hurt. Through those first few months when I really needed some help I got nothing, but they expected me to keep visiting them. Neither of them ever asked how I was or how I was managing except one time when I had the flu. They didn't make even the slightest attempt to understand and I think that they thought I was putting it on.

"I finally realized that there was no point in trying to please them; it was a lost cause. I wish I'd realized that years ago. I think trying to please them had something to do with my breakdown. I kept trying to help all my clients when so many of them were in such a hopeless situation. I really felt despair, as if it was my fault they were so unhappy. I don't blame them for my breakdown, but I think I had been striving to please all my life, and it started with them. I hadn't done too badly before but that last year, and a few particularly sad cases really struck me on a raw nerve."

Margaret's sister was more subtle in her condemnation because it was disguised in the form of helpful advice.

"I think Pat has always been really jealous of me, although she has much more money and a nice husband. But she has always had a chip on her shoulder, I think she was pleased that I had a breakdown. It showed that I had 'feet of clay.' She acted like she was really concerned, but instead of listening to me, she kept telling me what to do. She insinuated that she had all the answers. It wasn't so much the advice she was giving, it was the way it was done. She made me feel I wasn't doing all I could; she made me feel I was being weak.

"Pat would call me up and I'd be really upset and crying and she'd say, 'You really ought to get out more, Margaret, instead of sitting there feeling sorry for yourself' or 'Why don't you join a gym? You'd feel better if you got fit.' Every suggestion was a condemnation. Andrew kept telling me she was a bitch, but I couldn't see it at the time. All I know is that I would talk to her, and I would feel so much worse that sometimes it took me a day or so to get over one of our conversations. My dear friend, Ruth, made suggestions too, but with love, and she seemed to understand how I was."

Ruth was an invaluable friend to Margaret. She had the wonderful knack of being able to listen. Most of Ruth's suggestions really came from Margaret. Ruth would pick up on something Margaret had said and put it into a practical form, like arranging the stay on a friend's farm.

Jerry, the bank manager, was hurt by an old friend. One day at the golf club, his "friend" had said, "When the going gets tough, the tough get going. I guess you can't have been too tough, eh Jerry?" I was so close to punching his head in. I was really wild! My wife could see how upset I was, and she tried to smooth it all over. I couldn't look at him, and I started shaking, and I knew I was about a centimeter away from bursting into tears. Jan got me out of there and I can remember sitting in the car and just bawling. We've had no contact since then. I've got it all in a bit more perspective now. I know he was just trying to stir me. But it was still a really cruel thing to say."

Fortunately, such reactions are unusual. Most who have had a breakdown become skilled at sorting out who they can trust with their story. A look or a gesture is usually enough to give warning to shut up or to indicate that here is a friend. More often than not, someone who cares will be supportive, if they are given the chance. As Brendan said:

"Deep down I feel a bit of a failure, but I've got friends who like me, and they don't seem to think any less of me because of my breakdown. I've really needed them. It's a wonderful feeling when you know you have friends who support you and understand you."

Tom was very concerned about telling his parents about his breakdown as his mother had not been well for some time. Tom suspected that he was using his mother's illness to avoid any confrontation. He was very apprehensive about his parent's response. Both his parents had been on the land all their life. They were staunch conservatives, anti-union, anti left-wing teachers and they embodied the work ethic. His father had often mocked Tom in a lighthearted way about his easy life as a teacher: "You guys get good money, lots of holidays and everything taken care of, and you still go on strike at the drop of a hat." Tom could give as good as he got: "Damn farmers, you're never happy, always moaning. If it's not the weather it's the government, meanwhile you're driving around the paddocks in a damn Rolls Royce!"

In the months leading up to his breakdown, Betty had noticed these lighthearted encounters were getting an edge. Tom was getting angry with his father, and occasionally it finished up in a heated argument. It got to the point where Betty dreaded seeing them because of the unpleasantness it caused. Tom's mother was becoming visibly upset, which did not help her heart condition. Tom's father was just as stubborn as Tom, and they would finish up glaring at each other, toe to toe, just one step away from violence.

One day Tom rang them and blurted it all out. He told them a lot more than he intended although he did have the good sense to avoid telling the family that he was seeing a psychologist. Tom was extremely surprised and moved by their response: his parents were both concerned and relieved. Betty, who had been listening in on the extension, breathed a silent prayer.

"All we care about is that you're all right. We knew there was something wrong and thought it might have been to do with work. Just take your time and get better and if you need anything just sing out. We've got a bit of money put aside."

The subject was rarely raised again. Tom's father in particular avoided the topic because, as Tom said, "He's got enough on his plate, with mom's illness and all. I know he cares, and that's the important thing." Sometimes Betty would have to remind her father-in-law that Tom was still sick, but saying, "He still gets very tired" was sufficient.

Understanding

The key to helping someone who's had a breakdown is to be understanding, but that's hard to do. Those who have had a breakdown can find it difficult to communicate their experiences, especially if they sense some skepticism in their listener. Jennifer tried to describe her condition to an old friend in a letter.

"How would I explain it? My overwhelming feeling is that I've lost control of my life. I can't seem to be able to control myself physically or emotionally. I seem to have lost power over me. Does that make sense? I still get so tired. It's always with me. I don't seem to have any initiative left. My sense of humor has practically gone although, thank goodness, that's coming back a bit. It's not that I don't care anymore, I care tremendously, I'm just powerless to do anything about it, and I feel so dependent. I feel like a child again. I always have the feeling that someone is going to say, 'You've had long enough, off you go, back to work.' That's my worst nightmare. I couldn't do it."

Jennifer had great difficulty telling her family and friends face-to-face about her troubles and found that letters were the best way. She wrote long letters to herself too, trying to express her confusing contradictory, messed up feelings. Some fragments were very explicit.

"When I do feel good, I feel normal again. It's like clouds have parted and sun is shining through. When this tiredness sweeps over me, I feel very weak again. I can recognize it now, and I just walk away from whatever I'm doing.

"The hardest thing I've had to do is to forgive myself. Isn't that stupid? Why should I forgive myself? I haven't done anything wrong, yet I feel as guilty as if I'd committed murder."

While Jennifer was writing this, her friends thought she looked better than she had for years. She was going out, she was entertaining visitors and she was even able to laugh. She went to great lengths to keep her fragility hidden. Even her husband and children, who knew of her fatigue and her 'nerve storms' as she put it, could only guess at her despair and sense of loss.

Giving support

Family and friends who listen, care and try to understand are very precious. Margaret's daughter had a blazing row with Margaret one day over the state of her bedroom. Margaret burst into tears and fled to her bed. Half an hour later, a very contrite Hannah crept into the bedroom. Margaret pretended to be asleep; she didn't want another encounter. Hannah left a bunch of flowers on the pillow next to her mother's head, with a small note: "Sorry mom, love Hannah." Margaret kept the note for years and used to look at it when she was feeling her worst.

Family and friends can help in other ways by acting as a "minder," a go-between, an advocate, and even an interpreter. They can protect the person who's had a breakdown from other people and other situations. And they can indicate to others about the best sort of help to give.

Jennifer described with pride and gratitude how her very demanding youngest child had become more independent.

"She just had to really because I couldn't do things for her the way I had before. She learned to make allowances for me too. She told her friend's mother, 'Just write it down for my mom. She forgets things if you don't'."

Tom had a good laugh recounting his brief visit to the school on open day. At that stage, he was still inclined to push himself. His old boss had called him and asked that he come for a while to see their new building.

"I was walking along with Jan, who is the wife of Bob, my mate the technician. She was holding their baby and we were chatting. Suddenly I froze. Directly in front of me was one of my teacher friends. I'd heard he'd been spreading stories about me, calling me a bludger and a shirker. He came up to me and said, 'How are you doing? Enjoying your time off at the taxpayers' expense?' Before I could say anything, Jan handed me her baby, grabbed him by the arm and said, 'You come with me. You're going to get a few facts straight for a change.' I was bloody embarrassed at the time but glad, too. It's exactly what I would have liked to have done. I guess she went and told him a bit about what was really going on. To be quite honest, I didn't care much what she said, but it's nice to know you've got friends who'll stick up for you like that."

Betty often found herself explaining to others what had happened to Tom.

"I used to tell them that Tom's doctor said he had to have time off, something to do with high blood pressure. People can understand that. I usually suggested that if they came to visit they only stay for a short while and avoid the topic of Tom's work altogether. Some just wrote him a note every now and then, which was nice. He knew he was cared about then. I do remember a Get Well card from all the staff though. He just threw that in the bin. Some of them who'd signed it hadn't been helpful at all, and their hypocrisy really got to him. That's one thing about a breakdown; you find out who are real friends. Some who we thought would be really supportive came once or twice, and we've not seen them since. Others have been marvelous. One of our neighbors had a twin brother killed in a car accident, and I think that after he'd been through it all he was much more aware of what it was like to feel terrible and he's been great for Tom."

On using humor

Humor used in a loving way helps to distance the most disturbing symptoms. Jill found that when she told her boyfriend, Alan, about the horrible thoughts that were whirring away in her head, he could make light of them.

"He didn't ever ridicule me and was always really interested in them. Sometimes he'd say that he had those thoughts occasionally too and that made me feel better because I was scared I was going mad. More often than not at the end of it he'd have me laughing about them. Before, when I started telling him, I'd be petrified. Occasionally he'd just look at me and say, 'What's going on in there now?' Alan helped me to see that there was a pattern to those thoughts. They were always worse when I'd done too much or when I was under pressure. Now they make some sense to me: my tired old brain is telling me it can't handle the load."

Jennifer found that her two eldest children could help her to laugh at life a little. Before these little events seemed like major disasters.

"The most peculiar thing happens to me when I'm tired. I Start to talk mumbo-jumbo. The children call it 'talking in tongues.' They're definite words, but not English. The two of them are compiling a dictionary. I don't know whether it's good or not, but they're actually starting to decipher them. One of them says, 'What mom means is....' They are so considerate too. I didn't think they had it in them. When I start that sort of talking they just say, 'Mom, you've overdone it. Go and lie down; we can fix this.' They're really wonderful. One of them said to me the other day, 'Mom, your mind is like a bowl of spaghetti.' I laugh when I think about it because that's just what it feels like sometimes. If someone else were to say those things I'd get really upset. It's brought us a lot closer together."

"Hassle meter"

Tom's wife invented the hassle meter. She got sick of tiptoeing around the house to avoid Tom's wrath. He was so unpredictable: one day he was frightened and needy, which was okay by her; another day he would be coldly angry all the time. She couldn't talk to him, but if she ignored him he would blast her for not caring about him. She kept asking him to tell her how he was feeling, and sometimes that was successful, but on other occasions he would be angry with her for asking.

In self-defense, Betty invented the hassle meter. She went to a lot of trouble to make it like the authentic fire warning indicators that you see in the country, the ones that are used to tell people if they need to be careful of bush fires. It was a half-circle with four pie-shaped segments, ranging in color from green "NO DANGER", through to yellow "LOW RISK", orange "MODERATE DANGER" and red "HIGH DANGER". She had a pointer that could be moved to each segment. She hung it in the kitchen and when Tom got up for breakfast she would pick up his mood and move the pointer to the appropriate segment. The children quickly saw the value of this and would avoid Tom when the pointer was moving into the red sectors. Tom even started using it himself.

It seemed to make Tom's turbulent emotions more impersonal and enable everyone in the family, including Tom, to get some distance from his behavior.

On being alone

Besides giving support and understanding, there area number of specific ways in which family and friends can help someone who has had a breakdown.

People need long periods of solitude and quiet when they have had a breakdown, particularly during the early stages, but they also like to know that someone is around.

Betty found it very difficult to know how to behave when Tom went quiet or when he went off by himself for hours at a time. She didn't know whether to leave him alone or to try and boost him up. She was worried this might have been his way of asking for help, and she felt confused and worried.

"It was hard to work out at first. I felt so hurt when Tom would just go off by himself for hours and thought it must have been something I'd said or done. He finally explained to me that he just couldn't bear noise, people or activity. Those things made him uptight; he could feel it all coming in on him. I began to understand a bit better. I can see it for myself now and so can the kids, in their own way. He starts to get edgy and then he'll start saying things to other people that he doesn't mean. It's like firing off little explosions that release his tension. It makes our nerves worse though, of course. I realize now that it's better all round if he gets away when he feels like that. I still feel left out of things at times, but it helps him to get better, and that's the main thing."

Margaret needed solitude too, but was sometimes also afraid of it. "Although I was happiest when I was by myself, I also found I couldn't have too much of it. If it went on for too long I would start thinking about what had happened to me and I'd get worse. I remember that on some days I'd go out just wandering the streets to distract myself. For quite a while I was so afraid of being on my own for too long that I made myself worse with all that 'escaping' activity. I felt I was getting better when I could relax in my own company."

Restlessness

Although irritability is a daily occurrence for someone who is stressed or has had a breakdown, uncontrolled anger occurs much less often. Usually it's been building up for a while and although obvious to others, it is less obvious to the person who is about to explode.

Tom and Betty were able to discuss together how they should both handle his moods.

"When it got too bad, I'd do everything I could to keep the kids out of his way. I knew I could cope with it, but I worried about how it would affect them. I had to explain to them that he was like that when he was tired and that it didn't mean that he didn't love them anymore."

George, who became interested in pigeon racing, had at times been violent at home. His wife Nancy asked him to speak to his psychiatrist about it, but she saw little change.

"I finally got to the point where I moved out with the kids because I just couldn't tolerate it any longer. I hated to leave and worried about him terribly, but there was no alternative. I wasn't going to live with that threat of violence all the time. At the end of two weeks we met together, at George's instigation, and really worked on the problem. The shock of us leaving made him see that it couldn't go on because he was pretty hopeless without us around. I was determined not to go back until I thought he had really settled down. My Dad was an alcoholic and my mother used to put up with all sorts of stuff - punching, kicking and swearing - and I'd decided that I was never going to be anyone's punching bag."

Dealing with depression

Depression may be so severe that someone who has had a breakdown may feel that their family would be better off without them and they may even contemplate suicide. Although suicide is rare, the feelings themselves can be very strong and should be discussed with a therapist or doctor.

Betty's discussion with Tom, when he was at his lowest, helped him to see that going away or taking his own life wasn't an answer. She told him that they all still needed him and that no matter how helpless and useless he felt, the boys and her still loved him. Tom had become so self-absorbed that he wasn't even thinking about that.

Even in his worst moments George knew suicide wasn't for him. "I had a friend who committed suicide, and I was angry, resentful and yet envious of him. He found his way out, but I saw the effects on his family and friends. I don't think his wife or son will ever get over it. That was what made me mad. Having seen the effect on his family, I just couldn't do it myself. Now I'm glad I didn't, but at the time the thought often came to me about what a release it would have been for me."

Dealing with childlike behavior

One of the great difficulties for families when one member has broken down is that the usual roles and patterns in the family have been shattered. Dad was the breadwinner and now he's that sad, sometimes unpleasant figure in the front room. Someone who's had a breakdown is often unable to cope with the smallest demands of everyday living, and the family are called upon to take over and manage. They must manage everything including such matters as cooking, cleaning, finances, shopping and communication with others. The fact that coping can vary so much from day to day or even from hour to hour means that the family members have to keep their eye on the one who's fallen apart.

Stan's wife, Doris, found it especially useful to talk over her dilemma with the other two policemen's wives.

"Stan had always managed the finances before. He mended things around the house, did all the gardening, and used to be the main one to make major decisions, like holidays, big purchases, and so on. At first I felt lost, and I was horrified when the bills mounted up and nothing was done about them. I didn't have a clue where to start. Marie and Joan gave me a few ideas because they'd had to do the same thing. They were so good to talk to because they just accepted everything I said and made me realize that the problems I had were quite normal. It all had an unreal quality before I talked to them.

"Actually it was a relief to Stan when I did take over, but he was sort of resentful and ashamed as well because the better I managed, the more 'out of it' he felt. I surprised myself really with the things I was able to do, and it made me a more confident person, but I always try to consider him too. I made a conscious decision only to do the things that absolutely had to be done so that he could come back in and make some contribution when he could.

"For instance, our taxes were a shambles. The returns hadn't been done for three years, so I got an accountant to do that. I probably could have managed it, but I didn't want Stan to think we had taken over everything he used to do. Over the years he's been gradually able to do more but he still doesn't want to have to pay the bills!"

Providing support

Families and close friends are highly stressed and need to be particularly aware of taking care of themselves. Some, like Betty, find taking outside work a relief; others make sure they get regular breaks away from tension in the family by continuing their own separate interests and hobbies. The family members of someone who has had a breakdown appreciate the support they get from their own close friends more than they are able to describe.

"You find that your circle of friends shrinks. Those who stick by you are just wonderful. I felt like I was always going around to my friend's place and crying on her shoulder. I tried not to do it too much because I didn't want to wear out my welcome, but it was just fantastic to know there was somewhere to turn when I was at the end of my tether."

Coping with rejection

The work mates of someone who's had a breakdown behave in a number of different ways. Some, like Tom's 'friend' who ignored him in the street, seem to reinforce a sense of failure and rejection; others can be more actively hurtful and have the effect of deeply embittering the relationship, almost guaranteeing that going back to that job will be impossible.

Jennifer was particularly upset and hurt. "I went back to the school one Saturday afternoon with my husband to collect my things. There were just two cardboard boxes stacked for me in the corner of the room. Most of my books, aids and equipment had gone. They'd been stolen by the other teachers. It was like I'd died and they were dividing up all my worldly goods. I don't even think they were consciously aware that they were stealing my stuff. They had somehow decided that I was gone, I wasn't coming back and I wouldn't need it. I shouldn't have been surprised though. From the time I left work the only contact I had with them were letters about my sick leave and questions about how much longer I'd be off work.

"They messed up my sick leave too, and three times my pay didn't arrive. The first time it happened, I was writing checks, and there was no money in my account. The first I heard of it was when a check bounced and the bank called to tell me to put some more money in the account. What really made me mad was their attitude. They seemed to think it was all right for me to go without pay. 'It'll come sometime so what are you worried about?' was their attitude. I sometimes wondered if they thought I was lucky to get any money at all."

Jennifer's experiences guaranteed that she would never return to that school, and she was very uneasy about going back to teaching. Jill could not get through to her colleagues at the hospital that she was off sick and that she was off for a very good reason.

"The director of nursing rang me up to see how I was. She told me that the golden staph I had was a different strain from the one that caused the deaths, so it wasn't my fault at all. Then she went on for half an hour about staffing problems in the intensive care ward. In one way I felt better because it was nice to feel vindicated like that, but it brought it all back again, and I couldn't get her conversation out of my head for days afterwards. The charge sister who took over staff training rang up too. She wasn't even polite enough to ask how I was getting on, she just wanted to know how she could get in touch with one of the lecturers I used. Another time she asked me to come in and find some equipment for them. They were so matter of fact; they didn't really give a damn how I was feeling. After that my mother and father answered the phone, but I think mom might have told them that their calls weren't welcome."

A friend of Brendan's had also had a breakdown because of office problems. She was able to go back eventually because of the help she got from her friends at work.

"The manager was wonderful. He would drop by each week with my pay. If there were any problems he'd actually ring the pay office for me. He would ask how I was feeling, but he didn't stay too long. He'd let me know that they missed me, but he didn't make a song and dance about it. He'd tell me a little bit about work, but he'd steer clear of any sensitive issues. There was no pressure on me to come back, quite the reverse. He said that they didn't want me to come back until I felt I was ready. Later on, he told me that he'd had six months off work himself a few years ago, and that he had some idea of what I'd been going through.

"Although I didn't go back to work until February, he invited me to come into the office for their Christmas party. He said they'd look after me, and they did."

15

Getting Your Life Back Together

The storm has been weathered, you're not yet safely into harbor, but you can begin to see land, and you feel a restlessness within, an urge to get moving, to makeup for lost time. Your days are more tranquil now, and it's possible to look ahead with some confidence, the emotional furies are less frequent, and less intense. So, what happens now? What are you going to do with your new found stability?

Both Margaret and Tom looked for a new sense of direction. They recognized that their breakdown had provided them with new opportunities. Margaret was beginning to feel bored. This was a new feeling for her. Before, she was pleased to have a good day and was content to potter around her garden. On her bad days, it was a case of survival, of just getting through. About 18 months after her breakdown she began to feel restless.

Margaret had been very worried about driving. She was frightened of freezing behind the wheel and causing an accident, or simply getting lost. She hadn't driven for 12 months, and she didn't miss it at first, but she needed her transport to get into town; the farm was too far away to walk or ride her bicycle. Andrew and Ruth both helped and encouraged her and she began driving again in the lane leading into the property. After that she drove short distances on the road, gradually building up her confidence. She took it slow and easy, and gradually her old skills returned.

"I knew if I could drive again, I could do anything, so I knew I could do the pottery course. I spoke to my therapist about it a few times. She helped me to see that one of my fears was that I wouldn't be very good. Once I could see that, it seemed to be silly, and I could laugh at it. We worked out a plan of action to defuse my fears. I walked up to the community center a few days before the course started, I had a look at the pottery area and chatted to the teacher about books and materials, and that helped me to calm down.

"I was still very nervous on the first day, but I needn't have worried, it all worked out well. The teacher was good fun, and the other students were just as hopeless as me, which was a relief. At the end of the four weeks I felt really pleased with myself. I'd even been able to get there on time, which was pretty remarkable for me at the best of times. I couldn't wait to start something else, and over the next few months, I enrolled in a few other courses. I did calligraphy to improve my writing, and then a literature course, to get my brain working again. At one stage I got a bit carried away and started a word-processing course as well, but that was too hard, and I stopped. I could see that I wasn't quite ready, and I was pushing myself too hard. I have to be very careful about that."

A few months later, some of Margaret's old friends from her volleyball days asked her to play golf. She had never played before and was reluctant to go. Andrew encouraged her, rang Sue, an old friend of Margaret's, and suggested that they play golf together. Sue took Margaret under her wing, and Margaret was surprised how much she enjoyed the day.

"My week is getting a bit of shape now. I spend one day playing golf, one day visiting my mother, and one day doing a course at the learning center. I've gradually built it up, just making each commitment a bit harder. I'm trying to gauge whether I am ready or not. None of them are things I have to do, and I miss a day if I'm feeling bad, but I don't feel guilty!"

A few months later, another piece of the puzzle fell into place for Margaret. "I've always been interested in gardening and after the first year, when everything else was terrible, I'd go out and pull out a few weeds, or plant some seedlings. Sometimes I'd just sit in the garden, and just absorb it all."

As she improved, she began spending more time in the garden, weeding, digging, and planting. She did a course on plant propagation, and set up a little greenhouse.

"I made a bit of money selling some of my plants at the local market. A friend sold them for me, because I was still too scared to do it myself. A friend asked me if I could help with her garden. She offered to pay me, but I preferred to do it for nothing, because then I could do it on my terms."

Her friend had a large, old garden that had once been a showpiece in the district. She was keen for Margaret's labor and for her advice. Margaret agreed to help as much as she could, but she only worked when she wanted to, and she made sure there were no deadlines. Her friend had definite ideas and plans and wanted Margaret to make suggestions: some were followed and some ignored.

"I helped with digging, preparing paths, and planting. I look around that garden now and see what we've achieved. It reminds me of

how far I've come, just a step at a time. The garden changes month by
month, something lasting, and yet full of interest. I work at my own
pace, and I can have as little or as much contact with other people as I
like. It's interesting how well you can get to know people through their
gardens. There's a story behind so many trees and plants. The people at
the plant nurseries have been helpful too. They're happy for me to just
wander around. I don't know if I can make a living out of it, but I think
I want to do garden work."

Coping with setbacks

When he first broke down, Tom's search for help was frantic
and, for awhile at least, unsuccessful. It may have even made him worse.
When he found a therapist who seemed to know what was wrong with
him, he felt a great sense of relief, certainly Betty did. This therapist
could tell him what had gone wrong, in language he could understand,
and he made some simple suggestions to help Tom get better. The
therapist's explanation went over Tom's head a bit at first because he
couldn't take it all in, but he did hear that he had to rest. Tom was
frightened of giving up the struggle to survive. He thought the best way
to beat it was to fight.

"I felt that if I stopped I would lose everything and, in a way, I
did for a while. That was probably the worst time of all for me, but my
therapist kept me going with reassurance and the odd suggestion. I
think those pills he put me on helped too. They took the edge off it
for a while."

For a long time Tom was unable to look ahead at all. His main
concern was getting through the next few minutes, at first. Then getting
through the next hour; then a day. Finally Tom could look ahead further,
to the next few weeks and months. He began to see patterns emerging in
his behavior, and he felt a little more stable each day.

"I think you really just have to learn by your mistakes, and as
long as they're not too big, you're safe, even though it doesn't feel like
it at the time. When I first had those setbacks, they were terrible because
you didn't feel that you were getting anywhere. All those months, and
one little thing going wrong, and you were back where you started;
that's what it felt like. That was when I really needed my therapist. He
pointed out to me that each time I had one of those, I'd take less time to
get over it, that overall I was improving. He wasn't concerned by them
himself, and his calmness made me feel a bit easier about them too.

"Some of the setbacks I had really stand out in my mind. one
day, when Betty was out, I got a phone call from Jason's school to say

that he was sick, could I come and pick him up? I had to go myself, I didn't know when Betty was coming back, but I was petrified. It was the first time I'd been in a school for a long time. I almost ran inside to get him, and I got out again as fast as I could. What really upset me was how pathetic I felt. It was a different school, I didn't know any of the staff, but still I couldn't handle it. Two years later, though, I was able to go to an open day. I didn't stay long, but I did feel reasonably relaxed for a while, until I saw a teacher I used to know, who was now teaching at my son's school. I just bolted. I'll tell you about that another time."

Tom often tripped himself up by trying to do too much, too soon. After a year, he got restless and bored. He was fed up with being so useless, so he decided to repaint the house.

"The preparations were okay. I bought all the paint and moved the furniture out of the spare bedroom so I could start in there. Betty was really pleased that at last I was doing something constructive. Well, I started, but then I couldn't stop. For two days I painted almost non-stop; I became obsessed. Betty could see what was happening, and she was getting more and more worried; she even had to drag me out for meals. I yelled at the kids, I couldn't sleep and I was getting exhausted: all the signals I knew so well, but I couldn't see them. By the end of the second day, all my old symptoms were back, but I had to finish it. I worked until nine o'clock that night. The room was finished, and so was I. Next day, I stayed in bed, I didn't recover for about a week."

What made it worse for Tom was that, until then, he'd been feeling very well, but he hadn't realized that he only had a small margin of safety.

Most people find that they may feel well, but their stamina remains low. It's as if, after a breakdown, you have an energy balance sheet. Your energy level is just in the "black," and even a small expenditure of energy throws you into the "red." Pressure, especially time pressure, depletes your energy very quickly, and you find yourself back in the red again, back in the region of non-coping.

"I've learned that if I do things at my own pace, and don't put time limits on myself, I'm much better. If someone asks me to do something for them by a certain time, I just can't do it, but if I do it when I feel more energy, then it gets done."

Regaining your independence

Margaret had been concerned, for a long time, about her dependency on her family, friends, and therapist, Jane. She had little choice for a long time, but never ceased to find it vaguely uncomfortable and a little demeaning. She contrasted this with the pre-breakdown Margaret, who was so strong and independent. She discussed this with Jane.

"For a long time I thought that I'd have to see you once a week for the rest of my life. I needed you there to help me find my way again. For all those months you were my anchor, always calm, encouraging, and optimistic. You seemed to know what lay ahead. At first, I couldn't take in what you were saying, and I guess you had to say the same thing over and over again, sometimes in different ways, before I could understand what you were getting at. I relied on you; you seemed to know what you were doing with me, even when I had no idea what was going on. I don't think you realized how much I leaned on you."

Margaret's feelings about Jane fluctuated markedly during the time they were together. Sometimes she felt very angry and thought she was being manipulated by Jane. At one stage, she had the idea that Jane possessed the "secret" of "getting well" but was refusing to share it. As time passed, she could see Jane more clearly as a person who was trying to help her. She found more and more strength within herself, and her relationship with Jane became less important, although she hung on to the contact in case she fell apart again.

"Do you realize it's been nearly three months since I saw you? I haven't needed to see you. Isn't that wonderful? I can feel my old self coming back more and more, I've got energy, and I feel peaceful, not all the time, but enough. I'm not getting so upset and I'm starting to really like people; I thought I'd lost that forever. I'm almost leading a normal life, and I'm thinking about working again."

Margaret's life was much richer. She was mixing with old friends again, and she was making new ones. She had a great deal more energy, but never had the same stamina as she'd had before. She was still vulnerable, but she wasn't unstable like she had been. It was no wonder she was feeling better. Although the past two years had been so unpleasant and weren't high points of her life, nevertheless, she was determined to remember the lessons she had learned so painfully.

"I think I'd be risking another breakdown if I ever forgot what I've learned. I'm not over it completely. When my concentration goes, it's always a sure sign that I've been doing too much. I still can't concentrate for long but, even so, it's getting better. I can read again, and I can write, but I don't think I could work as a journalist again. I don't really mind at the moment. I can't be with a large group of people for long, especially not with noisy, overbearing people. Chatterboxes drive me mad and fighting upsets me. I have to walk away if people are fighting; even raised voices make me feel shaky.

"I feel in control of my life again, but I have to keep working at it. I take nothing for granted any more. I know, in a thousand ways, that my body has been damaged. It's all very subtle, but I know it's there. I keep asking my body how it's going. If I take notice of my body, I stay in harmony. Now, all those stress management techniques, like meditation, talking positive thoughts to yourself, and all the rest of it, really help me to stay on top of it, but I can't assume that I'll always be able to do that. I can't push myself like I used to. I still want to, but there are very real limits to what I can do."

Margaret was passing into the final stage of recovery. This is a time of restitution, of a return to normal functioning. If you have come to this point, you will have begun to learn a great deal about yourself, and about your strengths and weaknesses. You will have become more adept at 'reading' your body messages, and acting on them. Your symptoms will have become very familiar and, if not actually old friends, they have certainly become old acquaintances, whose messages cannot safely be ignored. You have become accustomed to your fluctuating moods. Your bad days are allowed to pass; your good days are appreciated, for you know that they may not continue. You can feel your old skills returning.

Margaret kept her diary, through good days and bad. At times she wondered why she bothered, but it proved to be invaluable in giving her a sense of improvement. As each month passed, she could see her progress.

"I look back over my old diaries, and I can see how much I've improved, with friends, for instance. When I read through some of the old entries in my diary, I can remember how it was. The first time I gave a dinner party was 18 months after I cracked up. My diary tells the story:

> September 3: Disaster! Hannah and her boyfriend, Phil, for dinner. Andrew too. Food overcooked. Soup cold. I was really tense. The final straw was when I dropped the fruit salad on the floor. I got really upset and I went to bed.

> May 23: Success. Ruth over for lunch! Made a light lunch with salad and cheese. It went well and I felt relaxed.

> September 4: Andrew's mom and dad over for dinner. Cooked roast beef, it was great. Andrew did most of the work. I felt okay, nervous at first but then I relaxed.

> December 8: Friends for Christmas drinks. I made snacks. I really enjoyed it. I can't believe how much better I feel.

"I have people over for dinner every few months now. I still have to write everything down. It doesn't come automatically like it used to, and I don't go in for anything elaborate. I'm more relaxed than I ever used to be about having people come to visit. I finally realized that it didn't matter if everything wasn't perfect. My guests didn't think any the less of me - it's actually more fun than it used to be.

"Christmas is a good example of how much I've improved. I don't remember much of the first one without Melinda. I think I spent most of the day in bed crying. I had started my diary, but must have felt terrible, because there is no entry for that day. I felt much better by the next Christmas, and I wanted it to be extra-special, to make up for the year before.

> December 26: Yesterday was a mess. I wanted it to be really special. I rushed around, last week, buying presents for all my relatives, so I got tired. Yesterday, I was exhausted, and shaky all day. Went to mom's. My sister was there with her family. Friends of mom's dropped in. I heard my sister telling mom's friend that I was seeing a psychiatrist, but that she wasn't doing much - because I was still so neurotic! That was the last straw. I just died inside. We should have gone to Andrew's family later, but I just couldn't go, and he went on his own.

> December 26: [next year] This year was much better. I bought all the presents months ago, and we spent most of the day at home, quietly. I visited my family for a little while in the morning, before my sister arrived, and, then, late afternoon, we went to Andrew's family for an hour or so. I felt really proud of myself, and I enjoyed it.

"I look back in my diary, which is several volumes now, and it's pleasing to see how much I've improved. Not many people would understand how all these little things add up. They're just things that other people take for granted. Talking to people, going out, household chores, driving. I remember when I couldn't even drive. I had so many near misses over those first two years, and I got lost so many times, it was as if I couldn't manage anything at all. It's starting to feel like a new beginning, and I'm back in control of myself again."

Recovery from a breakdown is always accompanied by setbacks. Margaret and Torn had learnt from these setbacks very early and were able to live within their limitations, but this was difficult and frustrating. Often they pushed too hard and then always paid a price. Others take longer to learn this lesson and seem to lurch from one disaster to another, improving a little, then allowing guilt, pride or simple denial to override any wisdom they have gained.

Sometimes they had to "crash" several times, doing them-selves a little more damage each time, before they were finally able to accept their limitations.

Some remain locked in by fear, living a shadow of a life, their recovery halted, as they withdraw more and more from the world. Their faltering attempts to reach out, to take risks, to try something new have failed. Rather than trying another way, or trying the same way again, their fears have become overwhelming, and they give up, and the more isolated they become, the harder it is to take anymore risks. They have not realized that recovery is a painful process. The pain is unavoidable, and has to be overcome if recovery is to occur.

Those who have supportive families and friends and widespread interests before their breakdown are generally better equipped to find a new direction for themselves when they recover. Those who have had led extremely limited and narrow lives, and have focused all their energies on work, find that task much more difficult.

Returning to work

During your recovery, you will have often thought about returning to work. If you can go back to work and stay there, then you know that you have really improved.

However, many go back to work too early, trying to prove to themselves that they can cope. When they fall apart, as they often do, they leave work feeling even more of a failure. This had been the experience of George, the fireman.

Despite warnings from Nancy and friends, George returned to his job just three months after breaking down. It was a bad time and sent George's confidence plummeting even further.

"That time back at work made me realize how bad I really was. It gives me the horrors just talking about it. I didn't know whether I was coming or going and I hardly slept at all."

If you are to avoid making the same mistake as George, you must ask yourself a number of questions before you return to work. Questions like: when will I be ready, what should I do, where should I work and with whom, and for how long each day should I work? The primary question is: how do you decide when you are ready to return to work?

You must be able to cope with your life when you are not working.

This means coping with daily chores, relationships, driving, shopping and socializing. You can test yourself in the months before you return to work by taking on more tasks and responsibilities.

The courses that Margaret and Brendan undertook showed them that they could cope with time pressures, mixing with new people, and concentrating for extended periods of time.

Some people on the road to recovery take on voluntary work, where they feel less pressure to perform and can leave when they are not coping. Others work for themselves part-time. Some people visit their work place to see how it now makes them feel. This was something that Tom was never able to do comfortably and it helped him decide that he could never return to teaching.

Many people find that anything that reminds them of their old job makes them feel bad. This feeling can last for years. These people should consider working elsewhere.

Like Tom, many people can never return to their old jobs: it has become too difficult. They must look to retrain or take on a job requiring less skill, responsibility and pressure.

An understanding employer can make all the difference in helping you return to work. If you are unlucky to have a boss who is unpleasant or even destructive, it is best to leave the job as soon as possible before any damage is done to you.

The attitude of your work mates is also a critical factor in returning to work. If you are going back to your old job, you may feel some initial embarrassment and even guilt because some of your colleagues may have seen you at your most vulnerable time. Their support will give you a great boost. If you are starting a new job, it is best not to be too candid about why you have changed jobs or taken time off work. Neutral explanations like "tired" or "needed a break" work best. Avoid being seen as "stressed" or "sick"; be circumspect about what you say, even when you have been there for some time.

You should also retain this attitude when going for job interviews. It is handy to do some interview practice with your therapist, partner or a close friend to prepare response to questions you are sure to be asked.

When you eventually start working, you will probably be dismayed by how exhausted you feel in the first days and weeks on the job. if you have made the right decision, this fatigue will pass as you become accustomed to all the strain involved in getting up early, commuting, doing the job and coping with work mates as well as time pressures.

Your recovery period will have taught you that you're still

vulnerable to strain and tension, so you must be aware of how you are coping with the job. You should try and avoid taking your work home and you will have to be assertive in informing your boss when you feel overloaded. Be clear about what needs to be done to relieve you of pressure. if your boss is unresponsive, then you should leave the job as soon as possible.

Keep in mind that you have fought hard to regain your health and it is too precious to squander.

16

How To Avoid Falling Apart

All agree that breakdowns are unpleasant, even horrible experiences and are worth avoiding, at almost any cost. Breakdowns impose a terrible physical and financial burden on individuals, their families and their communities.

Some of the ways of avoiding a breakdown will be self-evident. Even in circumstances that are suddenly overwhelming, it seems that post-traumatic counseling and community support can reduce the extent of ill-health among survivors. There is much that people can do to reduce stress in their lives and to increase their ability to cope with unavoidable stress.

When a breakdown seemingly can't be avoided

Some events are so terrible, unexpected and damaging that a form of breakdown is unavoidable. Such things as war, violent crime, serious accidents and disasters leave a trail of casualties even among those apparently unhurt. These "casualties" continue to have problems for years to come and may have to modify their lives considerably in order to lead a semblance of a normal life.

One thinks of the survivors of concentration camps during the Second World War, of violent crime victims (and families), of the victims of floods, bush fires or major accidents.

In recent years, counselors have been investigating ways of lessening the emotional impact of such trauma. As we have seen, there are wide differences in people's responses to a disaster. It also seems that, in helping people to come to terms with the effect of the disaster on their lives, what works for most people may be damaging for others.

What becomes obvious is that it is important to listen to what the person actually says and feels about their circumstances. Most people are helped, for example, by talking through what happened to them fairly soon after the event; for others, it awakens a nightmare they want to forget. Although some people will feel that they have overcome a fear by visiting the place where the trauma occurred, for example, there are others for whom the fear is so great that such a visit may precipitate a first or second breakdown and a prolonged recovery time.

200

Again, the timing of such interventions is important. One of the healing aspects of the Vietnam war veterans' marches, 20 years after the end of the war, was the ability of some to talk about events with comrades who understood.

If you are suffering as a result of trauma, your fears, sadness and anger need to be acknowledged and accepted. Being told that you are better off than other people doesn't help. Your feelings about what happened to you is what is important. Take the opportunity to talk about what happened when you can do so without too much distress and look for someone who tries to listen and put themselves in your position. You may have to give your friends and family the lead; they are likely to avoid the topic so that you and they don't get upset. This is a time to call on them for support. Most find that, if anything, others want to do too much.

Paul, a swimming coach in his mid-thirties, was slightly injured in a car accident in which his wife, Wendy, was killed; crushed by a truck that overturned on the taxi in which they were traveling. He was devastated and guilt-ridden at first. He was in hospital for a day or so. He needed time to grieve, to think, but he was overwhelmed by others wanting to help.

"There were times when I just wanted to be alone, to cry, to rage and just be myself. My parents came to stay for a while, but I just wanted to be with the kids. They didn't mean to butt in, but just by them being there, I felt I had to put up a front for them, and it was exhausting. They wanted to help, so I got them to cook for us and do the shopping and housekeeping. I also had to reassure them that I wasn't going to kill myself. I knew that was one of the things they were worried about. Some of my friends avoided me altogether and there were others who wouldn't talk about Wendy. I had to be the one to bring her up in conversation, and they seemed to relax then."

You might like to seek the help of a professional counselor for various reasons. It may be that your feelings are too personal or too frightening to discuss with those closest to you. Some are concerned that they are putting too great a burden on their friends. Paul saw a psychologist a couple of times. "It was good to be able to really say how bad I felt and to let it all out. I was quite frightened about my reactions at times, but he explained to me that what I was experiencing was a perfectly normal response to an abnormal event. Being told it was normal was the best part about it really. I just let it happen then and wasn't so scared by my own strong emotions."

Getting back into some routine and doing something purposeful is often a priority after a disaster. Margaret's friend Ruth was grateful to Margaret for getting her going after the bush fires and the death of her husband. "All that cooking we did, I wasn't able to keep going like Margaret did for hour after hour, but the couple of hours I put in each day helped me feel better about myself. Margaret saw strengths in me that I didn't think I had at the time. I suppose that's what I see in her too."

Some breakdowns can occur quite unexpectedly, and it is difficult to know what could have been done to prevent a breakdown. A sudden event may catch a person unaware and may get under their skin.

However, most breakdowns are avoidable. Our impression is that only two groups are totally invulnerable to breakdown: the totally corrupt and the totally spiritual. Most of us fall somewhere in the middle.

The totally corrupt are entirely self-centered and have little interest in relationships except for some form of monetary gain. They are cynical, manipulative and untrustworthy, motivated solely by self-interest. Preventable breakdowns primarily occur in those who are conscientious, hard working, trapped between the demands of self-preservation and the needs of their group. They are vulnerable to frustration and loss of hope. The saints, on the other hand, are profoundly protected by their intense spiritual belief and by their eternal sense of hope.

What can you do to avoid a breakdown?

Your resistance to breakdown is influenced by your history, the quality of your relationships and your experiences of the world. Above all it is determined by the success with which you have coped with the inevitable pressures arising from these varied influences.

You will be less vulnerable to breakdown if you can maintain your health and sense of well-being, learn new ways of coping with pressure by sensible risk-taking and, above all, by anticipating and avoiding fights that you can't win.

The development of successful coping styles involves a complex interaction between your inherent qualities and your experiences of life. Many of these experiences are beyond your control, are in the past and cannot be altered, such matters as your early life, your constitution, your health and "the slings and arrows of outrageous fortune."

Some of us are left with areas of vulnerability: old health problems which can continue to influence our life; damaging early experiences which may benefit from psychological help to free up some of the energy used in coping with past hurts; lack of emotional support from broken families and because of migrations.

All of these events use up emotional and physical energy which we may need in times of severe stress. They may also cut us off from sources of support. After some months of therapy, Brendan began to see that his mother's behavior towards him had made him feel he had to please others but also left him feeling suspicious and wary of being too open. He had lost many friends in the past because he had overreacted and had misunderstood comments or actions by friends. His extreme sensitivity had made him a fine social worker but a lonely person.

What you can do to avoid a breakdown

Our own areas of particular vulnerability (and we all have some vulnerable areas) help to guide us to those problems that are especially difficult for us. The aim of stress management is to make you aware of your own warning signs, to improve your coping capacity and to assess your areas of stress. Stress management techniques are useful before you are stressed or in the early stages of stress. If you are severely stressed, such courses are of little value. Beyond that point much more vigorous effort is required to avoid breakdowns.

You can build up your stamina by improving your health through a number of means. These include such things as having a more balanced diet, gaining adequate rest and exercise, reducing drug consumption, including alcohol and tobacco. It may also include obtaining a full medical check up and dealing with any latent problems that arise from this.

Reducing your vulnerability also comes from learning new ways of managing pressure. This is very important and difficult to maintain. We tend to keep to familiar paths and resist new ways. Taking sensible risks can lead to initial disruption, alterations in family and work relationships, potential changes in jobs and may at first increase levels of stress.

The other goal of stress management is to learn ways of examining and reducing stresses in your life. At first this involves exploration of all the different aspects of your life - your health, work, home, love relationships, family, interests, spiritual life - and making an assessment of your strengths and weaknesses in all of these areas. Once these stresses have been determined, you can make more realistic decisions about altering them.

Talking about stress management in isolation from all the realities of life is easy, but its practice is a different matter.

Margaret had managed the many stresses in her life, and these experiences had certainly given her strength. One of the problems was that because of this, she overestimated her ability to cope.

"I used to pride myself on my innate strength - I thought I was invincible. I seemed to be able to handle anything, my divorce, the bush fire, surviving with a young family. I delighted in my body, it seemed so strong and resilient. I'm much more sensitive to all those things now, and I think I'm not as arrogant and certainly much more vulnerable. I know I have a breaking point. I was lucky with so many of the things that happened to me. I had a good family and although bad things happened when I was a child, they never overwhelmed me, and I never had too many piling onto me at once."

During her adolescence, Margaret felt that she handled both disappointments and success in school work, sport and in her relationships. All that gave her confidence to cope with new pressures and new experiences. She looked on new experiences as providing fresh opportunities - she expected to succeed. She didn't just do this alone.

"I'd always known I had the support of my family, and I was lucky enough to have great friends. We all looked after each other. I took all that support for granted. I always expected to have someone for me. Even when my marriage broke up, my parents came to stay and to help - although it was a pain sometimes, there was also backing for me - someone to lean on when I needed help."

Margaret was also fortunate in that she had always been really healthy. She'd always had lots of energy, was able to eat anything and not put on weight, and she could go without sleep for long periods. She used to take long walks in the paddocks near home and would go for a run if she was feeling tense or irritable to burn off nervous energy. She'd come back physically tired but felt terrific and then slept well.

"As I got older, I knew I was slowing down, just a little, and I couldn't take quite so much for granted. I had to be more careful about my health. I cut out cigarettes and cut down on my drinking. As well, I was a little more careful with my diet. I had a more vegetarian diet, and I used to take some vitamin supplements, but I was pretty slack with all of that. I mean, what did it really matter? I still felt pretty good. I was just taking out a bit of insurance. Even so, I think I could have done more. I think if I'd been fitter and more rested I may have coped better with those last few weeks before I really crumbled.

"I couldn't do anything about my constitution, except change my parents, and I couldn't do a lot to change what happened to me, but I could have made sure I had more emotional support."

Margaret had been so busy over the last few years that she let a number of her friends slip away. The friends who remained were those who relied on her for support, but they disappeared when she really needed help.

"I should have been more careful about keeping my old friends. Some of the people I'd called friends were really amazing. Right in the midst of the whole disaster, one of them called me up in tears and got very angry when I told her I couldn't come around and have a talk with her. She was really offended. When she realized I was breaking down she had the gall to tell me that she had to be honest and she just couldn't cope with me if I didn't try to help myself."

Margaret made the mistake of taking her energy level for granted. Even when she was getting all sorts of warnings from her body she kept going.

"The other thing I did, which was really stupid was to keep pushing myself. I kept exhausting myself. A lot of it was wasted energy, but old habits die hard, and I was always pushing myself and assuming I'd cope, that I'd survive.'

Tom had allowed his work to take over his life and when things went wrong there, he was totally devastated. As he was less able to cope, he became even more single minded and tried still harder, becoming more exhausted.

"My basic mistake was caring too much about the department at the school; it was my baby. I let that become an obsession. It took over from everything else in my life, really to the exclusion of everyone.

"I've been over what happened to me again and again. I've tried to see where I went wrong. The seeds were sown years before I went downhill. My life had been unbalanced for a long time. I took my family life pretty much for granted, and I had a fixed view of what should be done at work. I had no patience with compromise, and I thought I could get my way by doing the right thing and pushing harder and battering through. I was totally unresponsive to the messages my body kept giving me. Sure, I did a stress management course, but it was the wrong thing at the wrong time. I think it would have been good for me before I started getting stressed. By the time I did the course I was far too far down the track to get any benefit.

"I've got an old friend who's a keen fisherman. He'll fish anywhere, anytime, doesn't matter whether it's a river or the ocean. He even likes sitting on the pier. He seems to switch into fishing mode and forget about the rest of his life. I put all my eggs in one basket and I couldn't switch off like him.

"The one thing, above all others, that I've learned from my breakdown is acceptance. I can't say I'm very good at it yet, but I feel it becoming easier all the time. I remember a prayer used at Alcoholics Anonymous. I think it goes: 'God, grant me the serenity to accept the things I cannot change, courage to change the things I can, and the wisdom to know the difference.' I reckon that just about sums it up. It makes me tired just thinking about all the things I used to do."

Avoiding a breakdown also means making a careful assessment of the external pressures you are experiencing and then doing something about them before it is too late - before your body and mind become too tired to respond or fight back. It is not unusual for people like those we have talked about to see with startling clarity, some time after the event, what they could have done to avoid their breakdown.

Jennifer: "Instead of asking for help I should have demanded it, but at the time when I needed the strength to do that, I had none. I thought at the time there was nothing I could do, but in reality there was a lot. I could have gone on sick leave, I could have walked out and demanded an inquiry or even resigned. Any of those would have been better than what happened."

George: "The hardest thing for me to do was to say that I was scared and that I needed a break. That was so stupid because the fire department is terrific with guys who've been in an accident or something like that. If you need help they'll do whatever they can. My problem was that I was too ashamed to ask for help."

Brendan: "I must have thought I was Superman. To think that I could become so involved in those kids lives and not only fight their battles for them but also my own in the department, and they were ones I was never going to win; was quite crazy. The wonder is that I lasted as long as I did."

Stan: "Let's face it, police work is damned hard. Hardly anyone I know has made it to age retirement but I thought I was different."

Tom: "In that last year my only chance of avoiding a breakdown was for me to have got out early before I was forced to leave. I was exhausted, and I could have fixed that by taking a break, maybe long service leave or even sick leave for a month or two. I was frustrated, and I could have fixed that too, if I'd had more energy and if I could have taken a clearer view of what was happening at work. I think being frustrated and being tired seemed to go hand in hand. Of course, the thing that was hardest for me to recognize, and especially to acknowledge, was that I was frightened. I was frightened of failure, I was frightened of getting out and starting afresh and I was frightened of facing the fact that I was cracking up. Maybe if I'd been able to acknowledge my fear and my exhaustion and my frustration, I think I could have drawn back from the brink, but by that stage I had totally blinkered vision. I'd lost any commonsense, and I got furious with Betty when she told me to slow down."

Many large organizations, particularly those where promotions are given because of seniority or political influence rather than ability, tend to carry people who are incompetent or lazy. Being competent in such a workplace is risky. The more capable you are, the more others expect of you. You then find yourself trying even harder to live up to both their expectations and your own. If you have low self-esteem, working hard and achieving success at work is a powerful motivating force but one which usually leads to exhaustion. If this is coupled with your employer encouraging such behavior by either deliberate intent or neglect, this is even more likely to result in severe stress-related ill-health or breakdown. It is worth taking a careful look at your workload in relation to both the work that others are doing and their allocated responsibilities. If you are doing more than your share, consider what your motives might be. Are you working hard to prove something to yourself - to prove that you really are a worthwhile person - or has your job become a way of avoiding personal issues such as loneliness or an unhappy home life?

These are the sorts of issues with which psychologists and psychiatrists commonly work and it may be advisable to seek professional assistance so that you can consult with them about these underlying risk factors.

We would not want to suggest that working hard is dangerous or that such work may be a cover for other problems. Many people are happy to work hard and are still able to strike a balance between their work and home life.

Tom felt that he had achieved this balance for some years but, when his plans were thwarted and he was getting no support, instead of leaving a position that had become untenable, he battled on, wearing himself out in the process.

The seeds of Margaret's breakdown were sown early in her life. Although she had a good family life, her mother was then rather vague and ineffectual, and Margaret was a "little mother" to her younger brother and sister.

"All my life I've looked after people, my brother and sister, my mom, my friends at school, my husband and kids, the community. You name it and I'd look after it. I liked to feel needed, it made me feel valuable and important. I was a born social worker. Of course, the only person I didn't look after was me. All my energies went outside and very little seemed to come back home to me. The hardest thing for me to change has been to see that I am worth caring about."

17

Gathering The Pieces - The Stories

Tom's underlying strength stood him in good stead during his lengthy recovery. He was unable to work for two and a half years. During that time he really transformed his life, became very fit and lost weight. His wife, Betty, had continued working after he stopped because both of them were concerned about money. She was doing office work for a solicitor who became a good friend to Betty and to Tom.

The solicitor was doing some development of flats and he asked Tom to help out with some carpentry work. Tom was very apprehensive at first.

"I was like a kid going to school for the first time. Betty made my lunch the night before. I couldn't sleep I was so nervous - silly, really. I was only going there for four hours.

"I got to the building site at 7:30 a.m. and introduced myself to the other fellas. They just said hello. I wonder if they knew how nervous I was. I had to do a bit of framing where they were renovating the walls of these old flats. It was easy stuff, I couldn't remember much, but I got the hang of it. I hadn't picked up a hammer for two years, and I was pleased I could still do it. Four hours was enough though. I was exhausted, but I'd got a lot of confidence."

Tom was able to stay working in the flats on a part-time basis. People didn't seem very interested in his past and just took him as he was. Some days he couldn't go, no one seemed to mind. He began doing a bit more and then even more. After a few months he was working every day. The solicitor, Ken, moved him to another project and wanted him to do some supervision, but Tom resisted the offer. He wasn't ready for responsibility. He'd lost a lot of his ambition and restlessness and felt curiously content with life.

Tom eventually received a lump sum settlement from his workers' compensation claim. He and Betty sold their home in the city and bought a small strawberry farm. Betty loved the life and started a small tearoom in their front room. Visitors paid a small fee to pick strawberries. Betty made superb strawberry jam and many people stayed for Devonshire tea.

"About a year after we moved in, I left the house at dawn one morning and walked to the small creek at the bottom of the paddock. I looked back at the farmhouse. It was like a ginger bread cottage, small, shining and neat. I could see my foot prints in the dew on the grass. It was a still crisp autumn dawn. The first rays of the sun caught the smoke from the kitchen chimney. Betty was cooking breakfast: homemade bread, farm eggs and bacon. I thought about all that had happened and I realized, unexpectedly, that I was happy, I was content. It was the first time I'd felt happy for years.

This idyll was broken six months later when Betty first felt the lump in her breast. She was frightened to mention it to Tom; she knew how he depended on her and how fragile he still was. She saw her local doctor who quickly arranged for her to see a surgeon. Tom had to be told and was quite devastated. He imagined the worst immediately.

Betty had breast cancer and both breasts were removed. She had radiotherapy and couldn't work on the farm. The pleasure of it had gone for Tom, and they sold it and moved close to the city so Betty could attend her radiotherapy. Betty knew she was going to die, but Tom could not bear to think about it. When it became clear that the radiotherapy wasn't helping, he began a mad scramble to find something to save her. Betty went along rather passively with his behavior; she knew it gave him hope. At her urging he made contact with his therapist again.

In the days before she died, the truth hit Tom at last. He was crushed, shrunken. He felt as if he was losing the most precious part of himself. His children treated him with great care. He fled to his flat after she died, but that was unbearable, it constantly reminded him of Betty. Many of his old symptoms returned at first but, after his acute anguish subsided, he returned to see his therapist frequently.

"I felt in despair and lost. Everywhere I went I saw reminders of Betty. But I'd felt worse when I broke down. Even the death of my closest friend did not make me feel as bad. Isn't that ironical. So much of what I'd learned recovering from my breakdown helped me grieve."

After a few months I was surprised to feel a sense of optimism and restlessness return as I left the black night of mourning behind me.

"I got in touch with my solicitor friend who got me some more work. This time I felt ready for some responsibility.

"Now I'm a building foreman. I like the work and I have a few friends. I've joined an amateur theater company again. One or two of the women there are interested in me but that can wait for a while. In a curious way I'm content."

Margaret's story

Margaret was to have one more setback. The trial of Melinda's murderer, the man Melinda had befriended, was mercifully brief, only six days, but they were days of great torment for Margaret.

"When I saw him in the dock, and he looked back at me, I knew I was gazing at the face of evil, evil that had been so well disguised. His stare was absolutely without feeling, there was no remorse, no victory, not even fear.

"I stayed out of the court room as much as I could. I would have liked to stay away altogether, but that was impossible. I had to be there for Melinda. I had to show that he had destroyed a beautiful person. This was my daughter they were talking about, not some abstract thing, but a real human being. In the months before the trial, I had deliberately refused to think about him, and about what he had done. Even at the trial, I felt weirdly detached, as though my legs and arms and mouth were moving, but they were not a part of me. I was able to give most of my evidence reasonably calmly, in that same detached way.

"The case was straightforward, he was given 18 years' jail, with a minimum of 13. I went home and fell apart again."

This time, Margaret knew she would survive, but she felt just as anguished as before. She experienced the same cycle of fatigue, crying, despair and emptiness. At first, all she could see ahead was more pain, but she had been down this road before, and she knew, this time, she would get better. She knew what was happening, she knew she wasn't going mad, and that there was a way out. This time, it took her about nine months to get back on an even keel again.

"The way back was easier this time. I knew where my supports were, I had found a therapist I could trust, and I had a better idea where I might end up."

She found a great source of peace in gardens. She loved sitting in her own garden for hours on end, she took to visiting public gardens, and soaked up their restful stillness, and their timeless beauty. She worked in her own garden and helped restore a rather grand garden that was overgrown.

"Ruth and I visited gardens that were open for display. I especially enjoyed the trips to the country places; Ruth drove the car and I relaxed. I joined the horticultural society and went to their monthly meetings. I met some really nice people and I began learning about pruning, herbs, growing indoor plants. I was really getting hooked. Ruth had been urging me to do a full-time course for some time and, eventually, I took the plunge. All these little courses at the community center had given me a great deal of confidence.

"I enrolled at the local horticultural college, and I began to study in earnest. After the first day, I came home and fell into bed, the excitement and stimulation was all a bit too much for me. It was really hard at first; I wasn't used to such intensive work. At the end of the first week I got the shakes, and I wondered if I had taken on too much, but I decided to keep going. I got through the first semester, I still loved it, and I found I had a real flair for garden design. Andrew was a great help; when I got down he would give me a massage, and a cuddle. The course took me three years, and now I'm a fully qualified landscape gardener. I've had some work already, and I have been really pleased with what I've done.

"I brief people before I start a job, and I refuse to take on work that has to be done within a time limit, those one-week jobs to do up a place for sale are not for me.

"I've gone back to writing, only this time, it's for the horticultural society newsletter. I've even been toying with the idea of writing a book, but I can't decide whether to do it on gardening or on breakdowns!"

Andrew and Margaret began living together when she was midway through her course. Andrew had wanted to live with her for a long time, but Margaret was very wary. She was frightened that she was still vulnerable, and she felt safer keeping him distant. She decided that someone who could put up with her still, after the way she had been for so long, could put up with anything, and she'd be mad to drop him.

"I still have bad days, they remind me that I am still vulnerable, and maybe that's not such a bad thing. Although I still wish none of this had happened, I've become reconciled, and I don't expect much to change. I think that there are some compensations. I'm a more sensitive person than I was, and I can see a different side to life now. Something like this has really made me see what matters in life, and what doesn't. I am very tuned in to other people. I can pick up on the ones who are in trouble. I can't say that I like it really; I'm still too close to my own breakdown.

"I've talked to a few people who've broken down, I told them what had happened to me, I think it gave them some hope to know that you can get better. I have to be careful not to get too involved, because it pulls me down. It's quite frustrating, at times, seeing people cracking up, feeling how hard it is for them, and yet not being able to fix it. Still, it's their life, and they have to make their own decisions."

Throughout her recovery, Margaret never lost the qualities that were uniquely hers. For long periods, however, they were buried under her misery and desperation. The quality that did show through was courage. Margaret never quit fighting. She tried new tacks, she stumbled many times, but she picked herself up and tried another way.

Her first priority had always been to regain her sense of self-worth, and only when she had achieved that did she feel she had really recovered.

APPENDIX

Breakdown - The Facts

What is a stress breakdown?

A stress breakdown results when a person's capacity for coping is severely damaged, and this damage is caused by stress. This leads to the development of characteristic symptoms and an inability to manage the ordinary demands of life, such as work and family. This damage is long term, and although most people recover, they are left with a permanent vulnerability to stress.

What is a breakdown?

Breakdown is a word that is used in three ways:
- It can mean someone experiencing any sort of mental illness. Someone with a schizophrenic episode might be said to have had a breakdown.
- It is used to describe any sort of sudden explosion of feelings, usually crying, especially by men.
- The third meaning of the term is the sense in which we use it. We prefer the term "stress breakdown" to make it clear which meaning we are attaching to the term and to associate the breakdown with its usual cause: stress.

What are the symptoms of stress breakdown?

Symptoms of stress breakdown are the result of damage that has occurred inside when outside pressure has become too great. Stress symptoms reflect the outside pressure, whereas breakdown symptoms are the result of internal damage.

Symptoms of stress breakdown are similar to those of stress, but they are much more severe, more global, continue even when the strain is past and are accompanied by feelings of powerlessness that are not a common feature of stress.

How can you tell if someone might have a breakdown?

Sometimes you can't tell because some people are so good at hiding their feelings. Generally, though, you have a good idea that someone is heading that way because they have quite a few of the symptoms we have already described.

The people we really worry about are those who are getting very exhausted, irritable and who seem trapped. The three danger signals are fear, fatigue and frustration. A combination of the three makes people vulnerable.

What can you do if someone is heading for a breakdown and ignores your warnings?

This is a common question and is always difficult to answer. No general answer will be really satisfactory. There are a number of things you can do, depending on your relationship to the other person and especially depending on the amount of power you have over them.

There are two key things that can be done:
- Avoid blaming the person you're concerned about, and try and listen to their worries before you offer any advice.
- Take a number of practical steps including:
  Make an appointment with a counselor or doctor and accompany them to the appointment. Talk to your friend's employer to acquaint them with your concerns (with your friend's permission). Try and reduce their load.

What is the difference between burnout and a breakdown?

"Burnout" is a term that is always used in relation to work. It usually means someone who is not coping well with their job. Generally people with burnout have to leave their job at least for a time. They maybe able to go back to that job soon or they may need to work elsewhere. Sometimes they may not be able to go back to any work at all.

You will notice that we are really describing the overlap between severe stress and a stress breakdown. The term 'burnout' can refer to either situation. The critical issue is the degree of damage that has occurred to their ability to cope.

Why don't people get better when they stop work, if work has caused their breakdown?

This is like asking why a broken leg doesn't get better when you get pulled out of the car accident. As in a car accident, there has to be some force that leads to a breakdown, but once the breakdown, or the broken leg, has occurred, the cause has become irrelevant. You have to deal with the consequences of the damage.

How long will it take to get better?

If you have had a breakdown, recovery generally takes place over months or years. This recovery is very gradual, so at times it can feel like nothing is happening. But most people recover, often despite themselves.

Sometimes people refuse to allow the healing process to occur. They make excessive demands on themselves and are surprised that setbacks occur. It's like taking off the bandage every 15 minutes to see if the wound has healed.

The rate of recovery can be delayed by further setbacks. Financial and marital problems often follow a breakdown and cause a great deal of extra pressure.

Recovery is always delayed by 'returning to the scene of the crime'. Such reminders may come from legal suits, revisiting the 'scene' of your breakdown, and well-meaning questions from friends, which bring up the past and other reminders.

Will I ever be normal again?

Most people recover from a breakdown. To an outsider they will seem to have recovered totally, but people who recover are always aware of a vulnerability. They are less effective in handling pressure and have less stamina than before.

Ironically perhaps, many people feel that their life has been enhanced by their experiences as they are much more sensitive to others' pain and savor life more fully, not taking their own health so much for granted.

Aren't a lot of people faking?

It's hard to fake a breakdown because the disruption to your life is so severe. The only reason to fake it would be to get money, usually from workers' compensation. Most people we have seen have impressed us with their degree of distress and their commitment to seek help long after their case has been decided.

What is the difference between stress breakdown and post-infectious fatigue syndrome?

Post-infectious fatigue syndrome, or Epstein-Barr virus (no relation), is a vague syndrome covering many different situations that all share the common feature of overwhelming fatigue. Some believe this is the same condition as myalgic-encephalopathy (ME), in which there is a combination of fatigue and muscular aching.

The syndromes mentioned above are not usually associated with high levels of stress. There is often a clear-cut history of a viral illness, like infectious mononucleosis and symptoms displayed involve high levels of fatigue. There are some mental symptoms such as memory and concentration problems but there are few problems in socializing, such as fear of answering the telephone and so forth.

Stress breakdown shares some of the characteristics of these conditions. In fact, when they were first discussed in any depth, we wondered if stress breakdown was a form of these disorders. We think there are some similarities. It may be that certain viral illnesses impose enormous stresses on our constitution so that the end result may be a form of stress breakdown. What is clear in both stress breakdown and post-viral syndrome is that the person's capacity is severely impaired.

We have wondered if many of the extra symptoms of stress breakdown arise from the fact that the stress leading to the breakdown has arisen from social forces, outside forces. Many of the problems of self-worth and interpersonal difficulties that are seen in stress breakdown arise from these noxious experiences and are an attempt to avoid them in much the same way as people who have been in a bad car accident later make very poor passengers.

What is the difference between stress breakdown and depression?

At times it is difficult to separate reactive depression from stress breakdown. There are two major differences we see. The range of symptoms with stress breakdown are much wider and include depressive feelings. These depressive feelings are reactions to the multiple losses that are part of a breakdown. The second major difference is the time course of both conditions. Reactive depressions generally resolve fairly quickly as the person adjusts to the loss. Thus reactive depression is an inevitable part of stress breakdown, and often exists as an isolated condition.

The depression of manic depressive illness is often quite profound and requires specialist treatment. The depression is very severe but effective treatment usually leads to rapid resolution.

What is the difference between stress breakdown and a prolonged grief reaction?

A prolonged or pathological grief reaction is a particular form of stress breakdown in which the cause arises out of the death of a loved one and in which the predominant symptoms are sadness and anguish. These intense symptoms often obscure the overall loss in coping capacity arising from a stress breakdown.

Is stress management appropriate for someone who has a stress breakdown?

The answer generally is no. Stress management is not only ineffective in stress breakdown, but generally makes people feel much worse. The whole premise of stress management is that you are still coping. It is like treating a fractured leg as if you had a sprain.

The point of stress management is to improve your coping skills, so these techniques may be quite helpful when a person has almost totally recovered from a stress breakdown and needs to improve their ability to deal with their life.

What is the difference between post-traumatic stress disorder and stress breakdown?

Like the term burnout, post-traumatic stress disorder refers to a spectrum of disorders ranging from a mild reaction to breakdown.

As its name suggests, post-traumatic stress disorder follows an acute trauma, whereas stress breakdown can be caused by either acute trauma or many small traumas over a period of time. Usually, post-traumatic stress disorder is a form of stress breakdown.

Further Reading

This reading guide is not exhaustive. It simply lists books and tapes that our clients, their families, and professional colleagues have found to be helpful.

Background reading:

Cherniss, C., *Staff Burnout- Job Stress in the Human Services*, Sage Publications, Beverly Hills, 1980. A thought provoking text with ideas for both workers and managers in human services.

Cherniss, C., and Krantz, D., "The Ideological Community as an Antidote to Burnout in the Human Services" in Farber, B., *Stress and Burnout in the Human Services Professions*, Pergamon, New York, 1983. This article suggests that hard work is not in itself the cause of a stress breakdown.

Mitchell, J., and Bray, G., *Emergency Services Stress- guidelines for preserving the health and career of emergency services personnel,* Prentice-Hall, New Jersey, 1990. Extremely useful information for anyone in a high-risk occupation.

Raphael, B., *When Disaster Strikes - A Handbook for the Caring Professions*, Century Hutchinson, London, 1986. Highly readable and carefully researched; mainly deals with the stress experienced by those who have experienced disaster or acute trauma.

Sacks, O., *A Leg to Stand On*, Harper Perennial, New York, 1990. Although the author describes his recovery from a physical condition, there are parallels between his experience and that of someone recovering from a stress breakdown.

Stress breakdown:

Farmer, R., Self-help therapy audio tapes, particularly "Nervous Breakthrough," "Depression," "Anger," and "Insomnia." Available from PO Box 118, Rozelle, NSW, Australia, 2039. Ron Farmer is a clinical psychologist who produced these self-help tapes as a result of his stress breakdown.

Stearns, A., *Living Through Personal Crisis*, Ballantine, New York, 1984. This book is particularly helpful in overcoming the grief and sense of loss that is associated with a stress breakdown.

Weekes, C., *Self-help for Your Nerves*, Signet, 1990. *More Help for Your Nerves*; Bantam, 1990. *Peace From Nervous Suffering*, Signet, 1990.

Claire Weekes's books have been used for many years by those who have suffered a breakdown. She gives clear, simple advice and is always optimistic.

Wilde McCormick, E., *Nervous Breakdown: A positive guide to coping, healing and rebuilding,* Unwin Paperbacks, London, 1988. An excellent book which will be especially helpful when you are looking at the causes of your breakdown and how you might avoid another one.

Stress:

There are hundreds of excellent books and tapes on stress, and we suggest that you look for one that suits you. Three books that give a good overview are:

Cooper, C., Cooper, R., and Eaker, L., *Living with Stress*, Penguin Health, London, 1988.

Girdano, D., and Everly, G., *Controlling stress and tension: A Holistic Approach*, Prentice Hall, Englewood Cliffs, New Jersey, 1979.

Hanson, P., *The Joy of Stress*, Hanson Stress Management Organization, Islington, Ontario, 1986.

INDEX